PRAYING AND PREACHING
THE SUNDAY GOSPEL

PRAYING AND PREACHING THE SUNDAY GOSPEL

Joseph G. Donders

ORBIS BOOKS

Maryknoll, New York 10545

The Catholic Foreign Mission Society of America (Maryknoll) recruits and trains people for over-seas missionary service. Through Orbis Books, Maryknoll aims to foster the international dialogue that is essential to mission. The books published, however, reflect the opinions of their authors and are not meant to represent the official position of the society.

Manuscript editor: Toni Sortor

Psalm 72:1–2, 12–14; Psalm 51:1–13; Acts of the Apostles 17:26–28 are from the *Good News Bible,* the Bible in Today's English Version. Copyright © American Bible Society 1966, 1971, 1976. Reprinted with permission.

Throughout the reflections, the author makes many references to Scripture that are his own trans-lation or rendition.

Library of Congress Cataloging-in Publication Data

Donders, Joseph G.
  Praying and preaching the Sunday gospel.

  Includes index.
  1. Bible. N.T. Gospels—Liturgical lessons,
English. I. Title.
BS2565.D675 1988   252'.6   88-17804
ISBN 0-88344-615-4 (pbk.)

Dedicated with thanks to
Robert N. Quigley,
who cooperated in the publication
of all my Orbis books.

Contents

LITURGICAL CYCLE B

*If Epiphany is not celebrated on the second Sunday after Christmas, see Cycle A, second Sunday after Christmas, "7. Does He Function?"

*If Epiphany is not celebrated on the second Sunday after Christmas, see Cycle A, second Sunday after Christmas, "7. Does He Function?"

REFLECTIONS ON SOME RECURRING CELEBRATIONS

Editor's Note

The three-year cycle of Scriptural readings is shared by the Roman Catholic and many Protestant churches, including the Episcopal, Lutheran, Presbyterian, and United Church of Christ. Lectionaries based on a common cycle promote a wider selection of readings from Scripture while emphasizing the living Word of God as the foundation for the life of the church. In concert with the liturgical seasons, the three-year cycle follows a continuous pattern. One year ends and another begins with Advent. The main selctions for year A are from the gospel according to Matthew; year B, are from Mark; and ycar C, from Luke. The Gospel of John is used for some Sundays in Lent and during the Easter season. John's sixth chapter is used for the seventeenth to the twenty-first Sundays in year B.

We commend this book to all who have enjoyed Fr. Donders' previous books, and to all who may encounter these reflections for the first time, that they may be drawn more deeply into the Word of God, and that we may all, as Fr. Donders asks us, feel God's spirit awaken within us.

Preface

In 1975 the World Council of Churches met in the new International Kenyatta Conference Center in Nairobi, Kenya. Some Christian Kenyan publishers wanted to offer the thousands of participants and observers a souvenir. Nothing was done about this until a few weeks before the meeting, when the local publishers, Gazelle Books and Lengo Press, took up the challenge. They published a booklet, "Expatriate Jesus," that contained fourteen gospel meditations given by me. The booklet was in a way ecumenical, as some of the meditations had been preached in Saint Paul's Catholic Chapel at the University of Nairobi, some at the Anglican Alliance High School in Kikuyu, and some at the interdenominational Saint Paul's United Theological College in Limuru.

Via American participants at the Conference, the booklet got into the United States, and through the mediation of Rev. John Wymes, an American Maryknoll Missioner, Orbis Books asked me to send a larger collection of gospel reflections. This resulted in the book *Jesus the Stranger,* containing fifty-two reflections, one for each Sunday of the year. In 1979, that book received the First Prize National Religious Book Award and was reprinted several times. Since then, Orbis Books published the gospel reflections given every year at Saint Paul's Chapel in Nairobi, and later, when I left Nairobi in 1984, those preached in Baltimore and the many places to which my new assignment brought me in America, Africa, Asia, Europe, and Australia. The result was nine other books, covering three times the three liturgical cycles.

The books proved not only to be appreciated in the United States, where they became best-sellers, but also in other parts of the world. There were Australian, British, and Philippines editions, and some were translated into Dutch, French, German, Korean, Portuguese, Spanish, and Swahili, while Polish translations are being prepared.

I was asked to select, from the over five hundred reflections published in the original American editions, the ones I liked most, one for each Sunday of the three liturgical years and for some of the more important feast days. As it would be impossible to publish them in their original sense-line format—the book would be too big and too expensive—all the meditations were reworked for the prose edition.

A choice had to be made. It was difficult to make that choice. Reading all those reflections again, I was reminded of so many faces, so many friends, young and old, so many events, conversations, discussions, and incidents. It reminded me also of a discovery I had made. A discovery related to what happened to them and to me when meeting Jesus.

A discovery I must have made before anything was put into print, because I expressed it—strange to say—in the very first reflection of that initial modest collection *Expatriate Jesus*. It was an intuition that grew with me, because I found it again expressed in the introduction to my last volume in this series of ten: *Liberation, the Jesus Mode*.

In that first sermon, I reflected on the two who walked with Jesus to Emmaus. They thought they were walking with a stranger. And he, Jesus, did not reveal himself to them. He waited until they recognized him! *It had to come from within them!* Jesus lived his life in a way that we would be able to recognize ourselves in him. He is a stranger. He definitely was in Africa where I gave most of these reflections. He was an expatriate, he came from another world, a Jew, an Asian from Asia Minor, but from Asia, he lived almost two thousand years ago in a totally different situation.

He really is an alien, but if you believe in him, then it must have been *you* who recognized something in him. And if this recognition comes from you, how could it be strange to you? That is what happened to the two friends from Emmaus. Jesus did not reveal himself. He did not tell who he was. He took bread, he broke it, and they recognized him. Him, the bread breaker, the universal companion. Emmaus was not the only time that he played that role of a stranger who had to be discovered. John the Baptist said: "There is a stranger among you," meaning Jesus. The woman from Samaria met him as a stranger, and so did Nicodemus.

This approach leaves it up to us to react to Jesus, and what he stood and stands for. He took that chance because of his respect for us, and because of his belief in us. He saw us all connected to our divine origin, interconnected in our human/divine family, and vivified by God's Spirit.

I chose the reflections that seemed to have reflected this approach best. Meditating on them, I hope you will discover your own depth and center and the richness of your human/divine relations. Communicating them to others, I hope you will witness them making the same discovery, as I so often did. The Kingdom of God is in us, it is in you, it is in me, it is in all, a hidden treasure, a forgotten pearl, a fish still in the water, but already caught, the yeast of the Spirit pushing up in the dough.

We in Western Christianity often seem too accustomed to those gospel stories. It often is as if we are tired and blasé. Telling those same stories to people who never had heard them before, who suddenly recognized in them the possibility of having their deepest hopes fulfilled, showed me their divine and human power.

In the Introduction we will have a closer look at this way of praying the Sunday gospels and of communicating our discoveries and experiences to others. It is the greatest thing that can happen to us! It will build the new world we all are hoping for. I hope that you will enjoy the reflections that follow, that they will widen your mind and your heart, at the same time healing and stimulating your body and all your senses.

Introduction

PRAYING THE GOSPEL

There is a beautiful text in one of the Preface prayers for weekdays. It is the fourth one. Maybe you never heard It, because it is for weekdays, and not so many of us have the time to go to Mass on weekdays. The prayer says simply that God has no need of our praise, our prayers add nothing to God's greatness, they are nothing but God's gifts, they make *us* grow in grace through Jesus Christ our Lord.

How would we be able to grow in grace through Jesus? How do we grow in grace? That question is not only answered by the gospel stories about him. It is answered by our everyday life. We all know the experience of someone being a grace to us. You have been a grace to others, I am sure. I do not know your experience in this, but I know about mine. Mine was not a special experience, I think it was a common one, and I hope you do not mind me telling you about it.

When I left the University Chapel in Nairobi, the priest who was going to succeed me came to me with a question. He asked me what I thought was the most important service I had rendered while being the university chaplain. I told him that I did not know, and that it would be better if he would come to the farewell evening the student community had organized for me. Most probably they would give an answer to his question. I told him that I myself was curious, too, what they would say. We went together to the evening. In the many speeches, one issue was made clear. The main thing they had appreciated was—as they said several times—that I had given them hope in life and themselves.

Reflecting on this, I understood that I would say the same thing about the ones I considered to be a grace in my life. Those who helped me most had been those who gave me hope. Not just hope like that, but hope in the context in which I lived. I am sure the same is true in your case. The ones who were a grace to you were those who gave you hope, who made you discover your own value. We all are looking for ourselves, we have a thirst for who we really are. A thirst we cannot quench on our own.

I remember how someone told me that she thought herself useless from almost all points of view. Unfortunately she had a family who strengthened her in that idea almost all the time. She felt a failure, even contemplated ending her life. Then she met a man who admired and loved her. It changed her life. He was her salvation, and she most probably his.

The people around Jesus must have had those same experiences in their everyday lives. It is an experience which is not limited to what a lover does for you. It is an experience you have every time another one is gracious to you. The person at the cash register who calls you back when you forgot your change. The taxi driver who looks with you for an address you cannot find. The person who runs after you with a bus ticket you lost. The professional who is kind to you. Those experiences are *legio*. Of course, there are other experiences in life, when others treat us in a way that shatters almost all hope in us. They are *legio*, too. There is, however, a difference. We all know that the hope-giving experiences are the ones that are *positive* and *good*, the hope-shattering ones are *bad* and *sickening*.

With great joy, we all look forward to so many gracious moments in human life: a wedding, a birth, a baptism, a feast, a church service, Thanksgiving, Christmas, and a party. It is not only a question of what humans do or do not do to one another. There are also hope-giving things like the warmth of a fire and the shine of the sun, the freshness of water and the softness of oil, the color orange and the sound of music, the brightness of a flower and the green of fresh grass, a gorgeous sunrise and the calm of the lake, the white of the beach and the sway of trees and palms, the pleasure of a meal and a glass of good wine. The gospel stories are full of those items. They brim with their energy, vitality, and sparkle. You must have an open eye, ear, nose, and touch to appreciate them. You must have an open eye, ear, nose, and touch to be able to appreciate the gospel stories, to let the richness of their imagery enter your imagination, heart, and mind.

The gospels tell us how these gracious moments touched Jesus. How he resonated or vibrated when seeing the sun, when smelling the grass, when standing in the wind, or preparing a breakfast for his friends. They tell us how he reacted when confronted with death, sickness, misery, poverty, hypocrisy, and despair. Aware of the negativity around himself, he was faithful to a vision where the Kingdom of God would be victorious and even death conquered. Many around him were so touched by him that their contact with him changed their lives.

How did that happen? We should know that, to really be able to pray the gospels. Obviously those who changed under the influence of Jesus not only remained observers of what he did. They were not only touched in that way. They became participants, they became sharers. It is not enough just to look, hear, smell, and touch; what is seen, heard, smelled, and touched should enter and shape us. It should come from within our own inner source of life. Or to say it in the words I used in the Preface: Jesus' life should be recognized by us as the life coming from within ourselves. He came to show us our own possibilities and potentialities. He was full of Spirit and life, the same Spirit and life that make us live. Full of hope and confidence, he wanted to show us who we are, and what makes us tick.

In our deepest inner being, we are all interconnected in our origin, God; we all get our lives from that deepest source in us. We are interwoven, interconnected as the threads in a piece of tapestry, as the threads of a spider web. When one thread is touched, the whole web vibrates. Praying the gospels, we should try to tune in to those vibrations in such a way that we resonate from within what comes from without. The source of our life is within ourselves. We should not only share, we should re-enact.

When you strike a tone with a tuning fork near a piano, the corresponding string picks up that frequency and starts to sing it from within itself. Did you ever hear the story of the old rabbi crippled by arthritis, who told his congregation how David was dancing in front of the ark? He got so caught up in his own tale, that while telling this, he suddenly was swept away and started to dance himself, despite his disabled joints. It is in that way that we should pray the gospel stories.

Reading the gospel we see, hear, smell, and even feel how Jesus acts and reshapes the world around him. There is also something else he does. Often he is apparently doing nothing. He is for forty days in the desert, he is endlessly in the mountains, he disappears from his company during the night to be alone. Those stories are so often mentioned that we better pay attention to them. The gospel stories are full of his acting, full of his making and remaking, but they are also filled with those moments that he simply concentrates on his being. It is in those hours and days that he touched the ground of his existence, that he was with God, with himself, and with all of us in the deepest sense. It is on that ground, on that fundamental experience, that the rest of his life seemed to be built. They are the moments of silence in his life. The time he resonated in God self, life at the deepest level. It was from there that his whole life, the simplest things, his breathing, his walks, his meals, his words received their meaning and their vitality. It was in that way that his whole life became a response to the Divine and the Humane. From that deep resonance with God, he resonated God's Spirit and love through his daily life, making so many around him vibrate in their turn.

How can we pick up those divine and humane vibrations and respond from within? One of the difficulties is that the gospel stories and parables have been heard so often they do not surprise anyone anymore. Most of them we know by heart. They have lost their bite and their sting. We are accustomed to them, we are immune. During a sermon, the attention of the listeners often slackens at the moment that a reference to the Bible is made. Another difficulty we meet is that the gospel stories we read or hear are overlaid by interpretations, transcriptions, explanations, and comments that are often outdated and refer to insights and experiences long gone. Their resonances of experiences do not lead us any further. It is as if they feed on themselves and have been doing that for ages. How to overcome this kind of gospel fatigue?

It's sometimes suggested that we should try to feel ourselves into the feelings and emotions, the thoughts and reactions of the persons around Jesus, Mary, Joseph, and the apostles, putting ourselves in their place. It seems a good suggestion. Yet, I think we should go further. We should not just remain at that level. We should react to Jesus ourselves, not by being sympathetic to him (neither by being antipathetic, of course), but by being *empathic*. We should be in accord, in harmony, in concert with him; of the same mind and heart and even of the same physique. We should ask ourselves: what did *he* feel and think when he met the lepers, when he was interrogated by his torturers, when he spoke about the good Samaritan, when he accepted the tuna sandwich from a small boy to feed the thousands, when he was confronted with the adulterous woman, when he broke the bread at the last supper, when he prayed on the mountaintop. Or, put in the words we used above: His life vibration should throb in us. His energy should become ours. Our imagination should be plugged into, and charged by, his vision.

Is that too pretentious an ambition as the outcome to our praying his life? No, it is not. It is his intention. It is the reason he came among us. He told us *to follow him*. He did not mean a literal mimicking, but an inner process of being vivified by the same Spirit that enlivened him. Paul meant the same when he said that he loved with the love of Jesus Christ, or, translated even more concretely in an older translation: "I long after you all in the bowels of Jesus Christ" (Philippians 1:8). This disposition should be the result of our praying the gospel. His life should be ours from within ourselves.

This way of praying is a question of establishing, cherishing, and nourishing an intimate relationship with Jesus. He is the main grace in our lives. He is the principal sacrament arousing God's breath and life in us. Jesus does not have that influence only on me. I am together with so many others around him. They, too, are feeling aroused by him. They, too, can be sources of grace to me, and I to them. We should be in communion with one another, forming communities and networks, linking our experiences as so many of us almost spontaneously do, when breaking his bread, sharing his wine, and being fed by his life.

Our community with others will not only inspire us but also help us to avoid self-deception, checking ourselves against the reactions of those around us and against those who went before us all through the rich tradition and history of the Church, from Paul to our own days.

We can learn a lot from one another. We all have in ourselves the same openness to the Infinite, to God; we all carry the original breath by which we are created; we all remember something of the melodies sung in Paradise.

I learned so much from the thousands I was privileged to live and pray with. So often they mirrored God's life to me. They made me feel and understand the depth and richness of life we can reach when God's Breath stirs in us while praying the story of Jesus.

Learning is not the correct word. It was more than that. It was a sharing of the emotions, of the life-throbs, we felt in body and soul, in heart and mind, meditating and reflecting together on Jesus' life, death, resurrection, and on the pulsing of his risen life in us, especially during our vibrant and life-giving celebrations. Those reflections, those prayers, were a grace to me. May they also be a grace to you, arousing in you God's Breath, the life of Jesus Christ.

It is in that way that together we will live his Body, his Heart, and his Spirit from within ourselves, engaging one another and the whole of creation—fire, oil, water, salt, yeast, sun, moon, stars, sky, fish, bird, every plant and animal—more and more, until God is all in all.

PREACHING THE GOSPEL

Praying the life of Jesus arouses God's breath in us; preaching the life of Jesus should do the same to the listeners. All is said in that one sentence. Preaching in such a way, however, presupposes a lot. There is the preacher, the Jesus story, and the listener. Preachers have to be faithful to Jesus, to their community, and to themselves. The preacher has to strike a balance between different poles. "Fidelity both to the message whose servants we are, and to the people to whom we must transmit it safe and sound, is the central axis of evangelization," is stated in the introduction to the mission encyclical *Evangelii Nuntiandi*. The term *evangelization* can be replaced by *preaching* in our context.

Preachers have to be endowed with two virtues: *bona fide* and *bona fiducia*.[1] It is our *bona fide* that makes it impossible for them not to listen to the people around them, when they are preaching. It is our *bona fiducia* that will keep them faithful to the Word and to themselves while doing it. The "Good News" has to be made relevant to contemporary man and woman.

How do you do that? Hundreds of books have been written on this topic. It is not the intention here to add to all those books. The purpose here is to give some simple and effective rules, suggestions in line with what we said on how to pray the Sunday gospels.

There are many theories on what a sermon is. There are preachers who give beautiful pieces of oratory. The listener is meant to be amazed by the learnedness and the never-ending flow of words hardly ever heard before. Other preachers give sermons in which God is praised and thanked and glorified and implored. It does not become clear why all this is done. Other preachers use their sermons to explain what certain Bible texts mean. They often are more interested in what those texts might have meant to the Corinthians or the Romans, than to the Baltimorians, the New Yorkers, and the Californians.

It is nice to assist at fireworks. Everyone wants to see them. They are spectacular, but also short and nonlasting. They produce lights and stars in the air. They whistle and they whiz. They trail tails of light through the dark, but after that, everything is as it was: dark. And people go home in that dark.

We expect more from a sermon. We expect sermons that help us understand. We hope they assist us in our understanding of God's revelation here and now. Sidney Carter, himself a preacher, once wrote: "So close the Bible now, and show me how the Christ you talk about is living now."

When we would like to make others react to life and the world in the way Jesus reacted, then we ourselves should be aware of a whole network of experiences. We should be able to feel ourselves into the emotions and reflections of Jesus and those of our hearers. This means that we deal with three sets of experiences: Our own, the ones of Jesus, and those of our listeners. This supposes in its turn that we pray, as suggested in the first part of this introduction, to get Jesus' life aroused in us, but also that we should be acquainted with what moves those who come to listen to us. They will only profit from homilies and sermons when they are able to link their grace experiences to those of speakers.

This might sound almost forbidding. It is not. Here, too, we may presuppose that listener and preacher are bound up in the same life-web of Spirit, grace, and life. Those links are there, but we should be made aware of those links; they should be discovered and revealed. It is what Jesus did in his preaching.

It is similar to what an artist does. He, too, has to meditate upon the world until he sees, feels, and understands what he is looking at. He then expresses this experience in his work of art, assuming that others will pick up what he sees.

It is a matter of communication. All through this process of communication, connections are made. Connections between the artist and what he sees; between the work of art he makes and those who connect to that, seeing what the artist saw, and seeing with him from within themselves.

The great Italian medieval poet Dante desired his poetry to affect the life of his readers in this way. He wanted to remove those living in this life from a state of misery, and to bring them to a state of happiness. His aim was practical, not a speculative one. He wanted to change the state of being of the reader and listener, to awaken their sensitivity to the feelings of others, to reveal the unity underlying his own nature, and to fructify and refresh through the integration of his psychology, his capacity for insight, understanding, and joy.[2]

The first thing the preacher should do is get Jesus' life aroused in himself. The second thing is to get his listeners inspired with the same life. To make them hear and see and taste and smell and touch and understand how God is at this moment with them in their everyday work and life experiences. To be able to do that, the preacher should know not only God but also his audience.

A good preacher is not simply someone who can talk well. Conversationalists can be found in any bar, club, party, meeting, or family gathering. A good preacher is not someone who reads his Bible well. Reading the Bible in public is not the same as preaching. The good preacher is a person who knows about our human experiences. He is "with us," he speaks our language, knows our problems, and manages to see us in a light that connects us with God, with Jesus, and therefore with our world and human history. It is concretely what people expect from him. He should be relevant. He should make us experience our lives as relevant, filled with meaning and hope. Preachers who are able to respond to these expectations of their audiences will grow from strength to strength every Sunday. Their churches will become too small. A point that is proved again and again.

It is interesting to see how all kinds of people bombarded Jesus with all kinds of questions. They asked him to speak about their issues and problems. Should we pay tax? What about the persons murdered by the regime? Who is the greatest? How should we pray? What is most important? What should we do? What about those people who died in that accident when the tower of Siloam fell over? What is going to happen to the woman who married seven times? Are the lepers punished for sins they committed? What happens after death? I am a rich man; what should I do? How often should we forgive? What about evil? It is also instructive to read how Jesus, as a preacher, spoke in the terms of the people around him, about water and wine, light and dark, fish and nets, wheat and harvests, vines and wine, water and sky, sowers and home-makers, rituals and cemeteries, and children sleeping with their parents in bed. He obviously knew his people well.

When he left Nazareth after thirty years, he lined up with the people in front of John the Baptizer. He identified with the policemen, soldiers, housewives, customhouse officers, and merchants who were looking for something more in their lives. He was with them in their search for a clarification of things human and divine. He could preach to them because he knew them, because he was one of them. They said of him that he preached with authority. That authority was not only based on his insight in Godly matters, it was also based on his understanding of them. They could not escape his words and his examples. His stories were made of the stuff they themselves were made of. They themselves felt connected to him and through him to transcendency itself. His listeners did not meet God in Jesus' theology or Bible reading. Through him they met God in their very own lives. He preached in a way that his human and divine vibrations aroused them from within their own minds and hearts.

So did his first disciples, the apostles. Think of Peter. Caught up by the Holy Spirit, he announced Jesus in such a way that the listeners—in their turn—caught fire, hearing what he said in their own tongue.

To have a heartthrob that concords with that of Jesus, and to have a similar connection with the people we preach to, is not sufficient. A third element has to be taken into account: the communication, the connecting of the listeners to God's Breath, the homily itself. There are techniques involved. True, to be able to preach is a gift. Paul even mentions preaching in his list of charismatic gifts. It comes from the Spirit. Consequently many tend to say that you either have it, or not.

This type of reasoning could lead to some lazy thinking. Both the ones with the gift and the ones without the gift might judge that they do not need to bother about the communication techniques involved. Those techniques are important, even for those who are gifted. And those who are not so well gifted can become quite efficient in their preaching, if they apply those techniques.

Thanks to all kinds of research, we now know a great deal about speech effectiveness. This material can readily be found and consulted, and that we do not need to repeat in this Introduction. Let me therefore restrict myself to some remarks that directly relate to the idea of praying and preaching as worked out above: the S-effect and the creative use of Bi-sociation.[3]

As we noted, one of the difficulties of using parables or other texts from the gospels is that almost all of them are too well known. Most of those texts have been heard so often that they do not surprise anybody anymore. Preachers aware of this difficulty have been looking for ways of overcoming it. Would it be possible to give the old "truth" a new vigor, a new dialectical push? They were looking for a way to make Jesus' saying: "Behold the Kingdom of God is in the midst of you" (Luke 17:21) alive and effective again.

One of their answers to this question is to bring the known text and truth out of the context in which their listeners were accustomed to seeing them. This approach is called by some the "surprise" technique; others call it the "alienation" method. I prefer to call it the S-effect, the surprise effect.

Jesus was a master in this technique. When people came with their usual questions, he never gave them the usual answers. Take the incident when he was asked: "Who is my neighbor?" (Luke 10:29). Instead of giving the answer everybody expected, he took a completely different approach. He spoke about a beaten-up man, thrown alongside the road and half-conscious, who saw a priest pass, and a Levite, and who was helped by a Samaritan. He gave the victim's point of view. He often turned the usual judgments upside down. The tax collector is justified, the Pharisee not. When they ask: "Who is the most important one?" he calls a child to the center of their circle. He uses the most astonishing metaphors, like comparing humankind with a woman giving birth.

His approach is always fresh, surprising, new, and unexpected. Consequently, it always provoked a direct reaction. What Jesus said was so strange, so alien, that it always worked dialectically. What he said was experienced as an antithesis of what had been held as sacred and true up to then. He shattered firmly formed convictions and beliefs. He often used nonreligious language, avoiding the religious language of his contemporaries, a language that had been used so long, and so often by so many people, that it had lost its meaning almost completely. He continually used examples from everyday life to express himself.

Jesus conveyed his experiences of God and humanity in stories. He had a creative imagination, and it is obvious that he used his direct environment, and all that happened to him and around him. He must have been a good listener, too. He had a great respect for his audience. He told his parables not because he underrated the intelligence of his hearers, but because he wanted to make things clear without imposing. He left the conclusions and decisions to the ones who listened. He rarely moralized after having told his stories. No wonder that his teaching made a great impression on them, because he taught and preached unlike the scribes (Mark 1:22).

In his S-effect approach, Jesus used bi-sociations. This is a term used by Koestler in his study *The Act of Creation.*[4] That sounds complicated. In fact, it is simple. Bi-sociation means that two aspects, words, ideas, or realities are brought together in a combination that nobody ever heard before. The new combination surprises. According to Koestler, all discoveries are made in that way. Things that had never been seen together are suddenly *seen* together, and there is a flash of new insight. Jesus used the approach when he compared the Kingdom of God with a seed, a net full of fish, a hidden treasure, a pearl, bubbling yeast, and so forth. It is those bi-sociations that have now lost much of their original freshness. The preacher has to look for new bi-sociations. He has to get contemporary flashes of inspiration.

This should not be too difficult. We have to associate Jesus' life with the life we are living nowadays, in any case. Our sermons should be steeped in those gospel stories, our Christian traditions, and the world around us. Good preachers have always been doing that.

The gospels were written in the same tension. They also try to mediate between the stories around the life of Jesus and people who had never seen him in the flesh. Luke, for instance, wanted to tell and interpret the story of Jesus to a third generation of Christians, people who were worrying about other things than the first and second generations. He had to explain to his readers and hearers why Jesus had not yet returned, how they should understand that the way to salvation is our love for God, and that our love for God should be expressed in our concrete love for our neighbors.

Luke not only registered stories and facts, he interpreted them, he tried to connect his audience to what happened to Jesus. He wanted to tell his story in the same way Jesus had told his story to the companions on their way to Emmaus. Once they had recognized him, they said to each other, "Did not our hearts burn within us as he talked to us on the road and explained the scriptures to us?"

It is the way the Sunday gospels should be preached to all of us on our road, that, challenged by Jesus' life and fire, our own hearts start to burn from within, the bread gets broken, the wine shared, and the warmth of his love will be known and felt by all to the glory and praise of God.

NOTES

1. *See* Kenneth Cragg, *The Christ and the Faiths* (Westminster Press: Philadelphia, 1987).

2. *See* William Anderson, "The Central Man of All the World," in *Parabola,* v. 13, 1 (February 1988), pp. 8–17.

3. *See* Ernest Henau, *Inleiding tot de Practische Homiletiek* (Cahiers voor Levensverdieping: Altiora, Averbode [Belgium]), 1976.

4. *See* Arthur Koestler, *The Act of Creation* (Pan Books: London, 1970).

PRAYING AND PREACHING
THE SUNDAY GOSPEL

LITURGICAL CYCLE A

1. The Troublers of Israel

Matthew 24:37–44

You can prepare for Christmas in many different ways. You can celebrate Christmas as something that happened in the past.

It was in the past that Joseph and Mary traveled to Bethlehem, where they could not find a place in the inn. It was in the past that they finally found a shed and Mary gave birth to her child. It was in the past that angels started to sing and shepherds came to find the baby and his mother. It was in the past that some wise men came from the East, and that Herod got upset about the announced news. It was in the past that Jesus was circumcised in the temple, where Anne and Simeon came to greet him. It was in the past that the whole family finally had to flee to the safety, security, and hospitality of Africa.

You eat and you drink—in a bar, a cafeteria, a restaurant, or even at home—as much as you can, and even a bit more, to commemorate that string of events that took place so long ago, once and for all, in the past.

You can also celebrate Christmas as something that happens in the present, meditating upon the graces given to you: heaven is opened again, new life is given, a savior is born, hope is regained. Alleluia, joy to the world!

Others celebrate Christmas by not celebrating it at all. They say that Christmas does not help, that it has no meaning, it never had meaning. They say nothing in the world ever changed: no new life, no salvation, nothing at all. They are—apparently—without hope, without expectation, without anything. Yet, they may be the ones who understand best what Christmas is about. They are the ones looking for an alternative, for a new beginning.

They seem to be the ones most in line with the expectations expressed in the three readings for today: the alternatives offered by Isaiah, Paul, and by Jesus himself.

Isaiah says: "Come, let us go the mountain of the Lord, let us walk in his paths, let us come together, let us hammer out our swords into plowshares, let us finish war."

Paul writes: "The time has come, the night is almost over, it will be daylight soon. Let us be awake, so that the light is not going to find us asleep."

Jesus says: "Be prepared, great things are going to happen, get ready, get ready!"

Those three appeals do not ask us to sit down and eat and drink, to celebrate only the past or merely the present.

We are urged to celebrate Christmas in a way that is directed to the future, toward a change in our lives, toward a change in the world. We are told to walk to the mountain of the Lord, to grow in goodness and community, to live in peace forever.

When we celebrate Christmas like that, we will be joined by all men and women of goodwill, forming a pilgrim people who are on the move.

We should not be settled in the past of this world, or in its present, either; we should be *the troublers of Israel*, a community of dissenters, in view of what Jesus came for, in view of what the angels sang about at his birth: "Peace, real peace, his peace, to all of humanity, to all of the universe."

SECOND SUNDAY OF ADVENT

2. John the Baptizer, an Old-Timer

Matthew 3:1–12

People wondered about John the Baptizer. They had reasons to be surprised by him. He came from the desert. He did not work, he did not own anything, he did not eat bread made by human hands, he did not drink wine pressed from the grapes. He ate nature as it fell from God's hands: grasshoppers, locusts, snails, and honey. He did not use an ounce of textile; he was dressed in a camel's skin, with a leather girdle made of another skin.

His teaching was remarkable, too, because it was hard-hitting and one-sided. He called his public—people who, after all, showed sufficient goodwill to come to be converted—a brood of snakes. He announced without any hesitation that, as far as he was concerned, God's judgment was very near, and everybody would be cut down like a tree and thrown in a fire that would never go out. He maintained that everyone should change his life, and quickly, without hesitation—policemen, soldiers, and housewives.

He was not clear about what would happen to those who converted. He was more clear on what would happen to those who would not. Their future would be God's wrath, God's anger, God's fury, and God's vengeance.

He did not exclude the possibility of being saved, otherwise he would not have asked people to be baptized, but he does not dwell on that theme very much.

His message was somber and grim, dark and heavy.

Later, Jesus would compare John's approach and the song he sang to a funeral song, a dirge, something belonging to last rites.

Later, Jesus blamed the crowd for not having understood, for not having wept.

Jesus understood, Jesus wept, and Jesus went up to John to be baptized. John got frightened. He said: "No, not by me!" Jesus said: "Oh yes, by you!"

Jesus was baptized to show that he shared the feelings, the prophetic inspiration, and the prophetic impulse of Saint John.

John was right; Jesus confirmed his opinion. But John was right in the old way, according to the Old Testament pattern. With John, the Old Testament closed.

Something else came to replace it. John's message was a message of doom. It could hardly be called: "good news."

After John, this changed. It changed when John baptized Jesus and the Spirit descended upon him, in a way She had never descended on earth before, to start something new, a new era, a new period. An era in which a father was looking for his son, a shepherd for his lost sheep, a housewife for her lost coin, a host for reluctant guests, and Jesus for all those who were sick and sinful.

Jesus made the difference very clear. He spoke about a complete break. He said: "Up to the time of John it was the law and the prophets; since then it is the Kingdom of God."

Saint John lamented; Jesus rejoiced. John sang a funeral hymn, Jesus an alleluia verse. John refused to eat bread; Jesus broke his bread. John refused to drink wine; Jesus changed all the water in the kitchen into wine. John dressed in a camel's skin; Jesus in a customized shirt without a seam. John warned; Jesus invited. They were, in fact, so different that they started to wonder about each other. John sent his disciples to Jesus to ask him: "Are you really the one?" Jesus answered: "You, John, are the greatest of the Old-Timers, but the smallest of the New Timers is greater than you!"

Something new had started—the Kingdom of God. We are invited into that Kingdom, the Kingdom of the new era. We are invited not only to profit passively from it, but to build it.

Jesus compared the people around him with children. He said: "You are like children, when John sang his funeral lament, you did not weep; and now that I am singing, playing my melody on my flute, you are not dancing."

We should be dancing because of the promises made, because of the Kingdom of God.

THIRD SUNDAY OF ADVENT

3. John the Baptizer's Difficulty

Matthew 11:2–11

The reason John sent those disciples of his to Jesus remains a much-discussed issue among those who study the Bible.

Some say John sent them because he was fed up with them. He had told them explicitly that he had only come to announce the coming of Jesus. He had told them very clearly that he, John, was *not* humanity's destination, that he was only a signboard along the road. Still they remained—like babies that do not want to be weaned—hanging around him. He sent them to Jesus with that question in hopes that Jesus would convince them to stay with himself.

There is also another possible explanation. In the text, there might even be an indication of where we have to look for what happened. At the end of his answer to John's supporters, Jesus asked them to tell John not to lose faith in him! So that is what John must have been doing in his prison cell. He was losing faith in Jesus. But why?

Was it because John had announced God's wrath, selecting and uprooting all sinners, destroying them with power and fire?

Was it because John heard, while he was suffering in prison, how Jesus was eating and drinking with those very same sinners, sitting with them at the table, conversing with prostitutes who washed his feet and dressed his hair?

I don't know, but there is another hint in the gospel about John's difficulty and his difference with Jesus.

Do you remember how one day some people came to Jesus, blaming him? They told him: "We don't understand you. You don't seem to do the right thing! John the Baptizer and the Pharisees teach their people how to pray, they tell them to mortify themselves, they introduce them to all kinds of spiritual exercises. But you don't do any of those things, do you?"

We should not forget that John had been a monk all his life, living in the desert, dressing in skins, eating insects, drinking dirty swamp water. John was accustomed to being far from the world, praying day and night. I think that John expected something to change drastically with the arrival of the Messiah. He expected Jesus to stress prayer, going to the temple and the synagogue, charismatic alleluias, rosary crusades, praise-the-Lord meetings, the public singing of psalms, and things like that.

When John read Isaiah, he read that after the Messiah came, all peoples from all nations would go up to the temple in enormous, colorful processions. But John might have overlooked where Isaiah said that this world would start to change under God's influence through the efforts of the faithful.

Jesus listened to John's messengers, then told them: "Tell John, that the blind see again, that the lame walk, that the lepers are cleansed, that the deaf hear, that the dead come to life, and that this good news is proclaimed among the poor." The wilderness is changing, the wasteland is blooming, and the glory of God is on its way.

The disciples went back to tell John the message. I hope John understood. I hope we understand, because I am afraid that we are too much like John. As Christians, we are willing to pray, we are willing to go to church, to say rosary after rosary, to be faithful to all kinds of spiritual exercises, build churches all over, plant statues on hilltops, and so on.

Is that one of the reasons that the people around us who are waiting for a change in this world are giving up hope in us? Aren't they saying to one another what John, for another reason, said of Jesus: "Are they really the ones, or have we got to wait for others?"

Churches might be full, but is there justice in the world? Even very dull spiritual exercises are faithfully kept to, but do our life decisions make the blind see, the lame walk, the dead rise?

Are we good news among the poor of this world? Are you?

FOURTH SUNDAY OF ADVENT

4. The Virgin Issue

Matthew 1:18–24

When you read the Old Testament prophets, you realize how intensely those prophets were on the lookout for a messiah and for a new beginning in their day and age. Those prophets were very aware of the appalling situation in which they lived. Their awareness of the evil in the world made them scan the horizon every morning to see whether he had come.

We are preparing for Christmas. We are looking forward to Christmas. We did our Christmas shopping to celebrate his coming, but are we really so very hopeful? Are we really so very eager? Are we hoping for something new? I wonder.

I think our lack of expectation is partly due to our blindness to the situation in which we live. We are blind to the thinness of the thread that keeps us together, bound to human life.

You all know a sick person who is not taking his medicine. You all know someone in your family who does not stick to her diet, even though it's necessary for her continued good health. And you say to these people, "If only you knew how serious your situation is, then you would be more careful. But you do not know, and you do not want to know!" And we don't know what to do, either.

I am not going to give you a picture of all the horrible threats that are hanging over this world. I don't need to do that, because they are shown to us every day. I am not going to tell you all the evils and sins in our lives: the jealousies, the envies, the betrayals, the indecencies.

But I would like to tell you that I now see—much better than before—how deep all that havoc is in this world of ours.

When I was younger, I did not know all this. When I was a child, I thought that what happened around Jesus was unique. I thought that he lived with people who were extraordinarily bad. I did not know that all the intrigues that went on around him are still going on all over the world all the time. I did not know that nothing unique, nothing unheard of, really happened when he was arrested, mocked, tortured, beaten, and killed for his sense of justice and peace. I had no idea that all this was going on all the time in the world in which we live.

Now I do know.

Now I know what sin is better than ever before. I know now how much we need a savior, a redeemer. We don't just need some medicine, some updating courses, a psychoanalytical analysis, Alcoholics Anonymous, or some reflection days. We need something new: a new life, a new type of human life.

When the prophets hoped for that newness, one thing became very obvious to them: There had to be a totally new start. A new strain of human life would have to appear. That is why they began to foresee that this life could only be virginally born. Not because they wanted to protect its mother against anything sexual or biological—they knew better than that—but because the life born out of her had to be new, totally new.

That is the life we need; that is the only originality that can help us. That is what we believe was born among us in Jesus Christ.

That was the life born in us at our baptism!

CHRISTMAS

5. In the Dark of Our Night

Luke 2:1–14

It is the middle of the night. Everywhere, it is dark. The dark has crept into all the angles and corners around the world. When we meditate on that darkness, we might be thinking romantically about its peace and quiet, about the sky unfolding God's majesty, full of stars, and eternally turning galaxies and planets.

That is what children think about in the dark of this night, full of expectancy about what will happen during this night and waking up to find their presents.

This is not only what we think, it's also what we sing: "Silent night, holy night, all is calm, all is bright!"

But, sister or brother, it is not because of this idyllic scene that we say, in the solemn blessing of tonight's liturgy, that the Son of God *scattered the darkness of this world.*

It is not because of the night's loveliness that we are called together in the middle of the night to celebrate the birth of Jesus.

Nighttime is full of terror. Its darkness is horrible when you are alone and cannot break it. No streetlights, no torch, no match, no light—only darkness—and within the darkest corners lurk the still darker shadows of menaces and threats. To step into that darkness is to step into danger; to step out of the light is to step out of safety. Every day you can read in the papers how many people are being robbed, mugged, and raped in the dark of the night.

The dark of the night can be a terror. It is the time that crime stalks about. It is the time that fear reigns. It is the time that nobody goes out without a good reason. Darkness becomes like a wall that separates neighbor from neighbor, friends from friends, and we only dare to pierce the dark with our cars, which we use as tanks.

Aren't you afraid of the dark? Aren't you afraid of its terror?

We celebrate the birth of Jesus in the middle of the night to indicate the darkness in which we lived and live.

It is only when we understand that darkness, that we can comprehend and experience what a wonderful thing the light was that was lit when Jesus appeared in this world.

Hope at last. Finally, a new beginning, finally a new start, a divinely good human life, a light to the world.

"The people that walked in the darkness have seen a great light. On those in the land of deep shadow a light has shone."

Do you remember, dear sister, dear brother, how once at your baptism a community prayed over you, asking that you might be like him: a light in the darkness that we try to survive?

Do you remember?

FIRST SUNDAY AFTER CHRISTMAS

6. Cut from the Same Cloth

Matthew 2:13–15, 19–23

They settled in a town called Nazareth, and there he spent most of his time, more than 90 percent of his life, with his family.

There are no authenticated and canonized miracle stories about that long period of his stay with us. We hardly know anything about it. We know that the years passed and that he grew from adolescence into adulthood. The difference between him and us during this part of his life was not made known. The difference made no difference.

In a sense, he was more *God-with-us* in Nazareth than later on. He lived the type of life—family life—we all know about. Yet even then he did not live exactly as we do, because we live in a society where being different always seems to make a difference.

We have to do better than others. We have to be first in our tests, we fight for grades, certificates, prizes, incomes, and degrees. In our self-esteem we depend too much on those *outstanding qualities* that make us different from all the others.

People who do not have those outstanding qualities look at themselves in mirrors all over the world and, seeing nothing special, they consider themselves to be nobodies.

"I am the first one in my class." We cling like schoolchildren to those aspects of us that set us apart from others: my skills, my insights, my sermons, my techniques, even my religious experience.

We become jealous, mean, anxious, insecure, envious, hateful, and we cannot form a community with others because we refuse to live in the world we have in common with others. We refuse to live, or even try to live, within the margins of our common existence.

In Nazareth, Jesus taught us that we human beings do not find our real identity on the edges of our human lives, where we can brag about our specialities and charisms. We find it in the center of life, when we recognize our basic human sameness, when we discover one another as sisters and brothers, cut of the same cloth as he, Jesus, was cut of.

He did not reveal himself as our redeemer as much by being different from us as by being the same, with a difference.

SECOND SUNDAY AFTER CHRISTMAS

7. Does He Function?

John 1:1–18

Christmas is a time when we give each other gifts. Everyone of us must have received something during this time: something small, a pencil, an eraser, a copybook, or a banana; or something big, a fountain pen, a new pair of trousers, a bicycle, or school fees for a year.

Christmas is, of course, a very fitting time for gifts. Aren't we celebrating the greatest gift that God ever gave to humankind, the gift that constituted us: human life? He gave his own offspring, Jesus Christ. And according to the rather mysterious beginning of the Gospel of today, even that first donation, our human life, was given to us in him.

Gifts are all over the Christmas scene, Jesus is a gift, his spirit is a gift, his peace is a gift, and the three magi came with gifts. In the long run, we risk getting so many presents that our house and our life run the risk of being overloaded by them. Take a good look at your home and in your garden, look around your street, go once through your room, and you will find that all those places are almost like cemeteries cluttered with unused and dead things on the way out.

Cupboards, wardrobes, kitchen table drawers are full of old gifts others gave to you, or you gave to yourself, presents that you never use, a miraculous potato peeler, a promising pasta maker, a special knife, some marbles from your youth, and so on.

You bought them, you got them, but they did not function. That is why they disappeared in the dark of your room or wardrobe. This might even happen with that gift from God: Jesus Christ. Why did he disappear out of the lives of so many? It is simply because they thought that he did not function. But why did he not function, was it because of the nature of the gift or because of the addressee?

If I do not want to see, I can throw my spectacles away, I can even have my eyes removed, but am I not destined to see? If I do not want to walk forward, I can throw my shoes away or, if I want to be radical, I can even have my feet amputated, but am I not destined to proceed? If I do not want to live in God's world, I can do without Jesus Christ, but am I not destined to live in his world? In his letter to the Ephesians, in the second reading of today, Paul thanks his friends not only for the fact that they received Jesus Christ, but also because he functioned in their lives. He wrote: "Having heard about your faith, about your faith in the Lord Jesus, *and the love you show*, I will never fail to remember you." That is how people around us should remember us also.

EPIPHANY

8. Three Wise People

Matthew 2:1–12

Three people came from very far to see Jesus. In the country I come from, they are traditionally called kings. In English-speaking countries, they are more often called wise men. I prefer the title wise men; I do not know exactly what to do with kings. I like to see these men as wise, and I think they were wise, very wise.

They were obviously seekers, and that, according to many reliable sources, is the beginning of wisdom.

They saw a star. You might say, that is not particularly wise; everybody can see stars, which is true. But to see stars you must look up, and not everybody looks up. When did you see your last star? When did you last look up?

They not only saw that star, they saw a message in it. They saw the star as a sign, and that means that they were not only living in the present world around them, like animals and insects do, who seem to think only about food, drink, and sex.

They believed in a beyond, a world behind this world, a world different from this world, and yet appearing through it. That is very wise, too. They did not believe their eyes; they could not believe that what they saw was all there was. They believed that there was more to it all.

They were religious people. Nonreligious people only believe their eyes. Religious people do not and cannot believe only their eyes; what they see presents itself as a further question mark.

Those three saw that star as a big question mark. It invited them somewhere, and they followed it, which was another wise move. Why did they follow that star? I do not know exactly. They must have had some hope or some expectation that something new was going to happen to this world, that the past and sin and guilt were going to be taken away, or at least taken over. I think that within the context in which they appear, we might suppose something like that. So they were looking for what some of us nowadays call salvation.

In looking for that salvation, they made another very wise decision. When they followed the star, they were convinced—and this is sure, because they themselves said so—that they were not looking for a learned book that might have the solution; not for a political system that might bring liberation to all; not for a sociological theory that might explain human behavior so it could be changed; not for a psychological gadget that might help psychoanalyze humankind; not at all. What they were looking for was a person.

They were looking for a child.

That was very, very wise, because, if you think about it, salvation can only come from a person.

I will explain why I think this.

Take Jesus, telling the parable of the prodigal son, about the father willing to forgive. A very nice story; a classic, without any doubt. Even its economy of words is remarkable. But that whole story does not help a stitch unless the teller can assure us that the father—that God the Father he seems to talk about— is a real person, willing to take that type of personal attitude.

We know the same thing when we go to a hospital. The hospital is full of the most wonderful intensive care and other units, full of pacemakers, iron lungs, artificial kidney rinsers, and who knows what.

We know that all that equipment is nothing, without a person willing to mediate between it and us. If there is no personal interest in us, it is all useless.

In school, it is the same. All the books, all the teaching aids are there, but it is the teacher that makes the school or breaks it.

A neglected child is not helped by a report, a plan, or a building. The child is helped by a hand and a voice that says: "I am going to help you."

Those three wise men knew that. They wanted liberation; they were looking for assurance from the other side; they were looking for a hand and for a voice—the hand and voice of God. They found it, and they went home different men, via another way.

If we think about it, we are in the same position. I am looking for several things. I am suffering under a guilty conscience, feeling dishonest, unfair, forgetful, stubborn. I feel that my hands are dirty from this world. I would like assurance that all this can be restored and forgiven, or better yet, even forgotten.

I am looking for a new life, for another possibility, for a greater integrity. To be able to find all that, I do not need a system, a moral code, a theory, a theology, a policy, a philosophy, or something like that. I need a *person*. I need Jesus.

SUNDAY AFTER EPIPHANY

9. Getting Involved

Matthew 3:13–17

The baptism of Jesus took place thirty years after his birth, but it is celebrated at Christmastime, immediately after his birth, his incarnation. That is correct, for his baptism, too, belongs to the beginning—the beginning of God's incarnation in this world.

That incarnation is a wonderful event. It gives the final and ultimate assurance that God is with us. That incarnation was a slow process. It was not only a question of being born, but also a question of the further steps to be taken, the further initiation rites.

First he was presented for circumcision. He got his name. He was taken up. Then, as a boy of twelve, he went to the temple. He got involved. He asked questions, he answered questions. He got embedded; he wanted to be involved.

Getting involved is a painful process. It is the hard way, a continuous effort.

A man knocks at your door. Do not listen; you will get involved. A child takes her thumb out of her mouth; do not listen, you will get involved. Your boss tells you about his temper, your son about his school, your daughter about her fears, your old mother about her loneliness, your friend about his frustrations, your aged father about his worries, your brother about his difficulties, your sister about her children. Do not listen; you will get involved.

Every time you listen, it is going to cost you time, energy, involvement, and very often money. It eats you, it needles you. The clearer things get, and the clearer you let things get, the more time it is going to cost, the more energy, the more of your personality, and the more of your money.

At the moment Jesus left Nazareth and stepped into the crowd, he got involved. Up to that moment, he had been hidden. They had been ignorant of him, and their ignorance meant his bliss. Up to that moment, he had been safe. Up to then, he had been secure. At the moment he stepped out in the open, he got involved. When he saw his son stepping out, God was so excited he could not keep his mouth shut. He shouted through all the heavens and the sky: "This is my beloved son, here he is, watch him."

Jesus, revealed in that way, "betrayed" by God, fled into the wilderness, to come out again, of course, to carry the burden of his involvement.

People did not leave him alone anymore. He got tired, very tired, and in the end, he died on the cross.

Modern authors have been much impressed by Jesus' involvement. D. H. Lawrence wrote a rather heretical book about it: how Jesus, after his death struggle on the cross, woke up in his grave, and how he scrambled back to life out of his grave. How he found refuge in the house of an old widow, and how he disappeared again, to live a different life, a totally uninvolved life.

His baptism, his stepping into the crowd, was a deliberate decision to get involved, to rub shoulders with all the others, to be with the crowd, to be with sinners, to be with all.

That is not our vocation. It is not your vocation. It is not my vocation, not with all and everyone. That's impossible.

It definitely is our vocation to be involved with those who may and should claim us: our children, those entrusted to us, those dependent on us, our direct neighbors, the people we meet on our way.

SECOND SUNDAY OF THE YEAR

10. A Lamb Misunderstood

John 1:29–34

When John saw Jesus coming, he pointed at him and said: "Look, there is the Lamb of God, who is going to carry all the sins of the world." He added: "The Spirit of God is on him!"

This must have sounded like a curse to his listeners, because they knew the lamb he was compared with. It was the lamb that in their tradition, but also in the tradition of so many African peoples, was slaughtered or sent into the wilderness after having been loaded and charged with all the sins of the community in which it had been growing up.

It is a lamb that can lead to very many misunderstandings.

Some theologians have developed a theory in which God became a kind of revengeful, bloodthirsty (if I may say so) monster, demanding, clamoring for the blood of his son. Sisters and brothers, it is not true. God does not want to see that blood. God does not want to see any blood at all. Even in the responsorial psalm of today, God makes that very clear. God does not ask for sacrifices and holocausts. God does not ask for a victim. From the very beginning, God has been interested in only one thing: our well-being. God created us to live, not die. God's will is the well-being of humankind and *nothing* else. God's Kingdom is the Kingdom of human life. You may call it grace, you may call it salvation, it all comes down to the same thing: God wants us to live.

It is that interest in human life, and nothing else, that makes up the Spirit of Jesus, because it is the Spirit of God. He was not just a lamb on which humankind, including you and me, can put our hands and unload our sins. It was nothing like that.

He said: "I am the light of the world," and that is what he was. He made the blind see and the ignorant understand.

He said: "I am the life of the world," and he gave the hungry bread to eat, and the thirsty water to drink.

He did not complain when they had no wine, but he, the greatest party goer of all time, gave them nine hundred liters of wine to drink.

He did not just say to his followers, "You should be responsible." He gave them his Spirit, so that they could be responsible by themselves.

He was not a mere lamb who fished them out of the troubled waters of this world to get high, dry, safe, and saved.

He told them to go out and change this world. He told them to overcome all the powers of death in this world: jealousy, envy, hatred, pettiness, racism, tribalism, poverty, misery, torture and violence, greed and lust, sickness and death, as he overcame them all.

We should not misunderstand God because of that lamb; we should not misunderstand Jesus because of that lamb; we should not misunderstand ourselves because of that lamb, either.

We have the terrible and deadening possibility of doing just that, of looking for someone else to rid us of our responsibility.

We are greedy because others are greedy. "It is their fault, not mine." We drink ourselves senseless because the society around us is frustrating. "It is the fault of society, not me." We run around with prostitutes because the campus is unsocial. "It is the fault of the campus, not me." We have a baby without a marriage because we feel so lonely in this world. "The fault is the world's, not mine." We bribe and we steal, we throw away food, because we live in a bribing and stealing and wasting society.

We speak about the rift between the rich and the poor. We enjoy it when others speak about that, too. We listen and we applaud, but how do we relate to the sweepers and the cleaners, the waiters and the night watchmen, the poor in the midst of us?

We have our lambs, our scapegoats for all we do.

One very faithful follower of Jesus said that as long as one person in this world cleans the toilet of another person, the world is no good. The man who said this is a man who changed the face of India in his time, according to the method of Jesus, by giving himself nonviolently in the interest of all: Mahatma Gandhi.

We should be lambs like Jesus, and in no other way.

THIRD SUNDAY OF THE YEAR

11. Followers of Jesus, Unite!

Matthew 4:12–23

The first thing Jesus did when he heard that John the Baptizer had been arrested was leave Nazareth forever. He chose a new home, his new headquarters, at Capernaum. The second thing he did was start to preach. His message was short and clear: Everyone should repent, everyone should change over, the Kingdom of God was very, very near.

Preaching is a strange thing. Preaching can be frustrating. As a preacher, I know very well what I am talking about.

You can preach and preach, people can listen and listen, and you just wonder what all that preaching and all that listening accomplish. I am afraid that very often they accomplish nothing at all. Something else must be added.

The pope can preach, the bishops can preach, the priests can preach, the laypeople can preach, even the politicians can preach. They can preach in parks, at railway stations, in streets, in churches, in the Senate, and in the House, but all that preaching does not accomplish anything at all if it is not followed by something else. Preaching is useless unless its listeners come together to do something in an organized way about the injustice, the corruption, the sins, and the evil in this world that their preachers preach about.

According to today's gospel, Jesus did a third thing. He left Nazareth, he started preaching, and he decided not to remain alone. He decided to associate, to unite himself with others. He called Simon, he called Andrew, he called James, he called John, and afterwards so many others. In our day, he even calls us, you and me.

This is normal and logical for anyone who wants to change anything in this world. When you want something to be done, you associate, come together, network, unite, and do it. That is what Jesus did.

If there was anyone in this world who might have been tempted to make his life a *one-man show*, it was Jesus. The temptation was there. The devil put him on top of the temple and whispered in his ear: "Be a stuntman, be admired by all, jump down and use your influence with your Father. Let angels carry you down on their wings. Show them a piece of good circus work, and your name will be on the lips of all."

He refused, just as he had already refused that other temptation to stay alone at home and forget about changing this world and its humanity.

When his family heard what he was doing, they came to tell him to come back home with them to Nazareth. "You are out of your mind," they said. "You cannot carry that load, you cannot change the world. Leave history to be history; come down with us. The coffee is ready."

He decided not to give in. He decided not take their advice. He decided not to go back to Nazareth. He decided to stay in Capernaum. He decided to forget about their coffee and their talk during the evening hours, evening after evening, sitting in the dark of their rooms and complaining about what went wrong and all those others who went wrong.

He left them and their fruitless talk, but he also took that other resolution, *not to remain alone*. That is why he picked Simon and Andrew, John and James, Mary Magdalen and the other Mary, you and me.

It was in that community that they went out and preached and healed and chased away evil and the devil itself.

There is much we could learn from all this. In fact, it is all so obvious that it hardly needs any further explanation.

We, his followers, are not allowed to merely stay at home, criticizing and complaining, accusing and backbiting somewhere in the darkness of our rooms during the evening hours.

We, his followers, are not allowed to remain alone, safe and secure, washed in the blood of the lamb, with clean hands in the ivory towers of our apparent righteousness.

We, his followers, are asked to associate ourselves with him and with one another in an organized and efficient drive to chase away the evils that terrorize our societies. We are called together not only to pray and to sing *alleluia* and *praise the Lord*. We are called together to heal all the areas of life where we live and work.

If we don't do that, if we remain alone, if we only pray, we belong to the deadwood of human history. The deadwood he, Jesus, carried to his death on the cross.

Please, sister, please, brother, don't remain alone, don't just criticize. That's too easy. Let us unite, let us come together in *his* desire to shape God's new world. Let us associate, let us move together with him in the direction of the Kingdom, which in that case, will be at hand, indeed. Amen.

FOURTH SUNDAY OF THE YEAR

12. Happiness Did Start

Matthew 5:1–12

Good news is bad news, and really bad news is good news. If I go to an office and I am treated well, and the person I need is polite, kind, understanding, and helpful, then I have nothing to tell my secretary when I get back to my office. She will ask: "Any news?" And my answer will be: "No, everything went well."

But if I go to an office and the person I need is a big, pedantic, proud stinker who shouts at me, and I shout at him, and we finally shout together, then I have quite a story to tell my secretary when I get back.

If you get a phone call with really bad news, you will easily be able to organize a group of willing listeners. They will listen exactly up to the moment that they know your story, and after that, they will run away, as fast as they possibly can, to tell your story to as many people as they can. Bad news is, indeed, good news. While they run, the terribleness of your news grows even worse.

If you get a phone call to tell you that all is well, you might even ask your caller: "Did you really phone me to tell me that?" Who is interested in hearing that all is well? Mothers, maybe.

We like to hear scandals. We love to be able to tell them. The real news is bad news. "How do you do?" "Very well, but. . . ." It is there that the real news starts.

The papers we read know that, too. The *New York Times,* the *Washington Post, USA Today*, their main stories are almost always about crime, rape, disaster, disease, death, murder, robberies, arrests, war, and people who shoot others straight through the heart.

We seem to love bad news. We thrive on bad news. Journalists turn up in great numbers only when things go wrong, and the more things go wrong, the greater their number will be.

It seems to have been the same around Jesus. Check the gospels. They are called good news. Listen to what he, himself, tells people: The king is an immoral man; the tax collectors and administrators are hopeless; the men are adulterers—the whole lot of them (they all left when he said, if any one of you is without sin, let him stay). His best friend, John, was in jail; the shepherds were hirelings and mercenaries. Housewives were losing their money; children were neglected, scandalized, sick, or dead; the occupying forces were murdering people in the temple; the priests were hypocrites. The disciples were without understanding; Judas was a traitor; the only tower mentioned fell, killing a lot of people; sons were lost; sheep were in the wilderness; and finally, he himself was arrested and killed. "How do you do?" "Very well, but. . . ."

It is in that context that Jesus, in the gospel reading of today, climbed onto a hill to get a better view. It was in that context that he said: "Listen! Listen carefully! We are deceiving ourselves. There is happiness, notwithstanding all the stories we tell. There is hope. Things are going on. The kingdom of heaven is establishing itself. Look around you everywhere: Look at the gentle ones, the comforting ones, the outgoing ones, the ones who do not hang onto what they have. Think about all the help given to sisters and brothers, sick people and helpless people. Look at the peacemakers, the merciful ones, the seekers of justice, the strugglers for wholeness. Happiness and bliss are everywhere!"

We tell one another stories of doom and corruption, about bribes and smuggling, about the big fish that go wrong and the small fry swimming in their wake. That is what *we* say. *He* said: "Do not forget what is really going on.

Do not forget that I, Jesus, dared to entrust myself as a baby with a frail human body and a wide-open, vulnerable baby skull to the human relationship of Mary and Joseph, happy, comforting, helpful, peaceful, and persecuted only in the cause of right.''

Let us pray that this Spirit, which you can find anywhere, will grow, and that it will cover over all the bad news in this world.

FIFTH SUNDAY OF THE YEAR

13. Of the Earth and of the World

Matthew 5:13–16

We are supposed to be the salt of the earth and the light of the world. Those texts are so well known and also very often misunderstood.

Christians will say, when using those texts: "We are the salt, we are the light.''

They do not seem to realize that being salt is a pretty hopeless affair. There was only one person in the Bible, a woman, who really could say: "I am salt!'' That woman was the wife of Lot, who turned into salt when she looked back on her past in Sodom and Gomorrah. She became salt, 100 percent salt, and nobody around her seems to have been happy about it.

Being salt is hopeless. There is nothing so useless, so unmanageable, and so inedible as salt by itself. You can't do anything with just salt. In a time of famine, you cannot eat it. In a time of drought, you cannot drink it. That would only make things worse. Salt by itself is no good. It makes the fields infertile. It kills life. It preserves death. It is heavy. It is useless.

Salt only becomes useful when it is used, as Jesus indicates in today's text, *mixed up with other things*.

We are not salt, we are the salt of the *earth*. We should be mixed up with the *earth*. We should be mixed up with the reality around us.

If Christians say or think: "I am the salt of the earth,'' they should understand that, as a consequence, they should be prepared to be thrown in the cooking pot of human affairs. They cannot just stand in front of the pot. They have to be put in that pot, they have to be mixed with the contents in that pot. They have to be boiled and smothered with it, practically disappearing in the process, but, nevertheless, making it all tasty and palatable.

Christians who are the salt of the earth do not need to immediately do all kinds of special things, though they might sometime be called to do special things. They do not have to join all kinds of organizations, though they might have to do that eventually. They do not have to organize all kinds of prayer groups right away, though they should pray. They do not even have to run out and do all kinds of social work, though that is very useful. Christians who are the salt of the earth should first of all be taste givers and taste makers in our human reality—in this world, in this life, in this street, in this town, in this city, in this country, in this world.

As long as salt is not mixed with something, it is too salty, too bitter, too sharp, too biting, too wounding, too hot. If salt is used by itself, it is like the salt torturers use when they beat people with a whip through a towel drenched in salt that is put over their bare buttocks. The salt that is beaten into live flesh and hurts for days on end.

Salt alone is unbearable and harmful.

Jesus also speaks about the light we are supposed to be. Again, very many Christians will eagerly call themselves *the light*.

They stand in their own light, just like a candle in an empty room or a light under an empty bucket stands in its own light, glorifying its own shine.

Light alone is useless, too. Light alone is blinding. Light alone does not make you see anything at all. Light alone is the light shone in the eyes of tortured prisoners to make them confess. Light alone hurts.

Light becomes useful when it makes us see things other than itself: the world around us. It becomes of use through us when it corresponds to what Jesus said of it: *You are the light of the world*. We should make things visible, we should light up possibilities, we should brighten our world.

This is our task and our mission. Every one of us who was baptized received a candle lit from the Easter candle: "Receive the light of Christ!" And in the older baptismal ceremony, it was for that reason, too, that everyone got a pinch of salt on his lips.

We should be the salt, but not apart. We should be the light, but not on our own. If we live and act like this, as Jesus Christ did, then we will be a consolation to others, we will be their salvation, their hope, and their comfort.

It is that salt and that light that you can find—thank heavens and thank God—all over this world, all over this country, all over this town: people hit and changed by Jesus' Spirit (see Psalm 112:4–6).

> They are the lights in the darkness for the upright,
> they are generous and merciful and just,
> they take pity, they give and they lend,
> they conduct their affairs with honor,
> they will never waver,
> they will be remembered forever,
> they have no fear of evil news,
> with firm hearts they believe in the Lord,
> with steadfast hearts they will not fear,
> open-handed they give to the poor,
> their justice will stand forever,
> their hearts will be raised in glory.

SIXTH SUNDAY OF THE YEAR

14. Not a Thing

Matthew 5:17–37

A small boy was kicking a doll. I could not see it was a doll; to me, it seemed to be only a piece of dark wood. A small girl was trying to get at the doll. She was shouting: "Don't kick her! It is my doll. It is Lucy, it is Lucy!" The boy kept on kicking, shouting: "It is not Lucy, it is only a thing, a thing!" and he kicked and kicked.

I saw a picture recently that showed a man on his face in the street, surrounded by a mob. Some policemen were guarding him. Under the photo was a caption that stated he was a thief, and the police had come just in time to save him from being beaten to death or lynched by an angry mob.

They had not come in time to prevent the crowd from cutting off one of his fingers. The man was lying flat on the street with an outstretched arm, looking at his hand in front of him. In the gutter was something that looked like the stump of a cigar: his cut-off finger.

Not far from here, a girl returning from a hotel was captured, stripped naked, and tossed up by the crowd like an ugly, despicable thing. A beautiful girl with body and soul, with spirit and content divine, tossed up like that, high up in the air, like a ball, to be manhandled by all.

It is about this type of event that Jesus is speaking today.

Jesus says: "Don't make your brother into a fool. Don't make your sister into a thing!"

One of the most horrible episodes in Africa's struggle for independence and self-determination was the freedom fight in North Africa. So many people were tortured, maimed, and killed, that some doctors, psychologists, and psychiatrists—Frantz Fanon was one of them—started to wonder how this inhuman behavior was possible.

They did some research and found that people don't just torture a human being like that without doing something else first. Before the police, the soldiers, the public start to kick and beat, before they even *could* start to beat, something else had to happen first: They had to declare their victim nonhuman.

They would shout: "Pig," and then they could beat. They would shout: "Dog!" and then they would be able to kick. They would shout: "Vermin" or "Insect," and then they would be able to kill, to crush under their feet.

In today's gospel, Jesus pleads: "Don't do that! Don't call each other names! Respect each other. If you don't do that, you are all going to be hurt, those who are kicked, and those who kick."

That was the very observation of Frantz Fanon. Being a practicing psychiatrist, one day he received a man who was upset, depressed, and low, who could hardly sleep during the night, and who, when sleeping, had terrible nightmares, all because he had been treated as a nonhuman, because he had been tortured as if he were a thing.

Another day, he received a man who was upset, depressed, and low, who could hardly sleep during the night, and who, when sleeping, had terrible nightmares, all because he had kicked others as if they were things, because he had *acted* as a nonhuman.

It is our sanity, our own dignity, our own health, our own existence that is at stake. "Don't do it! Don't make each other into things. Never!"

SEVENTH SUNDAY OF THE YEAR

15. On How To Be Treated by Others

Matthew 5:38–48

You remember that we were told last week not to treat one another like things? You remember how reducing one another to the state of things or animals—pigs, dogs, chickens, or cockroaches—must lead to disaster in our human relations?

Today's advice is about how we should treat those who handle us as things or commodities.

It is about those who take our eyes and our teeth; those who hit us, who take our shirts and our pants; about those who order us to accompany them, who want our money, and even our lives.

At first, the attitudes Jesus asks from us are baffling. He tells us not to offer resistance, not take revenge, to turn our other cheek, to lend out what we have, to go even further than people force us to go with them. He seems to invite us to be meek, humble, and naive. He seems to invite us to be passive and stupid: doormats over which the whole rest of humanity can walk without any difficulty. He seems to be preaching a kind of slave mentality in which we should not mind being exploited by others, staying passive and inert before injustice.

Some time ago in a meeting of our Justice and Peace Committee, someone told about a priest who had said he could not understand how he could have preached this kind of passivity for so very long—the kind of submission in which misery is tolerated in the name of the gospel.

He had discovered that Jesus had not preached that type of passivity. It is true that he preaches nonviolence, but it is not true that he tells us to be doormats.

In his own life we can find the true interpretation of what he wanted to say. He said: "If anyone hits you on the right cheek, offer him your left one." When he was hit himself, however, he did not—according to John—turn his other cheek, but he said to his attacker, challenging him: "If what I said was wrong, tell me. If I was right, why did you hit me?''

In fact, that kind of attitude seems to be the exact point of the whole statement on turning the other cheek. Did you ever realize how strange that statement is? If I hit someone in his face, I will normally hit him on his left cheek, because that faces my right hand. It is difficult to hit someone on the right cheek. We can only do that with our left hand, or with the back of our right hand, unless we're left-handed.

If you were to give someone a slap in the face, wouldn't you hit him on his left cheek, too? When we hit someone on his right cheek with the back of our right hand, our slap cannot be very hard. If we do it, it is always a sign of disdain, disrespect, scorn, or contempt: "Bah, pooh, who are you?" That is what such a slap meant among Jesus' contemporaries, too. Knowing this, we can understand what Jesus meant: "If anyone hits you on your right cheek, offer your left cheek, challenge your attacker, let him justify himself, don't accept being treated as an *object* of contempt, as a thing, just like that!"

That is what he did when he was hit on his right cheek. He asked for a justification. That is the way we should respond to those who degrade us: we should work at their changeover, at their conversion.

Being a doormat does not serve any purpose. Being a doormat is not going to help. A doormat does not care.

We should care for ourselves, but also for those who mistreat us.

If we love our enemies, as we love ourselves, we should hope for their changeover, for their conversion.

If we love our enemies, then we have to challenge them in view of their and our *salvation*.

EIGHTH SUNDAY OF THE YEAR

16. Like a Lily in the Field

Matthew 6:24–34

"Old King Solomon had a thousand wives." You know the rhyme, I'm sure, but do you know what King Solomon, his seven hundred wives of royal stock, his three hundred concubines, plus their combined staff, ate in one day?

The Bible tells us. In the first Book of Kings, we see one page out of the household book of King Solomon's kitchen: thirty measures of flour, sixty measures of meal, ten fattened oxen, twenty free-grazing oxen, one hundred sheep, plus deer, gazelles, roebucks, and fattened fowl. All this was eaten, the text says, from golden plates.

Solomon was the wisest human who ever lived. He composed three thousand proverbs, and wrote fifteen hundred poems. He could lecture on plants from a cedar in Lebanon to the simple hyssop growing from a wall. He could talk on animals, birds, reptiles, and fish. People came from all over the world to witness his astounding knowledge. He was pious and built an unforgettable temple; he was business-minded and monopolized the whole arms trade in his part of the world; he was a warrior who never lost a battle with his fourteen hundred war chariots, and his twelve thousand horses.

And yet Jesus says that Solomon in all his array was nothing in comparison to a simple bird, flying high in the sky, to the splendor of a flower out in the field, or even to a blade of grass.

Jesus does not set Solomon as our example, but that bird, that flower, that blade of grass. Like those things, we should not worry about what to eat, what to drink, how to dress, as Solomon must have done. We should be different.

Jesus does not say that we should not eat, drink, or dress, but that our splendor should not come from all that.

"Unbelievers are always running after these things, but you, you should be seeking the Kingdom of God, the Kingdom of God that is within."

Seek the Kingdom of God as it is in that bird, that flower, that blade of grass, shining forth from within. Anything you are running after, anything you chase, runs ahead of you, outside of you, and it will never make you shine.

Our splendor comes from what is within us: God and the Kingdom from within.

Be like a flower, a lily in the field, shining from within, from within God in you.

NINTH SUNDAY OF THE YEAR

17. Not the Shouters but the Doers

Matthew 7:21–27

You all must have heard about those martyrs in Uganda about a hundred years ago. There were many of them: Twenty-two were Catholics, twenty-three were Protestants, and two were Muslims. They died in different ways: Some were speared, some were beaten to death, most of them were burned on June 3, 1886. They were arrested after formally declaring that they wanted to follow the new way of Jesus. But they were not numb or stupid after their arrest; they resisted all attempts to make them fall back into their old ways.

One of them, Mbaga Tuzinde, was the son of the chief executioner, a man called Muhajanga. Mbaga had been baptized on the morning of the arrests. His father took him home for a week, to change his mind. He did not succeed.

While the fire was burning with thirty-one bundled-up young men in it, the executioners danced around the fire, shouting: "It is not we who are killing you: Nede is killing you, Mukasa is killing you, Kibaka is killing you, the spirit guarding the Eastern frontier, the great spirit of the Lake, the spirit of the war and the storm, are killing you."

The boys shouted from within the fire: "If that is true, you are the slaves, you are not free. You are their slaves, and we are free!"

They were free to escape from an older order in which they did not believe anymore. They were free to live in a new order, in a redeemed and saved order, the world of Jesus.

The fight between the old and the new is not only a fight between an old god and a new God, or between Christ and the anti-Christ, high up in the sky of our ideas and ideals on an apolitical battlefield.

It is a fight between the old and the new in *this* world, in *this* life. I don't exactly know how to say it, but when you read reports on South Africa, for example, it seems that many Christians over there refuse to analyze the real situation—the political situation of the oppressed people—because their fight is only in the air. Their fight is an ideological struggle between Christ and the anti-Christ, between the West and the East, between Christianity and Marxism.

The economic, social, and political struggle of millions and millions is reduced or elevated to a fight between Christ and Satan.

In today's gospel, Jesus says: "It is not those who say to me, Lord, Lord who will enter the Kingdom of Heaven, but the person who does the will of my Father."

Before he said that, he had indicated that will very clearly. He had started with the beatitudes, but after that he spoke about law, anger, adultery, divorce, vows, revenge, enemies, charity, prayer, fasting, justice, and human relations—all things to be done in *this* world.

Our fight is not in the air, between ideals and ideas. Our fight is here and now, as it was there and then for those martyrs who refused to cooperate any longer with the court because they knew them to be unjust.

It is not those who shout, Lord, Lord, Christianity, Christianity, Church, Pope, Bishop, who enter the Kingdom of God, but those who do the will of God by refusing a bribe, taking up a child, or establishing justice. They have a faith in Jesus Christ that will justify them and their world.

TENTH SUNDAY OF THE YEAR

18. Worship and Exodus

Matthew 9:9–13

While Jesus was walking, he saw a man called Matthew, a tax collector, a collaborator, a representative of the oppressive Roman colonial power. Matthew was sitting in front of the customhouse, receiving taxes and the obligatory extras he himself freely added.

Jesus said to him: "Follow me!" and Matthew got up and followed him. Up to that moment, Matthew had not been a free man; he had been a colonized man. He had been domesticated by the oppressors of his people. He had to sing their tune, and he had to continually express his loyalty to them, to enemies of his own people and himself.

Matthew was also not free in another way. He was a sinner. He was bound by his money, his career, by his deceit and his lies.

Matthew was so bound up from without and from within that he could not do what he wanted to do. He could not really define his own priorities.

Then Jesus comes along. He picks Matthew out of the small circle in which he was living. He invites him—he does not force him, but he invites him: "Come, follow me, get out of your strange prison, straighten things out, live the life you want to live, come."

He came.

He followed him. He came out of the hands of the Romans, out of the bond of money. A real *exodus*!

He started a new life, the one of Jesus, liberated, redeemed, saved.

That exodus reality is very important in the life of Jesus, and it should, therefore, be very important in our lives, too.

You know how Jesus waited until Easter to die. He instituted the sacrifice we are celebrating at this very moment during an Easter meal.

At Easter the Jews, and Jesus was one of them, celebrated the fact that they got out of Egypt, where they, as you all know, were exploited, colonized, beaten, and cheated.

With God's help, they marched out of their trouble, out of injustice, out of being unfairly treated, in the direction of a promised land.

When Jesus ate for the last time with his disciples before his passover, he was commemorating what God had told the Jewish people, who were paying taxes to causes foreign to them: "Get up, and follow me!" It was in that *exodus* spirit that he died on the cross and gave his last supper to us.

We should, therefore, today be celebrating an *exodus* out of all these bonds and chains that we call sin, and that are catalogued day in, day out, in the press of this world.

Is our celebration such an exodus? Do we get up like Matthew and follow? Liturgy can be celebrated in a way that is something completely different. Worship can be organized in a way that offers no exodus at all, that is only a consolation, a letting off of steam, a reason to do nothing at all.

The famous West Indian Frantz Fanon once wrote about the way in which colonized people dance and celebrate: "At a fixed hour, and at a fixed date, men and women get together and, under the attentive eye of the tribe, they lose themselves in pantomime, which looks rather like chaos, but which in fact turns out to be a very systematic head shaking, bending of the back, throwing up and backwards of the body. . . ." He explains that those people get rid of their frustrations, their violence, their anger, and their aggressiveness in that way. He adds that this dancing has an economic function.

When they come, they are tense, upset, impatient, and in despair. After the dance they go home released, satisfied, calm, peaceful, and willing to undergo more. The dance is a pacifier, an opium.

We, too, can celebrate this liturgy of ours, this exodus ceremony, this death and resurrection, this *new life*, this *get up and follow me*, in a way that resembles that dance described by Frantz Fanon. We get up, we sit down, we genuflect, we stand, we kneel down, we beat our breasts, we bow our heads on the very same spot all the time.

We should, however, get up and follow *him*, who, because of his pity and mercy toward us, wants to lead us out of the headlines of the Egypt in which we live, together with himself and that man he called today: Matthew.

FIRST SUNDAY OF LENT

19. The Old Enemy

Matthew 4:1–11

He had hardly been known, up to the moment of his baptism by John. Before that, he was only as well-known as you and I are, by our family and friends. Nobody paid any special attention to him. When he passed in the street, he passed in the street. When he broke his bread, he broke his bread. When he gave his opinion, he gave his opinion. When he sat on a donkey, he sat on a donkey. But, then, at that baptism, suddenly it all changed. Some learned people even say that it changed for Jesus, that he had never known who he was before that baptism, either. I don't know; I don't know how they know.

The others definitely had not known, and now, suddenly, they knew, because his Father revealed him at the moment he stepped in the water in front of John the Baptizer. Heaven opened, a voice was heard, the Spirit was seen. The Spirit was seen on him. He was revealed in all his power, with all his authority, with his mission to change this world into another one.

His first reaction was to run away, to hide, to put his head into the desert sand like an ostrich does in danger. He stayed in that desert for forty days, and then the Spirit that had driven him into the desert drove him out of the desert again, and his public life began.

Immediately he was tempted—not only then, but all through his life. He was tempted by temptations that are known to any of us who possess some skill, authority, insight, education, power, or influence. Any graduate who gets a job, any teacher, secretary, boss, specialist, lawyer, director, doctor, anyone among us has those very same temptations.

The old enemy said: "Use your skill and power and all that, to get for yourself bread, to get for yourself the dough that bread is really made of: money!" Jesus said: "But bread is not all." The tempter said: "I agree, but it is my most common trick, and the most common fall.''

The old enemy then put him on the temple roof, and said: ''Throw yourself into these temple affairs and angels will carry you, and people will applaud you.'' Jesus said: ''You should not put God to the test.'' The tempter said: ''I agree, it is the mistake I made myself, but many others still do; I only tried.''

Then he put him on a mountaintop and showed him all the political power in the world, and he said: ''What about this? If you won't fall for money, if you won't fall for honor, then at least fall for the thing they are all falling for; fall for political power.'' Again Jesus said: ''No. Not this world, not the actual world.'' He looked at Satan and added, ''because, indeed, it is too much yours, with its military budgets, its atomic bombs, its life-killing national-security priority lists. Not a world that's spending ten billion silver coins on bombs while saying: We are never going to use them, then forgetting that those bombs are exploding in the faces and lives of millions and millions of humans who have no food, no shelter, and no education, because the money was spent on those bombs that kill! Not this world, but another one, one full of justice and integrity, full of unalienated human life and dignity.'' Again he looked at Satan, that Prince of Death, and he said: ''I came to save, you know. I came to redeem, you understand.''

We all will be tempted as he was. He really was tempted as we are, as Saint Paul would remark.

Money, money, money is the name of the game, honor and glory, *our* honor and glory, without any alleluia or praise the Lord: power, political power, gunpow[d]er.

If we give in, this world will not change and we will not be with him. He will forgive us, he will understand, because he was tempted, too. But we will be the load which he carried on his shoulders on his way to calvary.

SECOND SUNDAY OF LENT

20. The March into a New World

Matthew 17:1–9

He overcame the temptation to be swallowed up—divine power and all—by the world. Now he shows those three hand-picked ones, Peter, James, and John, what the escape from the old world into a new one will bring.

This liberation story is introduced by the story of another deliverance, one of the oldest ones described in the Bible, the story of *Abram*.

Abram lived with his father, Terach, in a town called Ur. We know that place, since it was excavated not so long ago. There was a temple in Ur, where one venerated a god called *Sin* by the inhabitants.

That god was depicted as an old bearded man, bluish in color like the moon, seen by the farmers of that region as the symbol of all metaphysical power beyond this world.

On digging up that temple, a very gruesome custom came to light. Small children were sacrificed to Sin to promote fertility during times of drought.

We read in the Book of Genesis how Terach took his sons Abram and Lot one day and left that town. Why? Our Bible books do not give any further explanation. A noncanonical old Hebrew script, the Book of Jubilees, does. It tells us that Terach had to leave the town of Ur because his son Abram had offended—in fact, burned—that local god in his temple. They left for another town, Charan. But the same tradition existed in that town, and it is there that Abram is finally called to leave his country, his family, his father's house "for the land I will show you!"

Abram went as the Lord told him to do, and God blessed him because of his faith.

Together with Peter, James, and John, Jesus climbs the mountain, away from the world in which they lived, with its business, its quarrels, its competitions, its jealousies, its sacrifices, and its strange list of priorities. They climbed out of it all, higher and higher, until they were at the top. Then Jesus, who marched them out of the old into the new, started to shine, brighter and brighter, like the moon, like a star, and in the end, like the sun.

Heaven opened, and two other deliverance experts came to talk with him: Moses, who led the people out of the economic, religious, and political oppression of Egypt, and Elijah, who led his people out of the hands of the gods of Ur and Charan, whom they had started to fear again.

Four escape stories, four liberation reports, four deliverance accounts, four transitions from the old into the new.

By their combination, we are plainly invited to apply them not only in our own individual lives, but also in the life we live together communally.

We all know best where we are personally caught by the wrong list of priorities. Where we prefer wealth to integrity, consumption to equity, drugs to reality, and sex to human life. I am not going to indulge in working that out any further for you. *You* should!

We all know where we are communally caught by the wrong list of priorities in so many ways. Where a few oppress so many. Where 80 percent of all the edible oils are in the hands of one company, and practically all the grain in the hands of five others, not to speak of the armaments race, Star Wars, and so on.

We might even look for closer parallels and think of all the children's lives sacrificed nowadays—often even before they are born—to continue the old type of life and to be *blessed* in that old, cursed category. Difficult thoughts, painful considerations, disquieting visions.

Yet, Abram marched out and was renamed *Abr-a-ham* to indicate that what he did should be repeated.

Jesus walked away, and we, in faith and hope, should follow. We should be willing to be interested in that march, walking in the direction of that new light that started to shine on the mountaintop.

21. The Thirst at Samaria

John 4:5–42

The story seems to be a simple man-meets-woman story. It is the type of story you find in literature again and again. A man—a hero, a shepherd, a leader—arrives at a well and meets a woman who came to fetch water. There is the caring hand of the woman, the helping hand of a man, and everything that follows thereafter. In the Bible, the story is told several times.

Abraham, wondering about how to get a wife for his son, Isaac, sent one of his most trusted servants out to his original home country to look for that wife. The servant arrived at the well and made his camels kneel down, waiting for the evening, the time that local girls would come to draw water. Before they come, he prays: "God of Abraham, here I stand at this well, where the women will come to fetch water. God of Abraham, I will ask those women to give me a drink, and the one who cares, she will be the one."

The women do come. He asks for a drink; Rebecca obliges. Immediately he brings out his gifts, golden earrings and a ring for her nose, and the affair is settled forever after.

Then there is the story of Jacob looking for a wife. He meets Rachel at a well, a well that is covered with a heavy stone lid. The stone is so heavy that one has to wait until sufficient people are together to be able to take it away. When Jacob sees Rachel, he is in his admiration suddenly so powerful, that he—to his own surprise—can lift the stone alone.

Moses defended the seven daughters of the priest Reuel against the shepherds of the region who were harassing the girls at a well in the desert of Midian. He then took one of them, Zipporah, as his wife.

The fourth story is the one at Samaria: Jesus asking for a drink and a woman from Samaria asking him for the living water that will quench her thirst once and for all. The woman has no name; John does not give her a name. She is representing all humankind when asking her question.

The first story was a love story. In the second story, Jacob helps Rachel. In the third story, Moses defends those seven girls as their savior. In the fourth story, things are getting more involved. Salvation as such is discussed. Words like *Messiah* are mentioned. "Please, Sir, help us, we are thirsty. Give us the living, eternal water. If you are the redeemer, let us drink."

Redeemer and redemption, savior and salvation. What do those words mean?

That is very difficult and a much-discussed question. What is the redemption we are looking for?

Some reduce Jesus' message and mission to piety: peace of mind, being washed in the blood of the lamb, all personal sins being taken away, salvation.

Some reduce Jesus' message and mission to a social calling: It is about the poor, the abandoned, the disabled; it is about justice, equality, brotherhood, sisterhood, and development. He is to be found not in piety, not in praying fellowship groups, but in the inner city slums, in South Africa, in the plantations of South America.

Both groups have their difficulties. The first group, the group of the pious interpretation, has no difficulty with their Christian identity. They know what it means to be a Christian. They know what makes them different from others. They are witness to this difference day and night. That is not their difficulty. Their difficulty is their relevance. What is the relevance, the meaning of their piety to others, to Africa, to the world, to the oppressed and the poor?

In the second group, relevance is no difficulty. They are relevant to the communities they are living in. They are willing to work for the emancipation of the poor. They join in literacy programs, they will do all kinds of things like that. Relevance is not their difficulty. They have difficulties with their Christian identity. They are doing things others are doing, too. The others are very often doing these things even better than they are. It is within this frame of mind that socialists say: We have no need of Christ.

What should we do? What is our stand? What was that woman standing in for all humanity really asking for?

She was asking for redemption in many fields: She had no water, she had no husband, she asked about religion. Redemption should take place in all those fields.

Redemption in the economic field. It is here that the poor come in. Redemption in this world has to take into account that our differences are too great. The poor are starving, while the rich are overeating. Jesus said: "Break your bread!"

Redemption in the political field. In many countries, in almost every country, maybe in all countries, political power is not shared, it is too often used only to oppress the poor. Jesus said: "There should be no master among you!"

Redemption in the cultural field. All over the world, cultural minorities are oppressed. Women are treated differently from men. The rights of children are overlooked. Jesus took a child and put it in the center of their group.

Redemption in the ecological field. We should be liberated in such a way that the world, our earth, is going to be liberated, too; so that the animals and plants, pure water, and fresh air survive with us. Jesus said: "Look at the flowers. . . ."

Redemption in the field of final meaning. Even if all the above redemptions had taken place, even if this world were just, respectful to all, assuring equal rights in a healthy environment, one final question would remain: "So what? It all leads to final death!"

Our struggles, sufferings, efforts, and lives should have a lasting meaning, if only to enable us to find the courage to go on.

It is here that we should look at the cross. Not because the cross is the end, but precisely because the cross is not the end at all. He rose to the new life that is the only satisfactory answer to the question of that woman at Samaria.

We, participating in his Spirit, should be redemptive together with Jesus, and therefore with the Father, in the economic, political, cultural, ecological, and spiritual fields.

We should know, too, that by being with him in all this, we will be led to a cross, where the old world will die. We need to want that death to be able to be with him, the fundamental sense-maker and meaning-giver, Jesus Christ, forever and ever. Amen.

FOURTH SUNDAY OF LENT

22. He Began To See

John 9:1–41

First there was that woman at Samaria who had no name. He promised her that she would see. This Sunday there is a man, also nameless, who was standing in front of Jesus but did not see him: He was blind.

We all know what a blind man looks like. We all know how he behaves, because if we are not blind ourselves, we sometimes see him stumble or hesitate.

A blind man is surrounded by his world, by the things he needs. Everything is there: his room, his table, his chair, his bed, the handle on the door, even a mirror on the wall. But he does not see them. It is that man that Jesus met in the street. Jesus saw him, but he did not see Jesus, just as he did not see the children, the trees, the animals, the birds, and the flowers.

Jesus took some of the mud the Bible tells us the whole of humankind was originally made from. He put that fresh mud on the old eyes of that nameless blind man, and suddenly *he* saw everything, not only Jesus, the children, the trees, the animals, the birds, and the flowers. He saw much more, because almost immediately we hear him involved in discussions with the authorities about God, the Sabbath, sin and signs, Jesus and his belief in the Son of man. He saw it all, and they chased him away, because while he saw, they remained blind.

Many things could be said about a text like this, especially when it is written by that mysterious author, John.

Let us take one striking aspect only. That man said: "*He* put mud on my eyes and now *I* see."

He was in the dark, and now he saw himself.

In the case of this world, we all lived in the dark. Then Jesus stepped in and said: "I am the light of the world," a light that is going to clarify all.

That is both true and untrue. *He* came as the light in this world so that *we* might see. Sight is given to us, yet sight is still lacking in us.

Lord, make *us* see, and, like that man, judge and act.

FIFTH SUNDAY OF LENT

23. Dead and Buried

John 11:1–45

This is the last Sunday of Lent. The first Sunday, we saw Jesus tempted to think only of himself by Satan. The second Sunday, Peter tempted him to opt up and out. The third Sunday, a thirsty woman represented the whole of humankind. The fourth Sunday, he made a blind man see for us all. This last Sunday, his friend is introduced. This man has a name, our own name, *Lazarus*, which means "helpless." When the report starts, Lazarus is dead—though Jesus suggests that he is only asleep—and buried.

He is completely bound up: strings around his arms, cords around his legs, two stones on his eyes, his mouth gagged, a cloth around his head—lifeless in a tomb with a stone in front and the smell of decay inside.

Does Lazarus also stand for us?

Is that what the blind man saw at the moment he started to look around himself in this world? Is that not what *we*, too, would see, if we looked around our world?

Humankind is like that man *Lazarus*—helpless, frustrated, bound up, smelly, decaying, blind, deaf, at a loss, full of maggots—dead.

That is how Jesus found his friend, that helpless man, Lazarus, a man he had loved so much. When he got Lazarus's smell in his nose, it got in his eyes, as well. First there was a knot in his throat, but then that lump came up and he wept, he wept bitterly, and they said: "Look, how he loved him!"

He said: "Roll that stone away!" But Lazarus's sister said: "Don't roll that stone away. Leave things as they are. The smell would be unbearable." Just as we so often say: "Let us not touch this or that issue; it might explode in our faces."

He said: "Roll that stone away!" and then he called him, "Lazarus," and commanded him, "come out!" And that dead man came out and started to live.

Jesus wants to do to us—to humankind—what he did to Lazarus.

Let us step out of the tomb. Let us take the bonds from our arms and legs, remove the stones from our eyes, take the cotton out of our ears and mouths, and let us live with him.

PASSION/PALM SUNDAY

24. Armed against Hope

Matthew 26:14–27:66

In the beginning, they are enthusiastic: "Hosanna, Son of David, alleluia, king, prophet." There are flowers, trumpet blasts, nervous animals, dancing children, cloaks, colors, royal purple.

In the end, he is hanging on the cross: "Away with him, get lost, impostor, fall dead, perish."

Gall, pain, sweat, spittle, the dark smell of blood on the earth, wailing, mourning, and he himself shouting: *"Lama, lama sabactani?"* ("My God, my God, why have you deserted me?")

What a radical change, from the flowers to the mud, from the headlines to a cold, humid cave.

How often has this story repeated itself in human history? Is it not, in a way, our very own story, the story of every country, every presidency, of the whole world? All the good intentions at the beginning, the new life, the fresh start, the first blessings, are often hemmed in by betrayal and sin, pride and greed, lust and ill-will.

He underwent it all. When they shouted alleluia, even some in his company said: "Tell them to be quiet." He underwent it all when he stood before his judges. He underwent it all when they pressed his last drop of courage, his last drop of blood, out of his body and he shouted: "My God, my God, why have you forsaken me?" But there was no help that time. He bent his head and died.

What happens to us, in a watered-down way, happened to him in a very strong way. What happens to us, in a diluted form, happened pure and raw to him. Trying to establish good, he was overrun by evil; trying to establish peace, he was overcome by violence.

His last blood started to dry up. A tomb was prepared in a hurry, borrowed from a friend, but who is a friend in such an hour?

Darkness set in, hope was lost, and there was only a rumor left at the end of the day. They told Pilate: "This liar said after three days, I will rise again."

They got some guards. This world armed itself against any return of hope.

It was in vain; he would return.

EASTER SUNDAY

25. Up Will Prevail

John 20:1–9

Very early in the morning, as soon as the sun came out and they dared to go outside, they hastened to the tomb.

The first ones who came were the women, those who had loved him so very much. They were loaded with linen, oil, and perfumes, because they came to bury him properly.

The men only came afterwards, when the news about the empty grave reached them. They were running very fast, as fast as they could. John, being the younger, overtook Peter, but, being the younger, he waited for Peter to enter the tomb. They all gazed into the tomb before entering it, full of hesitation. They were all surprised, very surprised.

The story is, of course, about what happened to Jesus, and yet when you read it, it is all about them.

First it happened to Mary; then it happened to the other women; then it happened to John and Peter; then to the others; and finally to Thomas. *They* believed; something happened to them.

Certainly, something had happened to Jesus. That is what we are celebrating today. No doubt, he rose from the dead. Yes, he overcame darkness and evil.

But the story is really about what happened to *them* when they saw the empty tomb, when he appeared to them, a first time, a second time, in the house where they met, outside at the lake, seeing him walking over the sea, eating bread and the fish he fried for them.

The story is about them: *They* believed.

That is how we should celebrate this feast. What happened to Jesus is, of course, the main thing. It is the beginning and the end, the foundation and the pinnacle. But what we are asked to celebrate is what overcame them and what should overcome us.

What did they believe? What do they believe who believe in the resurrection, who believe in Jesus?

Some days ago, I talked with a very old lady, though she would not like to be called old. She told me: "As you know, life has its ups and its downs. The older you become, the better you know: it is light and darkness, sun and shadow, sweet and bitter, good and evil, sickness and health, virtue and vice, progress and regress, falling and rising, life and death, Good Friday and Easter!"

This is all true, but what they started to believe—at that empty tomb, as they ran home, when they saw him—is that good will overcome, that death will disappear, that light will triumph, that up will prevail over down, the *up* of the resurrection over the *down* of the cross.

They were not only willing to believe, they were willing to live that belief in their lives, themselves risen from all death. Amen. Alleluia.

SECOND SUNDAY OF EASTER

26. The Thomas Test

John 20:19–31

You just heard the story of how Jesus' disciples sat together after his death and resurrection and suddenly he appeared in the midst of them. They were amazed. They could not believe their eyes. To prove that they might be right, they gave him a piece of fish—a normal piece of freshly fried fish—and he took it. He put it in his mouth, he chewed, he swallowed. They looked very carefully. The fish disappeared. It did not fall through; it was taken up. He was real. He was not a ghost, not a spirit, or an evil dream.

They were satisfied and believed their eyes.

Thomas came later. Enthusiastically, they informed him, but he did not believe. He must have thought the others had been dreaming, that their desire to see him made them see him, as a hungry man dreams of bread or a man in the desert sees the water he is longing for in his thirst. They told him about the fish; he laughed at their fish. He disqualified their test. He put forth his own norms, another test, a more realistic experiment. He said: Let him show me his hands, let him show me his side, let him show me his wounds. If he has the wounds, I will believe, but if there are no wounds, if there are no scars, then forget about him, forget about your fish.

A week later, he appeared again. This time, Thomas was with them. Was he an impostor? Was he a tramp, a conjuring trick, a projection, a ghost, or a spirit?

The others looked at Thomas. He rose and approached the appearance, and he said: "Please, Sir, may I see your hands? Please, Sir, may I see your feet? Please, Sir, may I see your side?"

He saw Jesus' hands, his feet, his side, the wounds, the scars, and he believed, leaving us a test, the Thomas Test, a test you measure your Christianity with.

If you say you are a Christian, I ask you: "Please, Sir, may I see your hands? Please, Madam, may I see your feet? May I see your side?" If you have the wounds and scars, because of your interest and thirst for justice, honesty, integrity, and everything he lived and died for, I will believe. Then, but only then, you will have passed the Thomas Test.

THIRD SUNDAY OF EASTER

27. Bread Broken

Luke 24:13–35

First, let's set the scene. Cleophas and his companion walked from Jerusalem to Emmaus. That companion must have been Cleophas's wife, otherwise another name would have been mentioned in the context.

According to some experts, Emmaus was not really a village. It was a group of barracks, barracks of the Roman occupational forces. The two, being Jews, must have been servants in these barracks.

They had taken a weekend off to go to Jerusalem to celebrate the Passover. It is obvious from the story that they had heard that Jesus had been received as a king in Jerusalem the week before Easter. It is also obvious from the story that Cleophas and his wife had great hopes that Jesus of Nazareth would manifest himself as the Messiah, changing their whole world. Maybe it had been that hope that made them ask for the Passover weekend off. They had hoped he would end their endless struggle for justice, that the old glory would be restored to Israel, and that bread would be shared.

Now they were on their way home, and nothing had happened. That is to say, nothing they had hoped would happen had taken place. He had been arrested, tortured, and crucified. Maybe they had even seen him hanging on the cross. *They even knew about the report that he had risen.* But what they had hoped for had not taken place. The Kingdom of God had not been restored.

Jesus joined them on the road. He asked them why they looked so depressed, so they told him their story. He explained to them what had happened. They listened, but did they hear? They heard, but did they grasp what they heard?

Arriving at their shelter, he said he wanted to go on. They told him that he should not do that, because the night was too dark, and since nothing had changed as yet in this world, there were dangers everywhere. He stayed, and then, dear friends, he took *their* bread. Though he was the guest and they the hosts, he took their *bread, and broke it*. He gave a piece to her, and he gave a piece to him. The sharing had started. Then he disappeared from their sight.

There they were, with that piece of bread in their hands. . . . Suddenly they understood, suddenly they saw: From now on, it was up to them.

They rose from their table—after all, this is a resurrection story—and they walked through the night, which now was not so dark, to Jerusalem, where the victory had started, carrying that bread in their hearts.

Draw your own conclusions. What are we supposed to do? We must get things together—our vision and our techniques—to be sure this world is changed into a place where bread is shared by all.

FOURTH SUNDAY OF EASTER

28. He Is the Open Door

John 10:1–10

Did you ever, as a child, or worse yet, as an adult, step out of your bed on the wrong side in the middle of the night?

It is a horrible experience, because you are completely disoriented. You are looking for the light switch, but it is not there. You are groping for the window, for the small stool next to your bed, for your shoes, for the door, but you can't find any of them. And you start to scream for that door: "The door. Where is the door?" Finally, someone hears you and comes to open that door and bring you some light.

By itself, the door would not be sufficient. You must be able to open it.

French philosopher Jean-Paul Sartre wrote a play about four people locked in one room. There is a door in that room, but it is closed, and the whole situation turns into sheer hell. You must have heard stories about caves that fell in, doors of meat lockers that closed behind somebody, car doors that would not open, and about the ensuing panic, hunger, and thirst, the isolation and desolation.

But it is not only physically that people can be locked and barred in. We can be barred in so many ways: by a sickness, a rule or regulation, a complex or trauma, our family and friends, a car and a house, or by what we own and what we believe. All those things can lock us up and in. We are hemmed in. We don't know what to do, how to escape. There is no exit, no gate, no door.

And then there is that man from Nazareth, who says: "I am the door." Another time, he said: "I have opened a door in front of you, a door nobody will be able to close."

For thirty years he had lived in Nazareth. Nobody knows what he did there, but most probably he did the usual things. But then he escaped, he was free, and he set others free, too.

The paralyzed man who came through the roof because the door was blocked was told: "Your sins are forgiven, your legs are unbound."

The leaders of the people did not like that.

Levi, the tax collector, who was sitting in his office with his money and his intrigues, was told: "Follow me!" and he stood up without counting the money and the cost, without even closing the door behind him.

The leaders of the people did not like that.

They were all fasting; he was not fasting. They were all sticking to an absolute Sabbath rule, but he healed on that day.

The leaders of the people did not like that, either. They preferred all doors closed.

So many in our world think, like those leaders in his time, that things are settled, that we are caught once and for all. So many think our situation is desperate, without an escape hatch, that we are shut in on ourselves. But he said: *"I am the door, I am the door,"* leading us from the restrictions of a world so familiar to us. Leading us into space, into God, into transcendence, but also into a Kingdom here on earth, into him who said: "I was hungry, and you gave me to eat; I was thirsty and you gave me to drink," in every sense of those words.

29. Resurrection and Soup

John 14:1–12

It's Easter time, and we are listening to resurrection stories. Today's second reading is an unexpected one, but a very useful one.

The reading from the Acts is about a scandal in the early Church, a scandal in the earliest days. It is a scandal of favoritism, nepotism, discrimination, the scandal that would be called brotherization in Africa, or *apartheid* in South Africa.

What happened?

It was in Jerusalem, a town of many widows who could not help themselves. They were poor. They must have been looking for a support group. They found one, the one offered by the new Christian community, a community interested in all. Everyone in that community believed that we have the same origin, the same Mother and Father in heaven.

That community had started a soup kitchen, and every afternoon the widows came to get their portion. During the first days, everything went well. Everybody was happy. But then some of the Hebrew widows started to profit from the fact that most of the community members were Hebrews. They asked to be helped first. They did not come to the line in front of the house anymore. They were helped first at the kitchen door, and they got the thickest and the best part of the soup, the vegetables, the barley, and the beef. What had started as a good thing, as a real manifestation of what the followers of Jesus Christ stood for, had turned into the opposite, a countersign. It had become a scandal. It was divisive. It not only sowed hatred, it broke peace and brought war. Complaints were heard. They grew louder and louder, and finally the apostles came together and decided to arrange a better division of labor by delegating some lay people to be responsible for this type of work. They appointed seven deacons, ordering them to be impartial in the distribution of the food.

I think by now everybody understands why this story was told in resurrection time.

Over there in Jerusalem, they had been caught in that very old and yet so contemporary trap of dividing humanity according to color, race, and tribe. A division that always leads to war and *death*.

They came out of it.

They rose from that death by remembering how Jesus had said we are brothers and sisters and by having his attitude toward all.

That is what they did, and so should we.

SIXTH SUNDAY OF EASTER

30. We Will Have Done It

John 14:15–21

There are some experiences we all have in common. They are the same whether we live in the United States, Japan, China, or East Africa. One of these experiences is growing up. We grew up ourselves, I hope. We helped others grow up, I expect. And we have seen others grow up, I am sure.

We know the techniques involved. We know the skills. We know what should be done. One example will do.

Up to a certain age our parents took us to school, then they decided we should be able to go on our own. I remember being brought to school. Then one day my mother said: "You are big now, I can't bring you to school my whole life. Go on your own. Tomorrow I won't bring you anymore."

I still recall how proud I was, but at the same time, I was nervous; I was both glad and afraid.

I went. When I reached the end of the street, just before going around the corner, I looked back, and I saw my mother looking through the curtain of a window. When she saw that I was looking, she withdrew. She did not want me to know that she, too, was proud and nervous, glad and afraid.

Jesus had been with them for so long. He had done so much for them. Every time they were hungry, there had been food. Every time they were thirsty, there had been fine wine. Every time they were sick, he had healed them. Every time they were in debt, he had bailed them out. True, he had been sending them out, but they had always been able to come back, to sit down at his feet, listen to his counsel, and profit from his presence. They were responsible persons, fathers and mothers, professionals, but in a way, they had become too dependent, like children or teenagers following their leader in all things.

He spoke to them, and he said: "A little while, and I will be with you no longer; a little while, and you will be alone; a little while, and you will be independent; a little while, and you will have to stand on your own feet, and no longer on mine."

When he saw their frightened faces and the growing despair in their eyes, he added: "But I won't leave you alone. Another helper will be given to you, a helper from within you, the Holy Spirit. She will help you in everything; she will help you from within; she will help you to do all I did for you, and even greater things."

He asked us to walk on our own in his direction. He asked us to do what he had told us to do in such a way that, in the end, we would be able to say: "*It is we who did it. With him, that is true, but it was we. . . .*"

ASCENSION DAY

31. They Lost Their Head

Matthew 28:16–20

While the disciples looked up, they lost their head, and their heads, too.

He became smaller and smaller. A cloud intervened, and he was gone.

God had been with them in Jesus. They had become intimate with him. He had taught them, fed them, paid their taxes, fried fish for them, he even washed their feet.

He had promised them a new heaven and new earth, a Kingdom to come, and off he went.

It was as if all the doors of heaven that had been opened over the last thirty-three years closed again. Curtains were drawn. Shutters rattled down. Lights went out. A foggy cloud appeared: It took all vision away. They lost their head, and losing their head, they lost their heads, too.

They were dazzled. They remained looking. They were paralyzed, petrified on the spot.

Two angels had to appear to get them on the move. They stumbled down the mountain and found their way to Jerusalem. They, the beginning of the Church, the beginning of Christ's body, with their worldwide mission, locked themselves up in an upper room. Upper rooms are always safer than ground-floor ones, and they did not know what to do. They had lost their head. Their head was in the clouds.

You know how a man with his head in the clouds reacts. He sits down on chairs that are not there, and he hurts himself. He waits for buses that do not arrive. He makes a sandwich and eats his paper napkin. He wets a stamp to put on his letter, then sticks it on the table.

A man with his head in the clouds is useless, hopeless. His body stumbles along, falls, gets lost.

Those disciples, the Church with its head in the clouds at the right hand of the Father, did not know what to do.

There were no signals, no communication, so they sat down and waited behind locked doors until the signals suddenly came through again and contact was restored. Restored to the extent that there were sparkles everywhere: light, fire, noise, breath, wind, storm, enthusiasm, and SPIRIT, his Spirit.

They rose. They entered into the life of this world.

SEVENTH SUNDAY OF EASTER

32. Scotosis

John 17:1–11

People who think themselves learned very often use very learned words. If you go to a doctor because something is wrong with your foot, he will look at that innocent member of your body, and your foot is all at once no longer simply your foot, but an item in his orthopedic language. And while you say and think: "My foot," he seems to speak and think about something totally different. While normal people speak to enlighten you, doctors seem to speak to mystify you, to put you in the dark.

We should not only blame our doctors for that. When you look around, you will find many instances where people have a love of the dark. Many people do not want to know.

There is the child who puts her fingers in her ears when something unpleasant is told her.

There is the man whom the doctor told not to drink alcohol anymore, who simply does not seem to have heard the doctor at all.

There are those who cannot hear anything wrong about their children.

There are those who simply refuse to see the world as the world is, who escape from the outer drama of our human life to the inner drama of their fantasies.

They have ears, Jesus said, but they do not hear. They have eyes, but they do not see. They have hands, but they do not feel. They have a nose, but they do not smell. They have a mouth, but they do not taste. Learned people have, of course, a learned word for this type of more or less voluntary darkness. They call it *scotosis*, from a Greek word *skotos*, which means darkness. The resulting dark spot is called *scotoma*.

The word *scotosis* is used to indicate an unwillingness to see, an unwillingness to learn.

Scotosis occurs when people who are overrich and overweight discuss the hunger and starvation of others.

Scotosis occurs when students discuss justice and equality while hating their teachers or ignoring their fellow students.

Scotosis occurs when church people like us discuss the Kingdom of God while forgetting that God is present to us in the poor and the sick.

Scotosis occurs when parents work for welfare programs and leave their children alone at home.

Scotosis occurred so very often around Jesus. *Peter* did not see, and told Jesus that he would not suffer. *James* and *John* did not see, so they asked him: Can't we be the bosses? *Thomas* did not see, even in the end, and he said: I don't believe. *Philip* did not see and asked: Where is the Father? The *Sadducees* did not see, the *Pharisees* did not see, the *Herodians* did not see, his *own family* did not see. It is as if nobody saw.

In the reading for today, Jesus prays to the Father. He speaks to his Father, but what he says is also meant for his disciples. He prays: "Father, now at last they know. I have given them the teaching you gave to me, and they have truly accepted it."

That is what Jesus said about them. Their scotosis was over. Would he be able to say the same of us? Are we prepared to know the full truth? Are we prepared to understand our real situation? Are we willing to be informed? Are we ready to encounter ourselves?

When he left them after his ascension, they went back to Jerusalem, a short distance away. They went to the upper room, where they had been listening to his words. They joined in continuous prayer, waiting for the Spirit, waiting for insight, waiting for truth, hoping to be healed of all their remaining blind spots, or as a doctor would say, hoping to be healed once and for all of *scotosis*.

PENTECOST SUNDAY

33. The Spirit We Received

John 20:19–23

The feast of Pentecost, the feast of the sending of the Holy Spirit, is in a sense the only feast of the liturgical year that is really ours. The other feasts are all about what happened to others: Jesus' conception, birth, baptism, life, transfiguration, death, resurrection, and ascension; what happened to Mary, Joseph, the Apostles, and all the saints.

Today we celebrate a mystery that happened to us, to his followers. At least that is the intention of this feast. We can still act as if it is all only about others.

A theologian who understood that danger very well was Lutheran minister Soren Kierkegaard. He held that most Christians are not Christians at all. They only talk about it. When the bishop of his diocese of Copenhagen died, and everybody in the press spoke in glowing terms of this great Christian, Kierkegaard noted in his diary something like this: "He is dead now. And as he has been responsible for a very long period, it would have been desirable that one would have been able to convince him to end his life by giving in to Jesus

Christ, and to admit that what he represented among us was not Christianity but a compromise.''

Kierkegaard explained what he meant in his sermon about the geese. He compared his fellow Christians to domesticated geese. Those geese are always talking about flying: ''We have wings, we never use our wings, we should use them, let us fly!'' But nobody ever flies. On Sundays a big goose stands a bit higher than other ones on a pulpit, and he, too, every Sunday, exhorts the others, in the most beautiful words, to fly. But nobody does fly, and if one would start to fly, the preacher would be the first one to shout: ''Come down immediately!''

Pentecost is our feast.

It is the feast of our takeoff with the Spirit.

With that Spirit, we have to fly in all directions.

That is another difficulty: that variety in the Spirit.

She was given at different times: the third day, the fiftieth day, and every day since.

She was given in different ways: she blew over them, fire descended on them, and they got her in noise, light, and smoke.

She was given in different gifts: in the gift of peacemaking, forgiving, speaking in tongues, healing, administering, dancing, singing, playing, and praising the Lord.

The diversity is so great and the consequential difficulties so alarming, that even while we are celebrating all this today, Paul is quoted from his letter to Corinth, where Jesus' followers threatened to split up because they were all flying in different directions. Yet those in Corinth were at least flying. It is to those fliers that Paul wrote: ''There is a variety of different gifts, but always to the same Spirit. There are all sorts of services, but always to the same Lord. There are all kinds of ways, but it is the same God who is working in all.''

Let us belong to those who fly on the wind of that Spirit, and let us fly together into the dawn of the Kingdom to come.

TRINITY SUNDAY

34. Empowerment

John 3:16–18

A preacher is often tempted, especially on a day like this, when the theme is Trinity, to try to say it all, to try to say too much.

To say it all is impossible. To try to say too much is—at the end, sometimes for the second half, and in certain cases from the very beginning—boring.

So I will say only a little, giving, I hope, some idea, some inspiration that might be useful on the occasion of this celebration. Something that is neither a mere repetition of things we have heard over and over before, nor that is completely new and therefore unrecognizable. Something that helps us along, that helps us forward. An idea that makes us shift a bit in what we believe, what we hope, and what we love. A small modulation that, nevertheless, will help us all find some new enthusiasm and help all those around us, too.

That is why I would like to see us believe in the Trinity in a new kind of way, in a new light, so that even his command to go, teach, and baptize in the name of the Father, and the Son, and the Holy Spirit, might light up again in us with a new brightness.

Let me start with an experience that is very significant for me. I had this experience in Africa. Confronted with an alien Western culture, many felt powerless, frustrated, and diminished; they felt like nobody, unimportant and useless.

You can have people feeling like that right here, in this city, in this country. I am sure of that. I heard them. I saw them. I met them, and I smelled them.

At one time or another, all of us can be struck by that type of feeling when we read of the developments around us.

It is rather obvious from the reports of him that when God's Son, Jesus Christ, moved through this time and space, he had the same kind of experience. Day and night, he was surrounded by people who were blind, deaf, paralyzed, mute, and afraid. People who, in their own eyes, could hardly do anything at all, who were paralyzed like flies in the web of intriguing spiders, cocooned by political and religious ropes, strings, straps, shackles, fetters, and manacles.

You know what the Son of God and the Son of Man did to them. He always did the same: The blind saw, the deaf heard, the paralyzed walked, the mute spoke, those who were afraid got courage, and those who had been hardly anything at all in their own eyes were liberated and became prime movers in the history of salvation that he started among us.

They said: "There are no fish, what are we to do?" He said: "There are fish. You, throw out your net. I will make you a fisher of men."

They said: "There is no bread. What are we going to give them to eat?"

He said: "You divide what you have. There is plenty for all."

They said: "We cannot pray." He said: "Start praying like this: Our Father. . . ." And they who had thought that they could not pray, did pray.

In modern America, a word is used to indicate the strategy he applied: *empower*. He empowered them.

That is what he asked his disciples to do when he sent them out, saying: Baptize them in the power they have, the power of their origin, created by the Father; the power of their kinship, blood-related to Jesus Christ the Son; the power of the Holy Spirit in them.

That is the reality I would like us to meditate upon, hoping that it may cause in us, in our hearts and in our minds, that little shift that might make all the difference in our lives and in what we believe to be our mission in his name.

Do we feel empowered by him, in the name of the Father, the Son, and the Holy Spirit?

Are we, because of that empowerment, living and acting in such a way that those around us, maybe blind, deaf, dumb, and frustrated in their own eyes, are empowered, too?

35. First Cast Out, Then Cure

Matthew 9:36–10:8

The gospel of Matthew is often called the gospel of our mission. No gospel is so outspoken about what we should do as his. In the gospel of the tenth Sunday of the year, we heard how Matthew was called: "Come," and sent: "Follow me."

Today the group is larger. They are twelve, Matthew being one of them, and they receive power to cast out and to cure.

They were sent out not because Jesus wanted them to be *rich*. On the contrary, he told them: "Give without charge," because we all received without being charged.

They were sent out not because Jesus wanted them to *profit* from this world as much as possible. On the contrary, he told them not to take anything with them.

They were sent out not because Jesus wanted them to *rule* the world, but to serve it.

He sent them out because he felt sorry for the *crowds*, who were (and are) without help and lost, sick and diseased, harassed and dejected, terrified and frustrated.

He sent them out, and he gave them power to cast out unclean spirits and to cure, in that order: First, *cast out*, second, *cure*.

He did not ask them to organize a social-assistance organization to cure the sicknesses, hunger, thirst, diseases, and the other miseries caused by the gap between the rich and the poor.

He asked them first to reorganize all of society by chasing from it the evil of that gap. He wanted a society in which there are no masters and no servants, a society in which all use their talents to the full in view of that society, and in which all receive all they need, without having to ask for it. He wanted a society in which the human family is sitting around *one table*, and there is no first one, no second one, and no third one. A society in which the youngest, the child, is the center of all human interest.

He did not ask them to only organize a hospital-type service curing the effects of malnutrition, kwashiorkor, and tuberculosis. He asked them first of all to organize things in such a way that the evil spirit of irrational greed would be chased off.

He did not ask them to organize a clinic to heal venereal diseases, gonorrhea, and syphilis. He asked them to cast out the promiscuity that causes those evil ills.

First: cast out; second: cure.

He not only told them what to do, he told them where to start. He said: "Don't go to Samaria now; that will come later. Do not go to non-Jewish countries, do not go to Greece, do not go to Rome."

Scholars give us all sorts of biblical reasons to explain why he restricted himself and his disciples to his own people.

There might be a simple psychological reason. We all have the tendency to project evil outside our life and society. When those disciples heard they were going to cast out evil spirits, they, too, must have reasoned like that: "The devil? Where is the devil? Not with us. He is in Samaria, he is in the Decapolis, he is outside."

He told them: "Start at home, start among your own people. They are in need, they are harassed, they are dejected, they are oppressed, they do not know where to turn next. Start with them, casting out and curing."

Before Matthew's gospel ends, however, those same twelve are sent "to all peoples everywhere," and he added that he would be with them to the ends of the earth, and to the end of the age, casting out evil and sin and also curing their effects.

TWELFTH SUNDAY OF THE YEAR

36. In the Presence of the People

Matthew 10:26–33

The gospel for today is rather mysterious. It is about not being afraid. It is about things that are covered up now, but that will be in the open tomorrow. It is about light in the dark. It is about rumors and secret information. It is about those who kill and torture and imprison, but who cannot kill the spirit. It is about birds that fall from the sky but do not go unaccounted for. It is about the registration and administration of the number of hairs on our heads.

It is about all that, but it seems really to be about how to witness to him, Jesus Christ, in this world, *in the presence of people.*

Jesus promises that if we give witness to him in the presence of people, he will then witness to us with his Father in heaven.

Sometimes I have the impression that we Christians do not take those words of his seriously. Sometimes I have the impression that we are not willing to accept his list of priorities. We stick to our list, and our list is different.

He who healed said: "Give witness to me in this world," and some Christians seem to draw the conclusion that they only have to go church on Sunday to give proof of their belief in God.

He who fed the hungry said: "Give witness to me in the presence of people," and some Christians seem to draw the conclusion that they only have to go to prayer meetings or sermon-jam sessions.

He said: "Love one another," and some Christians seem to draw the conclusion that they should stand up in charismatic meetings to witness or contribute conspicuously to church-building meetings. They listen to the "epilogue" in the evening, and the "lift up your heart" in the morning, and the "daily service" every day.

Is that the witnessing he came to ask from us?

Did he come asking us to build churches in honor of him? He who did not even want to own his own house in this world, and who said very happily that he could not even call one stone his own in this world?

He who said to his disciples, while they were admiring the temple in Jerusalem, that he was going to destroy that temple? He who told that woman in Samaria that God was no longer to be worshiped on mountaintops or in temples, but in spirit and truth?

Did he come to give us an opportunity to organize church choirs or guitar-playing gospel groups?

He who told them that those who only shout: LORD, LORD, will not enter the kingdom, but that those will enter who *do* the will of the Father here in this world, leaving no doubt about that will?

He was not against praying; he even told us how to pray. He told us to call God *Father*, implying that we cannot reach him in our prayers if we are not first willing to relate to one another, as sisters and brothers with equal rights.

It is so easy to say "Father" to God and forget the family-of-God spirit he wanted.

Witnessing to Jesus in the presence of people is witnessing to that sister- and brotherhood.

He gave us a test.

When they asked him where we should start, he took in that world of ours, in which one-third of the children are sick and underfed as children, and he put that child in the center of their circle. He said: "This is your test. If you scandalize such a child by refusing to take care of it, God is not going to accept you, either."

He gave us a criterion.

On the last evening of his earthly life, he said to his disciples: "I am going, but if you want to commemorate me, if you want to witness to me, do this, as I do it now." And he broke his bread. He broke it and handed it around. He took his cup, and they all drank themselves into the same body.

That is the witnessing he asks from us: Everything is contained in that test and that criterion.

It is not singing "Alleluia, alleluia, amen, amen," that is going to save us and this world.

Salvation is in the breaking of the bread and the sharing of the cup: In the breaking of *my* bread, and the sharing of *my* cup. While doing that, we participate in the sacrifice he brought to save us all, and while doing that, we really should sing, "Alleluia, alleluia, amen, amen. We are saved through him."

THIRTEENTH SUNDAY OF THE YEAR

37. On Welcoming Jesus

Matthew 10:37–42

Being a lifelong refugee, the possibility of being unwelcome and not being received must have preoccupied Jesus' personality all his days.

It started in that very dark night when all were asleep, including Jesus, Mary, and Joseph, but not including King Herod, his suspect advisers, and his politicking cronies. They had heard about a newborn King, and that rumor made them fear for their rank, position, power, wealth, and reign. They decided, there and then, because of a star and the tale of some wise old men, to kill. They even decided to give themselves a very wide and secure margin, and they told one another: Let us kill all those under the age of two. Orders were passed on that very night. Officers were called out of their beds, and soldiers were informed very early in the morning that they had to swoop down and murder all the babies in and around Bethlehem, babies who at that moment were still innocently sucking their thumbs or the nipples of their mothers' breasts.

In the dark of that very same night, an angel appeared, this time not to give a message of light or hope or bring a morsel of heaven to earth. This time the angel did not refer to God or heaven, but to the chaos and disorder in this world. The angel said to Joseph: "Take up your child, wake up its mother, pack, and disappear to Egypt. They are looking for you, your wife, and the child. Move quickly. Travel in the dark only. Avoid any roadblocks. Quick!"

Joseph got up and woke Mary, and they decided to let the child sleep while they were packing their things, trying to decide what they would need and what they could leave behind. Finally, when everything was packed, they woke up the child, who looked for his mother's breast. In the middle of the night, they started the flight that would never again bring them back to their home in Bethlehem.

That story, that warning, that packing, that flight in the night, that fear, has been repeated so often since then, even in our days. It happens for all kinds of reasons: for reasons of color and race, tribe and religion, blood and land, ideology and justice, politics and history.

In the case of Jesus, all this was permanent, a lasting factor in his life. Even later, they would live in Nazareth, the small up-country hideout, though they wanted to return to their home in Bethlehem. But while they were on their way there, the angel appeared again to warn them, and they lived as exiles, as refugees, from then on in Nazareth, far from anywhere.

Even when he left Nazareth thirty years later, he remained like that. Who was willing—really willing—to take him in as a guest, not only for a day or two, but on a more permanent basis? Was he not always a security risk for his hosts? Did the police and the secret service, the security and the temple not always come, after a day or two?

It is often said in the gospels that he went into hiding in the mountains, in the forests, on the lake, in caves, in the desert.

Why did they want to kill him? Why did Herod try to destroy him, nipping him in the bud of his life? Why did he have to flee? Why did he have to hide? Why was he never safe? Why was he sold? Why was he bought? Why did he have to complain to the end of his life that he never found the rest of his own home?

It was always the same reason: Others saw him as a threat to their position, their wealth, their power plays, their greed, their type of life. They did not like the type of life and service he was talking about.

They did not like the type of togetherness, the type of community he wanted to start.

They did not like the type of sharing, the type of companionship he represented, and that is why they wanted him dead, once and for all.

If you come to think about those dynamics that caused his death, don't all those things lurk and hide in us, too?

It is our own lack of liberty, our lack of freedom, our lack of detachment about *our* possessions, *our* positions, *our* influence, power, and *our*selves that make us chase him away. We make Jesus a refugee, a chased and hunted person in our *world*.

"Those who welcome me, welcome the one who sent me!"

FOURTEENTH SUNDAY OF THE YEAR

38. His Burden Is Light

Matthew 11:25–30

Jesus speaks about a yoke in today's text. A yoke is a kind of stick that you put over your shoulders to carry a burden, or to carry two burdens, one on each side. Since hardly anyone uses a yoke anymore, it might be easier and more practical to stick to the second expression Jesus uses: burden.

Everybody knows what a burden is. All over the roads of Kenya, people are carrying burdens: food, wood, water, and their belongings.

Jesus says: "Take *my* burden, take the burden *I* want you to carry, because that burden is light and easy."

Jesus speaks about "my yoke" and "my burden," suggesting that there are other yokes and burdens we should (according to him) not carry. He explained what those burdens are in the gospel.

Jesus accused the priests and the Pharisees, the scribes and the "church" of his time of having put burdens on the people that should not be there—burdens that oppressed.

Did you know that according to their regulations, a Jew was not allowed to whisk away a fly that landed on his nose or his bald head during a Sabbath day? He had to wait until that fly finished its affairs—whatever those affairs were—and flew off. Those regulations even forbade Jesus to take the lameness away from a man on the Sabbath. Jesus said: "Throw that burden away, it is no good. Take my burden: love!"

Jesus accused the political powers of his time of having put the burden of submissiveness on the people. "You know"—and they all knew, since they all suffered under the same colonial power—"that your political leaders rule over you, calling themselves your masters. Throw that burden away, that is not how it should be with you. Nobody should be a master among you, weighing on the shoulders of others."

Jesus spoke not only about the yokes and burdens others put on our shoulders. He also spoke about the burdens and yokes we put on our own shoulders, on the shoulders of our terrorized and tired bodies.

When that rich young man comes to him, stepping out of his brand-new chariot or down from his beautifully groomed horse to ask: "What should I do?" Jesus likes him at first sight. He answers: "Take that burden of your wealth from your shoulders, sell everything you have, start another life, a new life; my burden is easy." We carry so many unnecessary burdens. We think we should drive a big, inconvenient, gas-guzzling car. When we are small, we think we should have a beautiful watch, even if we don't know how to tell time yet.

Do you know Samson Mwangi, a little boy who asked for a watch? He asked in the morning, in the afternoon, in the evening, and even in his dreams. Finally he got one, a beautiful one. He put it on his wrist and thought that he was very happy, and he showed his watch to everybody.

But then he walked through the street with his very fancy watch, and a big boy came up to him and tried to steal the watch. Mwangi had to run, and he didn't dare walk through the streets anymore, so he stayed home. Mwangi liked to play football, but now he couldn't because he was afraid his watch might fall on the ground. What a burden that watch became!

Things can become burdens in other ways, too. Advertisements burden us to eat a certain cereal at breakfast, even though it tastes like overcooked old newspapers. Advertisements burden us to buy very high, dangerous, and expensive platform shoes and other useless things like that.

They force on us the burden of being "with it." With what? Of being "in." In what?

Some of us have our diaries full of appointments. Others work late at night. Others labor so much that they are never at home. Their children do not recognize them anymore and ask during breakfast, "Who is that man over there?"

Jesus says: "Throw it off. Do not be burdened like that, religiously, politically, consumer-wise, and economically. Get free. Follow me!"

Saint Paul, in today's first reading, wrote: "There is no necessity for us, to obey our unspiritual selves; if you do that, if you burden yourself with all those things, you are going to be worried stiff, you are going to be overworked, you are going to end, you are going to die; put an end to all the strain you put on your body, eating wrongly, drinking wrongly, worrying wrongly, smoking wrongly, working wrongly. Shake off those burdens; *be merciful to your body*, and you will live." Jesus said: "Take my yoke, carry my burden: it is light, healthy, and joyful."

FIFTEENTH SUNDAY OF THE YEAR

39. Lost Alongside the Road

Matthew 13:1–23

The gospel for today is a complaint. It is a serious complaint, directed to us: God's word often falls dead on its soil. It is trampled, it is drying up, it is drowned, it does not grow.

The signs God gives in our lives remain unseen, unheard, unfelt, untouched, and powerless.

I am sure that some sign you wanted to give to another person has been lost along the way.

A young man had a misunderstanding with his girlfriend—a very serious misunderstanding. He was upset about it, because it spoiled their relationship entirely, and he liked her very much.

He tried to talk to her, but that did not work. He tried to phone her, but when he heard her voice, he did not know what to say, and he had to hang up. He tried to write a letter, but when he finished, he tore his letter up because he thought it sounded silly.

Then he remembered that she liked roses, dark red roses. He bought her a rose—only one, because roses were very expensive that time of the year. The man in the flower shop put some ferns with the rose and wrapped it in nice, thin paper.

The young man went to her apartment and put the rose down in front of her door at the time he knew she would come home. He then hid around the corner, behind some trash cans.

Then she came, as lovely as ever. His heart bounced in his throat, his mouth suddenly got dry, very dry.

She opened her purse and took out her key. She opened the door and stepped inside without having noticed his beautiful, expensive rose at all.

What a disappointment, what a horror, what a tragedy, what a missed chance.

It is in those terms that God, that John, speaks to us.

God gives us signs day after day, trying to get our attention: a flower, a thought, a dream, a child, a person, a fine feeling, sometimes even pain.

How often do we notice? How often do we stop and say: "Hello, thank you, my God"?

We live as those who have eyes and see not; as those who have ears and hear not; not only as far as God is concerned, but even as far as the people around us are concerned.

Isn't God trying to speak to us through others? Isn't that what God tried to do through Jesus?

SIXTEENTH SUNDAY OF THE YEAR

40. Letting Grow

Matthew 13:24–43

The disciples around him thought they knew all about good and evil, blessings and curses, virtue and vice, wheat and weeds; but, as far as we know, not even one of them was a farmer.

Most of them were fishermen who pulled in their nets and immediately sorted their catch. The good fish, the edible, marketable ones, go *here*, and the bad ones, the unedible and poisonous ones, go *there*.

"Lord," they said, "Lord, can't you destroy evil? Can't you do away with the bad once and for all, like we do on the beach, so only goodness and sweetness are left?"

He was not a farmer, either, but his heavenly Father was, as he himself had said. He knew about a field. He knew about his Father's field called the world, and he said: "You can't do that. You can't use fishermen's tactics in the fields of this world. If you did that, if you tried to separate the good and the bad like that, you would spoil it all. The two are so closely intertwined in their roots that pulling up one means pulling up the other. Let them both grow, trusting in God. Didn't the Father sow the seed that is good? Was it not the devil who sowed the seed that is bad? Goodness will win, light will conquer darkness. Don't be afraid!"

Today he is again surrounded by disciples who think they know very well what is good and what is bad, what is just and what is unjust, what is weed and what is wheat.

There is nothing wrong in that. On the contrary, we wish everyone knew it as well as they do.

Demonstrations, protest marches, sit-ins, and strikes galore.

But again, they seem to be like those fishermen who say: "Can't we throw the good ones *here* and the bad ones *there*?"

They forget that as in a field (didn't he call us God's acre?) goodness and badness, justice and injustice, blessing and curse, are so radically intertwined in us as persons that rooting up one makes the rest fall.

He said: "Don't do that. Let them both grow, but do take care that goodness wins. I am all for that until the end."

SEVENTEENTH SUNDAY OF THE YEAR

41. The Kingdom Is Human Life

Matthew 13:44–52

That mysterious Kingdom of his must have always been on his mind. In the New Testament there are almost one hundred fifty references to that Kingdom, and the more Jesus speaks about it, the more wrapped in clouds it seems to be. In today's text, he calls it a hidden treasure, a box full of golden coins hidden somewhere in the field. He calls it a precious pearl, a jewel found by a businessman who sells everything he has to buy it. He called it a fishing net full of fish, good ones and bad ones. Before, he called it leaven and light, salt and seed, a ripe harvest, a royal feast, a great banquet, an enormous party, a wedding feast.

All this is nice, very nice, but somewhere the question remains: What is that Kingdom of God here on earth?

Some think it is the actual world. Some think it is still to come. Some think it is heaven. Some think it is an ideal political order. Some think it is exclusively God's business, and that we only have to wait. Some think it is the Church. Some even think it is the town of Jerusalem. What is that Kingdom of God? When did it start? Where did it start? How did it start?

In the beginning, God divided the light from the dark. *Was the light the Kingdom of God?* God then divided the land from the water. *Was the land the Kingdom of God?* God then made the earth grow with weeds, climbers and creepers, bushes and trees. *Were those plants the Kingdom of God?* God made the seas and the oceans and the lakes crawl with fish. *Were those fish the Kingdom of God?* God covered the earth with animals of all kinds, he filled the air and the sky with insects and birds. *Were those animals the Kingdom of God?*

And then God made man and woman, you and me. He took the face of that woman, the face of that man, in between his hands, bent their faces backwards, blew spirit in the noses of the two, and said: "Live, you woman, live, you man, as I live. Rule over the world in such a way that you prosper. Rule over the earth in such a way that you may be well and joyful, and give life, your life and my life, to your children forever and ever."

That is the Kingdom of God here on earth: *human life.*

God's Kingdom is nothing else but God's will: Thy Kingdom come, thy will be done. God's will is nothing else but the well-being of people. Nothing else.

That is one way to explain that the Kingdom of God here on earth is human life.

There is a second way.

The people around Jesus recognized Jesus as the Son of God. Why, and how? I think they recognized him as God's Son because they discovered in him that very same exclusive interest in that divine issue: *the well-being of the people.*

Jesus always gave life. He seemed, in fact, interested only in that. When he met a deaf man, he said: "Stop being deaf. It is no good. Hear." When he met a blind man, he said: "Stop being blind. It is no good. See." When he met a paralyzed person, he said: "Don't be lame. It is no good. Jump." When he met a speechless person, he said: "Don't be dumb. It is no good. Speak." When he met a bleeding woman, he said: "Stop bleeding. It is no life. Get a child."

When he met that dead boy in Nain, the dead girl in Jairus's home, his dead friend Lazarus, he said: "Don't remain like that. Get out of your stupor. Live." They all stood up and danced with joy, because of their regained lives. Alleluia.

He gave life, he restored life, he repaired life, he stimulated life, he tuned it up, he recommended it.

He did not just do that in the physical or bodily sense. He also went to people who were spiritually blocked or psychologically frustrated. He identified himself with the poor, the wretched, the prostitutes, the adulterers, the widows, the orphans, the street boys, the aged, the crooks, and the vagrants.

He unbound and loosened Zaccheus, a greedy, mean man, so that very mean man, who only thought in terms of money, changed completely and became very generous, as God is very generous.

God gave life in the beginning, good human life everywhere. That is exactly what Jesus did from the moment he started. That is why they said: "He, he must be *the son of God*, because he is only interested in people's well-being, the Kingdom of God."

That is the second way to explain that the Kingdom of God here on earth is human life.

There is a third way.

Last week in Nairobi, representatives of all the bishops of Africa met. There were cardinals in red, bishops in purple, priests in black and white, and all kinds of other colors. They discussed the problems of this continent of Africa, of their countries, and of the world. What did Christians expect from those leaders who represent Jesus Christ on earth?

Did we expect a new hymnal? Of course not. Did we expect a new liturgical dress? No. Did we expect an organizational reorganization? We did not.

We Christians expected from them—because they are what they are—statements and, even more, initiatives on greater human justice, greater social equality, daily bread for all, the defense of human rights, the destruction of all weapons and wars that kill, a better family life, the plight of the refugees, and on other such *life* issues.

We expected this of them because they should have the interests of God and Jesus Christ at heart. We expected this because they should foster the Kingdom of God here on earth: a healthy human life for all, greater attention to that only gift God really gave to humankind, *life*.

But, sister and brother, we should not only judge them on what they say and do, or did not say and did not do, in the light of that Kingdom of God issue.

We should judge ourselves, too, in that very same light. Do we contribute in our work, in our decisions, in our education, and in all our activities, to human well-being? Or are we like Zaccheus before he met Jesus and before he started to live?

Let us invest in that Kingdom of God. It is the only investment that will last. It is guaranteed by God himself, who after the death and resurrection of his Son Jesus Christ, invested his own *Spirit* in our *common human life*.

EIGHTEENTH SUNDAY OF THE YEAR

42. To Be a Sacrament

Matthew 14:13–21

Everyone knows that time is very tricky. On our watches and clocks, every hour is an hour, every minute is a minute, and every second is a second. But that is only on watches, clocks, and the radio's time signal. When no mechanical spring or electronic gadget interferes in our counting of time and its duration, time is not like that at all. When you are suffering with terrible pain in the dentist's waiting room, when you are looking for a runaway child, when you are speeding a sick person you love to the hospital, when you are bored or very annoyed, then one minute, one second, one split second can last for hours, for days. Then time is everlasting.

But when the party is on and the music plays, the trumpets blow your inner feelings from your bowels, your partner is in your arms, all goes well, the mood is high, and you could dance all night, those many, many hours are like only one second, one minute.

That's how it must have felt for him and the crowd that afternoon. They had not been dancing, drinking, or eating; they had completely forgotten about all that. There were no drums, trumpets, or guitars. There had only been *him* and his voice, teaching—nobody knew how—the thousands and thousands.

He had talked, and talked, and talked. Even the children had become silent, gazing at him from the breasts of their mothers with their small, dark eyes, a thumb, or even three fingers, firmly planted in their mouths.

He had been talking about himself, about his reactions, his emotions. He had been talking about them, too. He had revealed their possibilities to them, their potentialities, their humanity, their dignity, their origin, and their destiny.

First they had been surprised, then they had become excited, and now they were captivated, understanding that more than a mere human being was talking to them.

They wondered about his authority. They wondered about his origin. They wondered about his destiny. And when they felt the life they had received from God stimulated and inspired within themselves, they knew and understood: In Jesus, God spoke to them.

The sun had not stopped to listen that day; it had run its course. The shadows had become longer and longer. Those shadows had almost fallen away in the growing twilight before the crowd woke up from its rapture and noticed how time had slipped by—as the text reads—*unnoticed*. They had to walk home with all their children, and they were hungry, very hungry, because listening, especially intense listening, eats your energy away.

He told them not to worry, but to sit down. They brought him some bread, and others brought some fish, and they started to divide up the food, handing it to the ones in the back, as he asked them to do. The bread kept coming, and so did the fish. There must have been plenty to drink, also.

Now they saw it even more clearly than while he was talking: Through him, God's generosity, God's self as the life-giver, the life-sustainer, broke into their lives.

They went home that night well-fed bodily and satisfied spiritually, singing and laughing all the way.

One of the things he must have told them that afternoon was that he should be a model for them. He had come to show them their own nature, their own content, their own deepest personality.

They realized that afternoon, better than ever before—or maybe for the very first time in their lives—that they should be sacraments of God's presence among themselves.

You know what a sacrament is: It is a sign that signifies and gives life. You know that many say there are seven. That is both true and untrue, because through those seven—through baptism and confirmation, through penance and communion, through marriage, orders, and the anointing of the sick—we ourselves should become, or are supposed to become, as he was: *a sacrament of real life* to ourselves and others.

That afternoon in the heat of the sun by the lakeshore, while they were all wondering about the disappearance and murder of John, God broke through *him* into their lives through his words and deeds. Sister, brother, how often did God break through you into the life of yourself, into the lives of others?

Are we like *he* was and is, a sign to others signifying and giving God's life, God's love, God's generosity to them? Are you?

NINETEENTH SUNDAY OF THE YEAR

43. Caught

Matthew 14:22–33

Peter was fishing. He sat in his boat. He felt safe. He knew his job. He caught his fish. He had his friends. He took care of his wife. He educated his children. He was not well-off, but he was not badly off, either. He had no hopes beyond the normal ones. He thought that nothing would happen to him that had not happened to his ancestors and his friends.

Then he met Jesus. It was as if he was bewitched, as if a spell had been cast over him. He did things he never thought he would do.

He left his boat. He left his wife. He left his children. In a way, he left his own life. In the gospel of today, he even steps out of his boat, straight into the sea. All the others must have thought him dangerously mad when they saw him go. Who had ever seen a thing like that?

But he went. He knew all along that he was not mad. From time to time, he had that strange feeling so many of us have, a feeling that the life we live is not the one we should be living, that the way we are is not the way we should be. We feel there is more to us than just that.

Very many of us know this—maybe all of us. Otherwise, how would you be able to explain our constant interest in Jesus?

In the year 1979, one-third of all the books in the United States were on him. The real best-selling books are never mentioned in the official lists in *Time* or the *New York Times Book Review*. It would be too monotonous, because the best-selling books are always on Jesus.

Peter was caught by Jesus, just as we are caught by him.

Peter stepped—in the name of Jesus—out of his boat onto the troubled waters of this world, just as we are prepared to step onto the troubled waters of our time.

When Peter suddenly felt the force of the wind, he took fright, he lost courage, and he sank deeper and deeper into the dark blue, treacherous, endless sea.

How often we feel like Peter: discouraged, disappointed, frustrated.

We hoped for a change, but it all remained the same. We hoped for a fire, but the evil was not burnt. We hoped for a storm, but the bad was not uprooted. We hoped for a flood, but sin was not washed away.

What did we get? Nothing, and like Peter, we took fright, we lost courage, and we are sinking deeper and deeper into the dark blue, treacherous, endless sea.

Elijah was like that. He was God's prophet, he had been very powerful, but now the king wanted to murder him, so he gave up. He lost hope. He went to hide in a cave. He, too, had hoped for a change, a violent one. He got that change—a terrible earthquake changed the face of the earth. He, too, had hoped for a storm. He got that storm—it uprooted all and everything. He, too, had hoped for a fire. He got that fire—it burned down all that was left. But God was not at work in the quake, in the fire, in the storm.

And then there came that gentle breeze, and Elijah understood. He covered his face with his cloak: *God was at work.*

Just as Peter, in the midst of the storm's violence, heard Jesus' gentle reproach: "Man of little faith, why did you doubt?" and was held by *him.*

Men and women of little faith, why did you doubt? Aren't we kept by him while overcoming the wind and the storm, the force of the troubled water, and the panic in our hearts, because of that gentle word from him?

TWENTIETH SUNDAY OF THE YEAR

44. He and Fascism

Matthew 15:21–28

You know what Fascism is. The word comes from the Latin *fascis,* which means a small bundle. It indicated a small bundle of sticks or arrows that was carried in front of Roman officers. The number of arrows indicated their rank and their importance, and their importance depended, of course, on the number of men they had power over. Nowadays we indicate those ranks, numbers, and powers with stars and stripes. The word *Fascism* stands for any attitude where a group of people isolates itself from the rest and discriminates against all others.

Fascism is the root cause of almost all the trouble in this world: racism, tribalism, nepotism, apartheid, and even national socialism, whereby one state organizes its welfare as if it consists of the only group of human beings in the world.

It is with that sinful situation that the gospel of today confronts Jesus, and the confrontation is a hard one. Jesus even uses the word *dog,* so common in Fascist jargon.

What happened? Jesus had left Galilee for a non-Jewish region around the towns of Tyre and Sidon. According to Mark, he wanted to be alone with his disciples. Suddenly a woman who had an uncontrollable daughter at home sees him. She recognizes him, and she starts to shout. "Sir," she said, then added, "Son of David." It might be that this addition upset Jesus even more than the fact that he had been discovered and his holiday was over.

Just look at the situation. He was in a foreign country and a stranger, a non-Jew, addressed him by the name of his people. She shouted: "Hey, Jew!"

If I were walking down a street and someone called behind me: "Hey, *mzungu*; hey, white man!" I would be upset, too. And if you walked in a strange region and they shouted behind you: "Hey, *Luo*," or "Hey, *Kikuyu!*" I am sure you would not like that, either.

Jesus did what I would do, what you would do. He did not react to a shout like that. He walked on. It is, in a way, degrading to be identified like that. Jesus did not react. He just walked on, trying to get rid of her. She continued following him, and the situation became positively embarrassing, so the disciples said: "Please, do something about her. Give her what she wants, so she will stop shouting behind us like that."

He told them: "I was only sent for the Jews," as if he wanted to say: "She calls me a Jew, so why should I worry about a non-Jew?"

Jesus, however, did stop. She came to him, and falling at his feet, she changed her tone and said: "Lord, please, help me!"

He then said those words that are almost unbelievable, coming from his mouth: "It isn't right to take the children's food and throw it to the dogs."

Sisters and brothers, I don't know exactly why he said that. There might be a much deeper, hidden meaning we don't know of. I would like to suggest that in speaking about those dogs, he just continued that rather awkward, discriminatory approach of the woman who called him by the name of the group she thought Jesus belonged to. Maybe he wanted to show her how unfair and unwise she had been.

As soon as the groups we belong to are the starting point for our human relationships, words like *dog, pig,* and so on are unavoidably used. Just check your own language. Listen to how we, how you, speak about others.

The woman must have understood what had gone wrong. She must have understood that she had divided humanity into groups and circles, that she had drawn lines that should not have been drawn and used categories that should not have been used. She said: "Sir, don't dogs have rights *in your house*?"

It is then, when she speaks in those universalizing terms, that Jesus says: "Your saying has deserved your wish to be fulfilled."

Her daughter was healed. At that moment the evil spirit that had been terrorizing her left. It left at the exact same moment that other evil spirit terrorizing her mother, and the whole of humankind, left the woman.

As long as she spoke discriminatory, Fascist language, he could not and would not communicate with her. When she spoke in terms of the one family of God, he spoke to her immediately.

That one house of God is mentioned by Isaiah today. The house of God, a house of prayer for all peoples, a home for us all, a home that should already be established here on earth among us, so that all racism, discrimination, nepotism, apartheid, and Fascism will disappear from our streets and a shout like: "Hey, Jew!" will no longer be heard.

The woman went home, and the girl she had left screaming in her house was screaming no longer. She was sitting peacefully on her bed: Humanity was rid of another devil.

Let it be. Oh, let it be!

TWENTY-FIRST SUNDAY OF THE YEAR

45. Divinity in All of Us

Matthew 16:13–20

They were surrounding him. They were simple people: his disciples, fishermen, people who did not think very much of themselves. People nobody thought very much of. Nobody ever asked for their opinions. Nobody ever paid much attention to what they thought or felt. The people who mattered looked down on them. They smelled of fish. The smell came out of their hair and out of their clothing.

And now he—whom they had followed as their model, whom they had imitated like children, whom they were surprised to be allowed to follow—asked them: "What name would you give me? Whom do you, people, say that I am?"

They could not believe their ears. It was impossible that he was asking for their opinions. That is why they started telling him what the scribes, the priests, the Pharisees, the political leaders, and the important ones were saying. They answered: "They say, those other ones say that you are John the Baptizer, others say Jeremiah, others Elijah, and again others one of the prophets."

Then he said: "But you, whom do you say I am?" They looked at one another. Was he really going to pay attention to what they thought? Again they looked at one another. They nudged Peter, who was obviously their leader, and he said: "I know who you are, we know who you are. You are the Messiah, you are the Son of the living God."

And then Jesus said something strange. He said: "Peter, how blessed you are because you do not say that of yourself. What you said came from God, God in you."

Sister or brother, what Jesus said of Peter, he also said of us. Don't we believe that Jesus is the Messiah? Don't we believe that he is the Son of God? Isn't that the reason we came together today?

That same God the Father who was in Peter must be in us.

We are charged with God's Spirit. We are full of the Son's Spirit. God is in us.

I invite you to stand in front of your mirror, once you are home again, and, looking at yourself, say: "Look at her, look at him, *charged with God, full of Spirit!*"

We often think of ourselves as totally negative, as nonparticipants in so many affairs, as in a sense good-for-nothing, just like his disciples did.

Others are important. Others are leading the world. We forget the good in us. We forget God in us. We overlook our potentialities, our dignity, our access to life itself.

I met an African bishop, who some years ago was described as a contemporary saint by the weekly magazine *Time*: Bishop Christopher Mwoleka, from Rulenge, in Tanzania. He said we need two types of confessional boxes in our churches, some at the right side and some at the left side. In the left ones, you confess your sins, getting as a penance going to the right side with the obligation to confess honestly the good you did, the good in you, the God in you.

That is what Jesus said of Peter: Blessed are you, Peter. God is with you.

TWENTY-SECOND SUNDAY OF THE YEAR

46. On Saving One's Life

Matthew 16:21–27

Jesus had called Simon Peter *rock, foundation,* and *key to the kingdom* because it was Peter who had received sufficient vision from the Father to be able to confess: "You are the Christ, the Son of the living God." That confession, that affirmation, made Peter the leader, and that avowal and acknowledgment changed his life.

But when Jesus says, as he does in the gospel for today, that the newness he brings also means death to the old ways and a loosening of the old ties, Peter says: "No, not that. We do want the new way, but not at the cost of the old way. We do want a new life, but not at the cost of our old life. We want to be a branch grafted on you, the new vine, but we don't want to be cut away from the old tree. We do want to bring forth fruits, but we don't want to die first in the earth."

Jesus looks at him. Jesus is, as he admits, tempted to listen to him, but he does not listen. He overcomes the temptation, turns against Peter, and hisses: "Get away, Satan. Get behind me. You are an obstacle. I called you rock, and now you are a stumbling-block, a stumbling-stone, an obstacle."

He *then* continues, saying: "If you want to follow me, you have to renounce yourselves as you are now; you have to lose the life you are living now. If you are not willing to do that, if you want to keep to the life you are living now, then there will be no newness, no vision, possible for you. My vision means passion."

Sister and brother, there are so many followers of Jesus Christ in this world.

The Catholics alone number 700 million. More than one-third of humankind is Christian. Their vision definitely changed the world. There is no doubt about that, and yet, why are things growing so slowly? Why is so much money spent on the defense of an old type of life style, while so many others are starving and, maybe still worse, thirsting?

Isn't it because too many followers of Jesus Christ want to have their cake and eat it, too? Isn't it because too many Christians want to cooperate in the establishment of the Kingdom of Heaven, while hanging onto the kingdom of this world? You really cannot live the old way of life and contribute to the new type of life.

You cannot overcome the old order, the hunger, the sin, and the injustices, by giving alms without dying to the old way of things.

Christ said: "Come on, carry my cross, help me carry it. The grain of wheat must die to flower and grow into seed a hundred fold."

TWENTY-THIRD SUNDAY OF THE YEAR

47. Appointed as Prophets

Matthew 18:15–20

Prophets speak in the name of God. That is what the word *prophet* means: *pro-phemi*, to speak for. Speaking for God, speaking in the name of God, was the role of a prophet. He said: The prophet has a mission to speak to the wicked. If the prophet does not speak to the wicked, the wicked will die. But the prophet who did not speak will be held responsible for their deaths. All this does not seem to touch us. We are no prophets; we are normal folks. We eat normal food, we dress normally, we transport ourselves normally; we are no prophets.

We know being a prophet is something rare. Being a prophet is something from another place and age, we think.

A year ago, a Spanish professor from a Roman university came to give a talk in this chapel. His talk was titled, "Magisterium, Conscience, and Morality." He told us that the gift of prophecy is very rare in the Church today. In fact, he suggested that it did not exist at all anymore. The time of prophecy is over. All is settled, the law is laid down.

That would mean that nobody speaks in the name of God anymore. Wouldn't that be horrible?

It would mean that Moses' desire that one day all people would be prophets (Numbers 11:29) remained unfulfilled and unheard. It would mean that Joel's prophecy (Joel 2:28) that one day all sons and daughters would prophesy, was never fulfilled. It would mean that Peter was mistaken on Pentecost day when he ran to the balcony to shout to the people in the street that Joel's prophecy had been fulfilled: All elders and youngsters, women and men had become prophets!

It would mean that when someone is anointed a prophet during baptism, in fact, nothing happens.

It would mean that the gospel for today would be meaningless, too. Because being a prophet and speaking in the name of God is precisely what Jesus asks us to do today.

The gospel reads: "If your brother goes wrong, if your sister makes a mistake, speak to them, in God's name, for heaven's sake, alone, or with two or three others, or with the whole community. Speak, speak, speak, don't keep your mouth shut. You will be held responsible for your silence and for the consequences of your unwillingness to speak."

We have all kinds of ways to escape from that duty. We say that is only meant for the Church's leaders; they should speak out. We wait until they speak. We are scandalized and even annoyed when they don't speak. We say that it is only meant for those who are specially called, and we might think about bishops like Oscar Romero, who was shot for being a prophet, or Helder Camara, or Mother Teresa, or a man like Martin Luther King, or Bishop Desmond Tutu.

The gospel does not say this. Peter does not say this. Joel did not say this. Moses did not hope for this. The prayers at our baptism do not say this.

We speak very often about what's wrong in the world, about what's wrong with the people around us. We gossip, we backbite, we criticize, we slander, we complain, we sigh, we weep, we rake mud. But do we ever *prophesy?*

Do we ever call a sister or a brother aside to speak to him or her; to have it out with them so their wrong ways will be renounced? Would we be willing to listen when others come as prophets to us?

Shouldn't we take up that role of prophecy more seriously in the face of corruption, injustice, the armament race, degradation, and violence? Shouldn't we?

Moses would say: "Please, do!" Joel would say: "Please, do!" Peter would say: "Please, do!" Jesus says: "You should!"

TWENTY-FOURTH SUNDAY OF THE YEAR

48. Restorative Power

Matthew 18:21–35

The question was: "How often must I forgive my brother, how often must I forgive my sister who wrongs me?"

The answer was: "How often would you, yourself, need forgiveness from him or her?"

In the story, the answer is strengthened by indications that we owe much more to others than others owe us. There is even a proportion given. It is, according to reliable experts on the economy of that time something like ten million to one.

The point of the story is not only that we should forgive, but also that *we are able to forgive!*

When we speak about the gifts of God or about the gifts of the Holy Spirit, we very often think immediately about the light and fireworks at Pentecost: the fire, the noise, the thousands in the street, the storm, the gift of tongues, the gift of foreign languages, prophecy and its interpretation, the laying on of hands, the healings, the evil spirits sprinting away, the streams of baptismal water, and all the conversions.

We overlook that other time when, very calmly (and was God not to be found in the gentle breeze of the Old Testament and not in its storms?) Jesus blew over them and said: "You can forgive, I give you the power to forgive. You *can absolve*, you *can forgive*, and you *can* set free."

If there is one gift of God we need in our days, it is that gift of forgiveness. It is only over the bridges of forgetful forgiveness that humankind—Africans and Europeans, Indians and Chinese, Jews and Arabs, Americans and Russians, exploiters and exploited, plunderers and plundered, old and young, fighting sisters and warring brothers—can be brought together in Jesus, who died for all in view of a Kingdom that will come to its fullness at the moment we all forgive, forget, and follow him.

TWENTY-FIFTH SUNDAY OF THE YEAR

49. He Said Friend

Matthew 20:1–16

The question last week was how often do you forgive your brother? The question this week is how much do you pay your sister?

These are questions on human relations, laws and regulations, the just and the unjust, rewards and fines, right and wrong.

He tells us a story about a landowner and his workers. Some were hired early in the morning, some at midmorning, some halfway through the day, and some at four o'clock in the afternoon.

He tells how the landowner paid them. *He paid them all the same!*

Of course, the first ones hired protested. This was impossible; had they not worked ten times as much?

According to human practice, justice did not seem to have been done. Wasn't it?

It was, but in a different way. With one word, Jesus changed the whole scene in today's story. The landowner does not treat his workers as servants, not even as sisters or brothers. The landowner addresses them in another way; he calls them *friends*.

We are accustomed to calling one another sisters and brothers in Jesus' name. In Jesus' name, didn't he tell us that we all have one Father, our Father in heaven? And aren't we all formed from the same Mother: God's earth? Aren't we descendants from the same ancestors: Adam and Eve?

Yet Jesus hardly ever calls us brother or sister, only once, maybe twice.

He called us, very explicitly, *friends*.

You can have a brother and not be his friend; you can have a sister and not love her at all. To be blood related is no guarantee of love or respect. The Bible is full of that type of relationship: Abel and Cain, Isaac and Ishmael, Jacob and Esau, Joseph and his brothers.

It was not for nothing that Peter had to ask, "How often do I forgive my *brother*?"

He calls us friends!

Of course, he is our brother, but what is nicer than having your brother as a friend or being the friend of your sister?

It is that relationship that changes all, even today's story. *What a friend we have in Jesus*!

As for the rest, aren't we all like workers who started at the very last hour?

TWENTY-SIXTH SUNDAY OF THE YEAR

50. Our Personal Responsibility

Matthew 21:28–32

The parable about the two sons had a very clear meaning in the time of Jesus. He had presented himself as a reformer of humanity. He had presented himself as the follow-up of everything that had happened before in the Old Testament. He had presented himself as God's final and definite word. He had presented himself as the Kingdom to come.

There he was, surrounded by prostitutes, tax collectors, and sinners of all sorts. They pressed around him, they called him their own, and those who before had only used the name of the Lord to curse now praised him loudly in his company.

Those who had been singing the praises of God since their earliest youth, those who had been to the synagogues and the temple while others were eating and drinking, stealing and fornicating, seemed to be completely overlooked by him.

This was not something that just happened. It was not chance or bad luck.

He had said very explicitly that he had not come for the saints, the yes sayers to the law, but for those others, the sinners, those who had said no to that very same law all their lives.

The "righteous" had always been envious of those who dared to say no and profited from life more than they seemed to do. Now they were angry and upset, indignant and furious.

It is at that moment that he tells them this parable about the man with his two sons who asked his boys to go work in his field.

The second one said: "Yes. Oh, certainly. No problem," but he never went to do any work at all. The first one said, simply and curtly, "No, thank you. No time. I am not in the mood." But afterwards he thought to himself, "Shouldn't I go?" and he went.

After the story was over, Jesus asked them: "Which of the two did his father's will?" They had to admit it was the first one, the one who had said no but had gone, nevertheless. They knew what he meant. They knew he condemned them by their very own words.

We could learn so very much from this parable. We might apply it in many ways. Even nowadays, a newly converted sinner seems to be more eager than we, the older cases. Even nowadays, we might get cross because those exsinners praise the Lord more successfully, while we who have been doing it for so long seem to be less blessed.

We might point to the fact that even nowadays, so many say yes in words and no in deeds.

There is also another message in this parable that might be brought out: The point that we ourselves are called to work, to do something about the Kingdom, and to account for that.

Maybe we have became too accustomed to overlooking that very simple fact. All kinds of tendencies and attitudes have caused us to have an attitude of blaming structures and systems for *our* unwillingness and incapacity to work at the Kingdom.

We blame the system. When we live in a capitalistic country, we blame capitalism. When we live in a socialist country, we blame socialism. We blame the international *order*, the political situation, the existing corruption—any number of things—for all that is overcoming us: our greed, our licentiousness, our lack of interest in God, the breakdown of our family life, our divorces, our abortions, our babies found in latrines, our corruption, and our sins.

Every time any of those ills are discussed, we tend to say they would not happen if we lived in a different world! Before anything can change, we say— and it is said almost every day—"*structures*" should change.

It is true that those structures should change. There is no intention of denying that. It is true those changes are even part of *our* Kingdom work in the field of this world.

Those changes however, will not come by themselves. Those changes depend on human decisions. It is often exactly at the point where we know we should say yes to those changes that our consideration stops.

Reports are written, studies are made, hopes are raised, but nothing ever seems to happen.

All the experts agree that the situation should change. They all say yes, and it all remains no in the reality of our lives.

In the gospel of today that man, that father, has some work to be done. He does not address his family, his community, or a crowd. He asks his sons personally, one by one, whether they are willing to work. Aren't you invited like that by him?

TWENTY-SEVENTH SUNDAY OF THE YEAR

51. The Earth Is Ours

Matthew 21:33–43

A young Ethiopian refugee stood in front of me. He had black, blazing eyes. He looked very thin and wiry. He told me about his hunger and his country. He asked me for help, but at that moment I could not give him the help he sought.

He asked for a piece of bread. I gave him a piece. It was not much, but I hadn't any more. Suddenly he got very excited. He knelt on the ground and, striking it with his fists, he said: "This earth is not yours, it is not mine. This earth is God's, this earth is ours. Your food is not yours, your food is not mine. All food is God's, all food is ours. Not yours, not mine, but God's, *ours!"*

Then with a softness in his eyes I had not seen before he said, "You know, I am Jesus. I came back to this world." And wrapping the piece of bread in some brown paper, he left, and waved to me from the corner of the street.

I thought: "The hunger got into his head." But had it?

We, in the West (or, if you prefer, in the North) live in the best vineyard of the Lord.

All goes well. Plenty of sun and rain, excellent seed that grows beautifully, and corn-fed cattle that supply plenty of beef, very rich milk, and much too much butter. Sheds and barns, warehouses and silos are overflowing with enough food for years and years.

And what we don't grow here, but like to eat or drink, we import from the East or from the South.

But now there are those people at our doors from that East and that South, hungry and miserable, poor and wretched, asking for their share.

Are they his servants, the one of the parable today?

Or maybe, maybe are they *he*? Is he in all of them?

TWENTY-EIGHTH SUNDAY OF THE YEAR

52. Invited Together

Matthew 22:1–14

From the very beginning, it had been God's intention to bring them all together in the end, gathering them from all over the earth in their parental home.

This dream was maintained in spite of the news about Abel and Cain, Noah and his sons, Babel and its tower, Jacob and Esau, Joseph and his brothers, the Jews and the Pharisees, the overlooking of women, World War I and World War II, the holocaust and apartheid.

Hadn't God given each of them her and his genius, his and her talent? Hadn't God given each of them part of the human heritage?

This dream was so often expressed by God's prophets who sowed its seed indelibly in the hearts and minds of all those faithful to God's will.

Isaiah foretold how one day all nations would come together, climbing the mountain of the Lord. They would share and celebrate, tear away all veils that hide us from one another, tear the webs that keep us apart. All the tears that were ever shed would be dried. All differences and discriminations would be removed, bringing them together to a banquet, a feast rich in food and choice wines.

Jesus told them then, and he is telling us now: "It is time, the food is prepared, the bullocks and the corn-fed cattle are killed, everything is ready, come to the feast!"

But we say: "Not yet. We are not ready. I have to tend *my* farm. I have to look after *my* business. I have no time to socialize with others. I am not willing to share. I am not prepared to let go. I am not going to come. I certainly am not. I am not going to sit down with all those strangers."

We laugh at those among us who say we can't go on living as we are now. Acting as if we don't belong together at all, acting as if we have nothing in common, neither God our Father, nor the earth our Mother. Acting as if there are walls between us, the blacks and the whites, the young and the old, the rich and the poor, men and women. Discrimination and apartheid everywhere.

He told us the whole story. I don't know at what stage of the story we are now. I do know that the meal is ready. I do know where we will be if we do not accept his invitation to be together. We won't be here at all.

TWENTY-NINTH SUNDAY OF THE YEAR

53. A Tax That Is Not Yet Paid

Matthew 22:15–21

Some Pharisees and Herodians came to ask Jesus a question. At least that is what they pretended to do.

They came to ask him a very good question. In fact, it is one of the burning issues that has been worrying many Christians and others all through human history. Should one pay tax to a political organization that is unjust, that exploits, that oppresses, and that has no respect for human rights?

It was a good question in Jesus' time, when the Romans were exploiting the Jews. It is still a good question for any Christian living in South Africa, where tax money is spent to subdue and frustrate the majority of the population. It is a good question in this country, where it has been decided to spend tax money on the development of nerve gases, on the improvement of atomic warheads, and on all kinds of anti-human-life and *consequently*, anti-Kingdom-of-Heaven devices.

Those Pharisees came to Jesus with that question. They did not come because they were interested in his answer. They had the answer already in their pockets, because they carried with them the coins a Jew had to buy to pay his taxes, coins with the head of the emperor on them.

They did not come for an answer at all. They came to trap him. If he said: "No, you should not pay," he would be caught by the Roman police. If he said: "Yes, you should pay," he would be caught by his own people as a collaborator.

They wanted to catch him, as they did afterwards, when they shouted from behind his back to the Roman governor, Pontius Pilate: "Condemn him, crucify him, he told us not to pay your tax!"

They did not come for an answer at all. They had not listened to any of his answers up to then. They had asked him: "What should we do?"

He had told them: "Sell all you have, give it to the poor, and be like me!" They had only walked away laughing.

They did not come for an answer to liberate the oppressed and the poor. They were the oppressors of the poor. Jesus accused them, those Pharisees and other religious leaders, of despising the poor, of looking down on them, and of laying on their shoulders extra burdens they were not willing to carry themselves, but from which they profited scandalously.

That is why he told them: "Hypocrites, you only came to set me a trap. You don't care a fig, but I will give you my answer. Show me one of those tax coins."

One of them was naive enough to do just that. He put his hand in his pocket and produced one.

Jesus took the coin, tossed it head-side up, and asked: "Whose face is that?" The man answered: "It is the emperor's head."

Jesus threw the coin back and said: "If that is the emperor's head, give to the emperor what is of that emperor," and he then added his real answer, an overruling answer: "and give to God what is God's; give to God what carries God's face, give to God what is created in God's image!"

With that answer, a whole new world opened up. What is created in God's image? What is imprinted with God's face? What does God expect us to give him?

Not a church, not pieces of gold and silver, not all kinds of prayers, not the tickling of guitars, the songs of competing choirs, not even four Our Fathers, signs of the cross, or endless Hail Marys.

All that is good. All that can help. But what he wants us to give him is a well organized *human life* for all. That is the worship he wants, that is the tax we have to pay to belong to his Kingdom here on earth.

As long as there are starving children and refugees, sick people who are not helped, poor people who have no means of being educated, rumors of war, plague, AIDS, and so forth, we should not rest. Our worship is not complete. We did not render to God what he wants us to render to him: a fully developed human life for all.

Our tax to him is not yet paid.

THIRTIETH SUNDAY OF THE YEAR

54. Our Neighbor Nowadays

Matthew 22:34–40

It was a hot afternoon in Thika, a small Kenyan town. Schoolchildren were going home, playing as children do. Some children were throwing a ball made of some old papers kept together by a rubber band. They were playing alongside the barbed wire fence of the enormous pineapple plantation owned by one of the largest transnational fruit companies in the world.

As far as you could see, those purplish fruits were coloring the hillsides.

The girls did not look. They were accustomed to the sight, and they heard too many sighs from their parents because of those fruits. They were playing with their ball. Suddenly, an unexpected gust of wind blew the ball under the wire fence.

Just at that moment, some of the plantation guards with their fierce dogs came from behind a bush. They saw the girls creep under the fence to get their ball. They let loose their dogs, who attacked the girls. Shouts of fear and anguish. The dogs were called back. They came, reluctantly, licking their mouths with rosy tongues.

One girl—let us call her Jane, Jane Wanjiku Chege—a beautiful one, her family's hope, thirteen years old, was bleeding to death. Another kept her mauled face in her hands.

That night the usual train left Thika's railway station with its freight of canned pineapples for the European market.

One of the canners was Chege, the father of Jane Wanjiku, who was working as a day worker, just as 9,000 out of the other 10,000 fruit canners and plantation workers do. That way, the company can pay less than the minimum national monthly salary of about thirty dollars and avoid any further social obligations. It keeps the prices very low in our world, and very high in their world.

Some weeks later, there was a birthday party somewhere in Europe. A girl— why shouldn't we call her Jane, too?—was turning thirteen, a beautiful girl, the pride of her family. She had been allowed to choose the dessert for the party, and she had chosen pineapple with whipped cream.

Before they started to eat, Jane was asked by the guests to say grace, and she prayed:

> "O, almighty God,
> who in your goodness,
> gave us all this food,
> and especially these fruits,
> as a sign of your goodness,
> we thank you for your bounty.
> *Amen.*"

The prayer was not heard in Thika. Maybe it's a good thing. But it should have been heard, nevertheless, just like the story of Jane Wanjiku wa Chege should have been told to the celebrating Jane.

One day, it may be widely told. Today it was told here. All of you heard it. And even that is not the full story.

Do you know why they grow pineapples for us in that African land that can hardly feed itself? Because that giant fruit company got into trouble with trade union tendencies in the Philippines. They had gone to the Philippines because they had the same trouble before, in Hawaii, and even before that in this country.

There is no doubt about that.

Do you see how we hang together?

Do you see who your neighbor is in this, our world?

Do you understand the impact of the words of Jesus, the man who saw all this in his divine human heart so long before anyone else?

Love your neighbor as you love yourself, in the name of God, who loves all of us!

THIRTY-FIRST SUNDAY OF THE YEAR

55. Where Are You From?

Matthew 23:1–12

It was in the dark of the night, the dark of the darkest night about two thousand years ago, that a remark was made that had often been made before. It is still made innumerable times every day, but it never should be made, with him among us.

It was a harassing scene. Jesus had been arrested. He was standing in front of a set of judges.

Outside in the dark it was cold, very cold. People were sitting around fires with their hands outstretched toward the fleeting warmth of the flames.

It was then that a busy maid, selling her wares, pointed at Peter and said: "Your accent betrays you. Where are you from?"

She tried to classify him. She tried to localize him. She tried to place him. She tried to pin down his descent, his blood, his land, his tribe, and his nation.

Peter denied knowing Jesus. He denied the truth. Peter should have denied something else. He should have denied that he was any longer classifiable as a Galilean, as belonging to one group, to one land, one nation.

That is what the gospel of today is about.

"Do not use any classification by descent, blood, land, tribe, or nation anymore. That time is over. Those divisions are gone."

From now on, it is all of us—one descent, one blood, one land, one people, and one nation. "Only one is your Father, the one in heaven!" Only one is your Mother, the earth, God's womb, from which the Father begot us.

How often it has happened to me. How often it has happened to you. Wherever you were, people said what that maid said so long ago in the dark of the night, the darkest of all nights: "Your accent betrays you. Where are you from?"

Where am I from? Where are you from? Where are the others from? The answer Jesus gave is for all of us: *"Only one is your father, the one in heaven!" You belong together, you are brothers and sisters, you should be friends.*

Only when this answer is given by all to that *treacherous* question will we be at home together here on earth, and in all time to come.

Only this answer can break the dark of the night in which we are still sitting with our hands outstretched in the fleeting warmth of some fire.

THIRTY-SECOND SUNDAY OF THE YEAR

56. Kingdom Now

Matthew 25:1–13

It's quite common that a bride is late in this chapel in Nairobi. In fact, the bride is practically always late, anywhere from ten minutes to three hours. I think they all want to make a point.

It is rare that the bridegroom is late. He is usually on time, and he is always the person most worried about the lateness of the bride. He usually waits here in the chapel, nervous, with his flower falling from his buttonhole, consulting his best man, sending messengers, and sitting in that first pew over there, praying very hard for a rather obvious intention: that she may come soon.

It would be unimaginable that she would be so late as midnight, however.

There are other strange things about today's story.

Where is the bride? She is not even mentioned. Who are those bridesmaids? What does the bridegroom enter? How was it possible for those bridesmaids, the foolish ones, to follow the advice from the wise ones to go and buy oil at midnight? Were there in Jesus' time local gas stations open twenty-four hours a day?

This strange story is almost always used to warn us that we should be ready to die at any moment of the day.

That is, indeed, a very wholesome thought, and a very necessary one, too, in our day and age. Nevertheless, it does not seem to be the gist, the point, or the message of the story, because it would not be like Jesus to suggest that the Kingdom of Heaven (and that is what the story is about) comes to us only at the end of our lives. It might come in its fulfillment at the end of our lives, but that fulfillment will come only insofar as we stayed awake in view of it during our lives here.

That seems to be the message of this parable: During our lives here, we should not fall asleep. We should keep awake and ready, in case Jesus wants to invade our lives with his Kingdom.

You know what that Kingdom is. You know what heaven is supposed to be. You can describe it in different ways.

For a hungry person, it is food. For a thirsty person, it is drink. For a homeless person, it is home. For a learned person, it is knowledge. For a blind person, it is light. For a deaf person, it is music. For a lonely person, it is communication.

It is always a total fulfillment of our human capacities—psychologically, physically, spiritually, and humanly.

The Kingdom of God is human life to the full: The type of life that appeared in Jesus.

Boris Pasternak said this beautifully in his book *Dr. Zhivago*:

And then in this tasteless heap of gold and marble HE came, light and clothed in an aura emphatically human, deliberately provincial, Galilean, and at that moment Gods and nations ceased to be, and MAN CAME INTO BEING.

57. Jesus and Gold

Matthew 25:14–30

The experts agree that Jesus used stories he heard around him in his preaching. That throws a very interesting light on Jesus. It means he not only sat down for profound and deeply spiritual conversations. It means that he also sat down to listen to what went on around him.

The story was simple. There was a rich man who had gone on a far trip to organize a business deal. Before he went, he gave his capital to some servants he trusted. He had more confidence in some than he had in others, and that is why he gave his servants different amounts of money to work with.

Two out of the three worked very hard. They doubled their capital. The third one was afraid; he buried his money somewhere deep in the earth. You heard what happened when the master came back: The two money makers were praised, and the one who had made no money at all was thrown out into the darkness.

The point of the story seems obvious: We should work with the talents we have while we are here on earth. We should double our initial capital, we should work as much as we can. Is that all?

It cannot be all. If that were all, Jesus would be just like all the others: asking us to increase our wealth quantitatively, overlooking further, more personal considerations, just as the master of the story did when he praised those two and threw out the third one.

Jesus must have been telling the story just as he heard it!

He told them that story to make his *own* attitudes and intentions better understood. He must have told them that story in view of the Kingdom to come. He told them that story in view of his vision.

He often showed his amazement at the way people who were interested only in money, and not in his vision, worked at money-making day and night. Keeping their shops open at impossible hours; cheating and deceiving; traveling through the dark of the night like wild animals; missing their sleep, their food, and their drink; all in view of some gain while overbooking their diaries day after day, risking their health and their lives.

Jesus often expressed his surprise about the way people who had made gold their master were willing to serve their king.

He admired—in a way—their relentlessness, their astuteness, but he condemned them—definitely—as *children of darkness*, children of death, murderers, and killers.

You cannot serve God and money. You cannot serve gold and humanity. Hundreds of years ago, a scholar saw this very clearly during a period when Christian invaders from Europe occupied what is now called Latin America. They killed thousands and thousands of the original inhabitants of that continent, and they made the survivors slaves on their own land. Protests against all this were very rare. One came from a theologian of that time, Bartolome de Las Casas. He wrote to the people responsible:

> I don't say that they directly want to kill, but I do say that they want to become rich, they want to swim in gold, through the work and the sweat of the tortured and in-misery-living natives, by using them as if they were dead means and tools, with as unavoidable consequence the death of all those people.

They did not murder because they were bad. They did not kill because they were aggressive. They killed because gold was their priority.

That kind of dialectics, that kind of logic, that kind of dynamism, is still with us.

You must have heard how over the last month in this city of Nairobi, landlords burned down whole slum areas without any warning to those who lived there. They did not do that because they were bad—though at least two people died in the fire. They did it because they wanted to replace those shanties with permanent buildings. They did it because their priority is money, not humanity.

This is the lesson of today's gospel: Just imagine that we, his followers, were to work with that kind of energy for the realization of the Kingdom of God, where humanity is tops and money a means—the Kingdom of justice and peace that we have been reflecting on so often over this ending year of grace!

Wouldn't we organize ourselves better and more efficiently? Shouldn't we spend our talents in that direction? Only in that way we will find the happiness promised and given to the faithful servants of God.

THIRTY-FOURTH SUNDAY OF THE YEAR

58. Jesus Christ, King

Matthew 25:31–46

Something strange seems to overcome Jesus, he who had always been serving others. He who had run away when they wanted to make him a king. He who had washed the feet of his disciples. He who had called a child the most important issue in this world. He who had told his disciples not to rule, not to be masters over others. According to Matthew, at least twice he calls himself King.

Very many people say the time of kings is over, and that is true now. In the Old Testament, that was not true at all. The word *king* is one of the most frequently used words, appearing over twenty-five hundred times in the Old Testament!

In that time, one expected much from a king. Those expectations were very often expressed.

In Psalm 72:1–2, 12–14, one prays for the king:

> Teach the king to judge with your righteousness, O God;
>> share with him your own justice,
> so that he will rule over your people with justice
>> and govern the oppressed with righteousness.
> he rescues the poor who call to him.
>> and those who are needy and neglected.
> he has pity on the weak and poor;
>> he saves the lives of those in need.
> He rescues them from oppression and violence;
>> their lives are precious to him.

This is what one expected from a king. It was in that line of thought that Christ called himself King.

Think of that day in Nazareth when he took the Old Testament to explain himself, when he rolled that scroll down to this passage in Isaiah:

> The Spirit of God is upon me,
> [that is what one had prayed for in Psalm 72]
> he has anointed me,
> to assist the poor,
> [again an echo from that psalm]
> to heal the contrite, to liberate prisoners,
> to help those in trouble.

So King he was, and yet, when we take the reading of today, something like a transfer takes place, because in the description of that final judgment, we do not come together to judge whether he has been a good king.

He is judging *us*, on those very same issues.

He, the King, is judging us in how far we have been king. He turns the roles completely around and says: "What did you do when you saw anybody hungry or thirsty or oppressed or in need or in prison?"

In that change of roles, he even goes so far as to identify himself with those poor.

Sisters and brothers, at this feast of JESUS CHRIST KING, on the last Sunday of the liturgical year, we are supposed to understand that it is up to us, to all of us, to rule as the kings in the Old Testament were supposed to rule. It is not in vain that we, all of us, were anointed priest, prophet, and *king* at our baptism.

Those kings were supposed to be life- and hope-giving. They were supposed to make others grow. They were supposed to widen their hearts and their minds. They were supposed to liberate and save, to open and develop.

Sisters and brothers, do you live like a king or queen? Does justice roll from you over the mountains and over the hills of the whole wide land?

Because that is the question he is going to ask you in the end.

Have you ever been like him, our King?

LITURGICAL CYCLE B

FIRST SUNDAY OF ADVENT

59. Two Thousand Years Later

Mark 13:33–37

He was born almost two thousand years ago. All the time before, people had been hoping for him, with each sigh, at each misunderstanding, before each fight, after each departure, at each death, all that time, all the time. . . .

Each child hanging its empty stocking or putting its empty shoe under the chimney (even if the flue is not really there anymore) before Christmas is still an expression, a symbol, a sign of the everlasting hope that gifts will come down from above and that all desires, hopes, and wishes will be fulfilled. Even though it might mean to that child only getting a Cabbage Patch doll or a robot.

Christ was born two thousand years ago, but humanity's desires have yet to be fulfilled.

There are 150 million starving people in Africa—the continent he knew so well as a refugee—who are looking into the sky each day, hoping for some relief, some beans, some corn, and some oil.

Christ was born two thousand years ago, but for many, it is as if nothing happened that night.

In a town like Chicago, two hundred fifty thousand human beings will sleep in the streets, looking for some shelter, as his parents did before he was born.

Christ was born two thousand years ago, but there is less peace in the air than when the angels sang that night. The sky now is full of warplanes and satellites that threaten not only newborn babes in Bethlehem, but all of us.

He is obviously away, like the man in the gospel of today who left for a far-off country, a man traveling abroad.

He had been speaking about returning to his Father, that's true, but hadn't he assigned them their tasks? Hadn't he entrusted his home, this world, to those who followed him, to those who seemed to have understood that they had been equipped, as he was:

> to fulfill all desires,
> to heal all wounds,
> to bring all together
> round one table?

Hadn't he told them, and us, that he would be back soon, hoping to find us not *asleep*?

Isn't that what we are: asleep in a world that needs to wake up?
That is why, again, we should prepare for him.

60. God's Hope in This World

Mark 1:1–8

The gospel of Mark starts by saying: "Good News about Jesus," but immediately after that trumpet blast, not Jesus, but John the Baptizer is introduced to us.

John in the wilderness, with his uncombed hair, clothed in a set of skins, with uncut nails, a very long, uncontrolled beard, and the smell of the insects he ate all over him. John, with a message of sin, repentance, and looming doom that definitely did not mellow his voice, notwithstanding the honey he ate.

Yet, even John was the bringer of good news. That must have been the reason people came to him. First two, then some more, and finally hundreds and thousands, Jesus included.

In the disastrous world in which he lived, John preached hope to those who were the cause of that disaster. John said: "You are not bound up by the world in which you live. There is a power in you with which you can escape from that world, overcoming it. There is hope, there is life."

There are at the moment some very strange stories in this country about people who were so sick that everybody around them said: "You are going to die. You are not going to make it. You are hopeless, your disease is terminal." Doctors said so, nurses said so, surgeons said so, relatives and friends said so.

Some of those people, however, did not accept that verdict. They said: "We might be condemned according to you; we might have no hope in your world. Let us try, then, to get out of your world to save ourselves." They tried, and some succeeded.

There is the report of American professor Joseph Chilton Pearce. His rather young wife became pregnant, but her pregnancy also released in her an extremely malicious disease. She suffered from cancer. She was operated on again and again, until the surgeons said: "This is the end, the end of your road. We can't do anything anymore."

It was then that she and her husband decided to try to escape from the world in which she was condemned to die. They reasoned: There is in every human organism, in any living organism, the power to heal. Let us tap that power. They isolated themselves in a far-off farm. They only spoke to each other about health. They prayed, and they influenced each other only in positive ways. They talked day and night about that possibility of healing that is given with the body.

It was on the thirtieth day that she suddenly felt something happening in her. She was healed.

She healed in the alternative world they had constructed around themselves. A world in which she did not die.

Would it not be possible to understand the message of John—that voice in the wilderness of our world—in that way?

You know the enormous difficulties under which we live. We seem condemned to die—socially, economically, and family-wise—in a world where uprightness, honesty, and integrity do not seem to count at all.

You know how sick humanity is according to all kinds of diagnostics. So much so, that in a diabolical way everything good seems to be turned into something very evil.

I'll give you one example. During a recent energy exposition here in town on the occasion of an international meeting on alternative sources of energy, some "sun collectors" were shown. In those collectors, aluminum foil is used to catch the sunlight in order to make your water boil and your bread bake. It is one of those hope-giving developments in an energy-poor world, helping it to be a better place. But did you know that some are thinking about a sun collector orbiting the world as a source of energy? And that others immediately saw the military possibilities of such a generator to burn their enemies out of existence from the sky?

It is in this world of ours that John's message gives hope, because while preaching repentance, he pointed to the possibility of change in us and the possibility of changing the world with ourselves.

An alternative world is possible. A new humanity can be built. There is hope in the world. In Jesus, God's hope entered this world.

THIRD SUNDAY OF ADVENT

61. Hope We Need

John 1:6–8, 19–28

Isaiah says: "Listen, justice shall be done." Paul writes: "Christ will come." John preaches: "He is already among you."

All three want to give us hope.

You might say, what is hope? Hope does not help. You can't buy anything with hope. Hope is nice, but it is so thin. It only means that you don't have the thing you would like to get.

Hope is very important, and we know that well.

There is someone seriously ill. You love her very much. She is so sick that she was taken to a hospital. The doctors say that she might come through, if her attitude were positive, that is to say, if she would desire and hope to live.

Every time you visit her, she turns her face away from you when you enter her room, and she says: "Don't bother. Get away, leave me alone. It is too late, it is finished, I am finished. You better start forgetting about me, this is the end, I feel it."

You speak about things you would like to do with her, a party, a dinner, a visit, a trip overseas, even a pilgrimage, but there is no interest, no reaction at all.

The doctors say: "We are afraid that she is slipping away from us. There does not seem to be any will to live in her, no hope."

Every day she is weaker, thinner, and paler. She really will escape from you, and from the world, if she does not pick up her spirit and hope to live. Without that will from within, operations, chemicals, radiations, surgery, pills, powders, injections, and pep talks will be to no avail at all. She will linger and die.

In the same way, we need hope in our world and in our lives.

I am not going to give you a long list of all the things that are wrong in our lives and the lives of so many others.

Think of the starving in Africa, the homeless in American towns, the prisoners of conscience and others in so many countries, the neglected youth all over the world, the difficulties in your own family, around your very own kitchen table.

Even without a full list, we know that we are sick, that we suffer many ailments.

John preaches: "It will change!" Paul writes: "He is faithful!" Isaiah says: "Justice will reign!"

We should hope so. We should believe it. That hope and belief will make us pick up our spirits and do from *within ourselves* whatever we can to heal, to survive, and to be thankful for life regained in that birth we are going to celebrate at Christmas. Amen.

FOURTH SUNDAY OF ADVENT

62. Mary's Vision

Luke 1:26–38

Mary must have been a very remarkable woman. No wonder Jesus was her son. Yet, even she needed some time to understand what happened to her. The earliest reports say she was initially very confused. Even in the presence of that archangel, she had some questions. Once she understood, she made her decision immediately. She closed her curtains. She closed her windows, her doors, and her house. She did that not to lock herself up, considering herself a kind of living tabernacle with that treasure in her womb, putting (so to speak) two candles and some flowers in front of herself, meditating day and night about her privileged position. No, she closed her curtains, her windows, her doors, and her house to do something else. She went out to visit her Aunt Elizabeth. What happened to her was not going to be only a private issue.

When preparing this sermon, I read several commentaries on this gospel. They all say, and very rightly so, that Mary gives us an example of how we should discern the Spirit of God in our lives. They all say that Mary gives us an example of how we should say *yes* to God's call in our lives.

Her *yes* was the beginning of all and everything that would happen to her during the rest of her life. Just like our *yes* will be the beginning of all and everything that will happen during the rest of our lives.

Mary, however, gives a wider example. Mary is not trapped in that beginning. Mary does not restrict herself to purely personal attitudes. Mary understood, as the angel had told her, that there was more, much more at stake.

Hadn't the angel given that new growing person in her womb the name Jesus, meaning "savior"? Hadn't the angel spoken about a reign, his reign, that would last forever and ever?

She must have been thinking of all that, visions of the prophets spinning in her head, while she was walking the long way to her Aunt Elizabeth. She must have been thinking of all that while she saw the normal human scene about her in the streets and on the roads. Soldiers accompanying their Roman officers, chasing everybody else in the ditches alongside the road to let those gentlemen pass. The rich, full of contempt, avoiding mixing with the poor. She, herself, an up-country girl, being pushed and looked at by the men all around her.

And then, in the middle of the road, with her savior in her womb, with the prophets filling her head, she suddenly got that flash of insight.

Before she reached her aunt, she understood what that kingdom of his would mean. She suddenly understood what it meant that she, of all persons, was carrying the seed of all change in this world.

She understood that this would mean a real beginning for all and everyone, and the end of all that had and has power in this world.

Did she, seeing this so suddenly, laugh out aloud?

She was now at her aunt's house. Elizabeth came out to greet her. In her womb, John gave her his push, and Elizabeth cried out aloud: "What an honor that you came, the mother of my Lord." And all at once Mary, who had had no one to talk to since the angel appeared, erupted in a vision so wide that she could not help but sing: "Look at what happened to me. In me it is clear that God is going to change the whole order of things. It is through me that God showed that his world is going to change!"

Sister or brother, that is what we should learn today from her. God is not only going to change private hearts. God is not only going to assure peace of mind. God is going to do all that, but only because God is going to change all structures in this world.

When Mary said *yes*, she not only opened herself to receive him in her womb. She opened herself to that vision, as we should in all we do.

What she carried in her womb gave her a vision wide as the world and as lasting as human history.

It is not for nothing that she is called the mother of all, queen of the universe.

63. Christmas Presents and Christmas Lights

Luke 2:1–14

We often use symbols that have lost their meaning, signs without an obvious sense.

Somewhere in the north of Holland there is a church where all those who entered used to bow down in the direction of a whitewashed part of the church wall before settling in the pews. Nobody knew why. They had been doing this from generation to generation, and no question was ever asked.

Then, one day, the parish council decided to clean the walls. While doing this, they discovered some traces of a painting under the whitewash on the wall. Very carefully they started to peel off the chalk, and they uncovered a centuries-old painting of Jesus on the cross.

Nobody remembered that picture. There was no description of it to be found: the painting had been lost from human memory. It must have been painted over centuries before. But the sign of respect had remained.

They finally knew why they were bowing their heads before sitting down. The sign had been there, but its meaning was forgotten. Nobody knew the story of the origin of that sign, nobody could tell its tale.

Driving through the towns and villages during this Christmas night, one sees lights everywhere—red, orange, green, yellow, blue, and pink. Driving like that, you will be driving alone, because everyone is at home, giving presents and gifts to one another, millions of them.

Those lights brightening up the darkness of our world, those gifts fulfilling so many wishes and desires, are obviously signs and symbols, too.

But who would understand them, if the Christmas story were not remembered and told?

The story about how they had been looking for him all through the ages. How even today so many are hoping for a redeemer. And how finally he came from God, God's gift to the world, a light brightening its darkness.

You should tell this story to yourself: How in your own world, which often seems so frustrating and lonely, new life was born. You should tell it to those around you, to give them the hope they need so very much. But you should especially tell it to your children, just as your parents told you the Christmas story.

It is the nicest story in the world, if you come to think of it, about God starting a new life in the midst of us. It is in this way that we can recapture the meaning of the lights we light in the night, of the gifts we give one another, fulfilling our desires.

That is why we came here together in the middle of the night, to start the new life he gave us.

FIRST SUNDAY AFTER CHRISTMAS

64. Beyond the Family Circle

Luke 2:22–40

That morning, Mary washed her baby Jesus with extra care. Joseph went out to buy two turtledoves for the sacrifice.

It was a very homely scene, those two caring for the third; those two fulfilling the law; those two walking together the considerable distance to the temple, taking turns carrying the child.

No wonder that long ago, pious authors saw that family as the model for all human families.

I don't want to be sarcastic, but I wonder if that family was so easily seen as a model because we know so very little about them.

Did Joseph work at home, or was he an absentee male? Did Mary stay the whole day with Jesus, or did she work as a charwoman for one of the richer families in town, in order to feed herself and Jesus? We don't know.

We might dream about the three of them, piously and comfortably together as we see them on holy pictures and in the imagination of so many who believe in the sanctity (and rightly so) of that type of family.

But what can you really do with that model when social and economic situations make it impossible? I know a priest-sociologist here in Kenya who started to study and discuss with his people their family difficulties. He had made the hypothesis that those difficulties were all due to the personal irresponsibility of the fathers and mothers involved: their drunkenness, their faithlessness, their adulterous promiscuity, their lack of restraint, their fickleness. But in doing his research, he had to change his original assumption. The real underlying cause for most of the difficulties was the situation in which those people were obliged to live.

Research at the National University of Nairobi proved that 65 percent of the families in Kenya are without the father at home. Because of that and some other reasons, 70 percent of the men in Kenya feel very frustrated and like nonparticipants in their own society! Not to speak of all the difficulties those mothers and their children have without their husbands and fathers at home.

How did those three in Nazareth live?

Were they living in their own house, or were they packed together with two or three other families in one small room, taking turns sleeping on their one bed?

Again, I don't know. You don't know, either.

One of the things we do know is told us today by Luke.

When Joseph and Mary came to the temple, they were met by two old people, Simeon and Anna. It is rather strange that we don't hear anything about the temple officials they must have met. Not a word is mentioned of what the priests said, but what that old man and old woman said was never forgotten.

Simeon said: "Finally salvation, salvation for all peoples. You see this child, he is destined for the fall and rising of many. Destined to be a sign that is rejected, so that the secret thoughts of many will be laid bare."

Then that old lady, Anna, took over. She was eighty-four years old, but she spoke about the future, about the deliverance and liberation of Jerusalem. Those two old people praised Mary, they praised Joseph, they praised that holy family, our model. But they saw that family and the relationships in that family in view of greater things: in view of a larger mission, in view of the crisis, the change, the justice, the peace, and the Kingdom Jesus had come to bring.

Sisters and brothers, the virtues and love necessary for a good family life are very often threatened these days. Aren't they threatened because we don't see our families in the light of what Simeon and Anna said to Mary, Joseph, and Jesus?

Aren't our families living under those threats because we in our families aren't sufficiently interested in that crisis, that change, that justice, that peace, and that Kingdom he came to bring?

EPIPHANY

65. They Followed the Star

Matthew 2:1–12

When the star appeared, those wise men must have been living a certain type of life. They were teachers or kings, philosophers or sages—nobody really knows. One thing we do know: When the three in our story saw the star, they decided to follow it, to interrupt their routine, to stop whatever they had been doing, to risk something new. They climbed over the edge of their existence and followed that star.

We might think that was easy for them. It was not easy at all. All through human history, there are reports and stories on how difficult it is to change. When, in the enormously popular best seller of some years ago, *Jonathan Livingston Seagull*, Jonathan explains to the other seagulls that seagulls can live a much higher, fuller, wider, and further life than they do, the others did not want to believe him. When he shows them that it is really possible, they throw him out of their circle and ban him.

Do we really need this story to know how difficult change really is? Even the most common changes in our lives are difficult. To repair a leaking tap, to start a more efficient computerized bookkeeping system, to rearrange a room, to clean a cupboard, to go to the doctor, to write a letter, to come to a reconciliation and shake a hand—these things are often not done. Though the light appeared, the idea flashed, the star shone, it was not followed, and nothing happened. All remained the same.

Those three men were wise. When they saw the new star indicating a new life, a new king, a new ruler, a new child, they followed faithfully, notwithstanding all the risks.

Let us follow it, too, until we arrive.

Some time ago, I met a priest who had been working for forty-five years in this country, following that star faithfully for all those years. He asked me very sincerely: "What was the use of all I did? Did things really improve? Did we come nearer to God? What did it help?"

He forgot, during that moment of depression, that a baby was born, that a seed had been sowed, that a growth process had been started: an evolution, not a revolution.

God could have given the tree, but God gave the seed. God could have delivered us as already processed saints, but God wanted us to grow. God could have flown those three wise men over to Bethlehem by the angelic-air-express God sent in any case, but God gave them a star, which they followed slowly and surely until they arrived where the star stopped, to find what they had been looking for: a new child, a new rule, a new king, a new life.

SUNDAY AFTER EPIPHANY/THE BAPTISM OF THE LORD

66. Stepping in the Mud

Mark 1:7–11

Jesus stepped in the mud of the river Jordan in front of a large crowd and his cousin John. He wanted to be baptized, he said. John, his cousin, was horrified to see Jesus bent before him in the mud. To understand the horror of John, we must know something more about that mud.

Do you remember the report of Noah, his ark, and his days? In those days, the Bible reads, people did not do anything but fashion wickedness, all day and night long. Do you remember how in those days people perished with all their sins, their works, their children, and their ambitions in the mud under the flood of water that lashed out over them for forty days and forty nights without any interruption?

When the ark rose out of the water, it was surrounded by that mud, stifled with sin.

Do you remember the report of Moses and his days? How the Egyptians pestered his people day and night. How they made them work without sufficient food, frustrating them even in their family life. How they killed, murdered, arrested, and detained, and how all those Egyptians finally ended up stuck in the mud under the water of the Red Sea that engulfed them, their chariots, their horses, their weapons, and their evil intentions? And how Moses and his people rose out of that mud, glorious and triumphant, alleluia?

When Moses and his people looked back over the sea, they saw the mud in which Pharaoh and all he stood for had perished. A new order was born, a new life started, a new covenant was made.

It did not last, because John in his days again felt the need—a divinely inspired need—to push the Jews of his time in the mud of their own sinfulness, to get them out of their evil.

That evil is so evil. Human evil is so irresponsible. It is so stupid. We know sufficient examples. Our whole life is one example. But let us take a glaring one.

In the year 1916, on a line of about seventeen miles, one million human beings killed one another over a period of eight months. That is an average rate of four thousand men killed each day.

The mud of human evil is very deep. It stinks forcefully. It is full of dangerous gases. And there was Jesus in front of John, asking to be allowed to bend down in that mud. No wonder John hesitated.

But Jesus went down, and when he came up, the mud still streaming from his ears, over his eyes, out of his hair, over his nose and mouth, *heaven opened.* A voice was heard. A Spirit, a new Spirit in people and a new heart were announced, glory, glory, alleluia.

He was bathed in light. He was drowned in God's voice. He was full of Spirit.

What about the mud? Was he going to forget it? Was he going to overlook it in the new light? Was that Spirit going to cover up evil? Was she going to work as a kind of consoling anesthetic, a kind of opium, cocaine, ether, or chloroform?

She was not.

Once he got that Spirit, he was driven by her into the desert, and again out of the desert, to do his work in this world, to struggle with evil in us and in this world, in order to overcome it.

SECOND SUNDAY OF THE YEAR

67. The Home-Life Test

John 1:35–42

John and Andrew were the first ones who started to follow him, first almost on the sly, very shyly, but slowly from nearer and nearer, until he noticed them. He stopped, turned around, and said: "You are following me. What do you want?" They said: "Where do you live?" He said: "Come and see. You are welcome!"

They went with him to his home, the house where he lodged. They stayed with him, and during their stay at his home, they started to believe in him. So much so that the very next day, they told others: "We have found the Messiah, the person sent to save us."

They discovered this at his home from the way he acted, reacted, and interacted *there*.

During a meeting of the World Council of Churches some years go, a famous liberation theologian came from North America. He spoke in this very chapel about oppression and liberation, about social justice and other justice. He spoke about "God is with the poor" and "God is not with the rich."

At question time, a listener stood up and said: "I hear that you are very rich, that you own four houses, one for each season, each one in a different part of the States. You spoke very nicely, indeed, but what about your own life, what about your own home, which side are you really on?"

Those remarks did not do away with the force of the speaker's arguments, but they did away with his personal credibility. In his life, in the way he acted, reacted, and interacted at home, he was not going to be of any help in this world.

About a year ago, a bishop came to address the students on this campus. His topic was "The Role of the Christian in Politics." He developed a whole plan on how to build a just society according to the spirit of Jesus Christ. At question time, a student stood up and asked why the bishop owned so many houses, including the one the student's family lived in, and why he had increased the rents of his tenants so pitilessly. There was no answer. The student's remarks did not invalidate the bishop's arguments. But that bishop could not be taken as an example of how to help this world become a better, more human, more divine place.

Their home lives betrayed them.

In the case of Jesus, his home life did not betray his words. It was precisely his home life that made John and Andrew say: "*He is the savior!*"

Sister or brother, John and Andrew taught us a way we can test others. They also taught us how we can test ourselves, the sincerity of our intentions, the honesty of our being.

The way we treat others at home proves our faith in him.

68. Total Overhaul

Mark 1:14–20

Jesus started his preaching. He could not postpone it any longer. John had been arrested; he had to step in, in his place. He had to take up the task assigned to him. He went to Galilee and started to speak. What he said seemed to be simple: "The right time has come, and the kingdom of God is at hand, repent and believe the good news!"

His preaching is not in vain. His words do not fall on the ground without bearing fruit. Several people hearing his voice and his message leave everything they have to follow him. Some are mentioned: Andrew, James, John, and Simon.

Within a few days it was clear that the old world was disappearing and a new world was coming. The expectancy turned into fulfillment, the hope into excitement. The world as they knew it was passing away, all problems would be tackled, all issues solved.

That was two thousand years ago, among totally different people in a foreign culture, in a very small part of the world's population.

It's touching to see how their excitement spilled over into our days. It's wonderful that the story is still told.

Aren't all fairy tales that way? Aren't all nursery rhymes immortal?

How can we take that type of preaching seriously in our day at a university among scholars, in between our research and our lectures, our analyses of the situation and our project planning? How would we be able to take that simple message: "The Kingdom is at hand, repent and believe!" as a tool for all the work that should be done to solve our social, medical, economic, scientific, or logistical problems? What can we do with those words in view of food, water, security, the population problems, refugees, the exploitation of people and nature all around us?

It's nice to think about Jesus. It's nice to dream about Jesus. It's nice to pray to Jesus. It's nice to see films on Jesus. It's nice to have a picture of Jesus. It's even nice to write Jesus' name on walls and car bumpers, but isn't all this at the same time rather naive and childish, perplexing and bewildering?

What did he mean? What can he mean to us? What did he want? What does he want from us in our modern day, when we seem to be at the point of solving all our problems rationally and scientifically? Isn't that what we are taught, not only at this university, but at all universities and schools?

Isn't solving problems only a question of a better analysis, more correct statistics, a more integrated interdisciplinary approach, and a few more seminars, workshops, conferences, symposiums, and congresses?

I once met an American at the Faculty of Commerce here. He said that he, too, was waiting for a new world, and he added that it will come when we have it all reasoned out and computerized.

What did Jesus know about all this in his time, in that tiny part of the world called Galilee?

No wonder people laugh at us, his followers, saying we are misfits, reactionary, stupid, old-fashioned, blind, fruitless, and dry. And yet, the more science progresses, the more technology dazzles us with its tremendous developments, the more we might notice that something seems to be lacking. All those developments seem not only to be a blessing, but also a threatening curse.

It is as if something is missing: the right direction, the right intention, the right meaning, an underlying principle.

It is in that context that the message of Jesus does count today, and counts very heavily.

The time has come, he said. The Kingdom of God is close at hand; repent and believe the good news.

This was the start. Later he showed what he meant.

He showed that it is possible for a human being to live with a changed heart, with outgoing love, interested in the welfare of all life around him.

He showed that his love will work out healing and restoration, fulfillment and invigoration. He showed how God's gifts to us, including science and technology, should be used for the benefit of all. He showed how we can break through sin and greed, ignorance and stupidity, egotism and shortsightedness.

He showed how the direction of the human will can be changed through the power of God.

It is that possibility of repentance and change that is good news, indeed, for the whole of humanity.

It is the start of a total overhaul, the beginning of God's Kingdom on earth, a changed human life.

FOURTH SUNDAY OF THE YEAR

69. An Object Lesson

Mark 1:21–28

They waited until the Sabbath and went with him to the synagogue.

He spoke. He taught. Everyone was impressed and amazed. They looked at one another and said: "Where did he get it? Unbelievable, and so self-confident, such an authority!"

Simon was the one who told all this to Mark, who was either his son or his clerk. He does not seem to have remembered what Jesus said that day.

Most probably, Jesus talked the way anyone talks who wants to change the human situation. He must have given an analysis. He must have drawn conclusions. He must have suggested some recommendations: words, words, words.

Simon had no interest in those words at all. He passed right over them. His interest was in something else, and it was that something else he asked Mark to note down. He was interested in what Jesus did.

There was, he reported, a man in the synagogue that day who was possessed by an evil spirit. That evil spirit talked. It shouted: "You want to destroy us? Do you really want to *do* something about us? I know who you are, you are the Holy One of God!"

Jesus told the spirit to be quiet and get out. The evil spirit got quiet and wriggled itself out of that man, who with a loud cry was liberated and free, there and then.

It was at Puebla, ten years after Medellín, that the Latin American cardinals and bishops met again. One of them, Dom Helder Camara, said: "Medellín produced beautiful statements, an excellent analysis, and very good recommendations, but," he added, "nothing really happened. The church is still with the rich, in order to be able to help the poor who are poor because of those rich!"

No evil spirit had been chased away. After all those words, everything remained the same or worse than ever before.

When Mark wrote his gospel, he was not interested in what Jesus said or taught. There are hardly any references to anything of the kind. He was more interested in what Jesus did. He chased an evil spirit away as a demonstration, an object lesson, showing what he had come *to do*.

We, his disciples, should *do* the same. We should, through our studies and words, locate evil, but once that is done, let us not repeat those words again and again. Let us chase evil *out*.

FIFTH SUNDAY OF THE YEAR

70. Healing and the Kingdom

Mark 1:29–39

He had just started, his heart and head full of great ideals, foreseeing and wanting a total change of the world: the introduction of the Kingdom of God. That morning it all ended up with some cups of coffee, as it so often does.

What happened?

He came from the synagogue where a devil had been chased away. He went to the house of Simon Peter, most probably hoping for some breakfast, as all of us would.

The lady of the house was sick. Simon's mother-in-law was in bed with fire in her bones, as the text reads. That's a nice way of saying she had a fever. Jesus went up to her, took her hand, and healed her. She got out of her bed and started to wait on them. In no time they were sitting in front of their breakfast.

Or, translating this into the realities of today, in front of their cups of coffee.

In the meantime, the story spread all through the place: He was healing. However, the day remained calm. Nobody was allowed to move, since it was a Sabbath. But in the evening, when walking was allowed, they came from all sides in droves, carrying, pushing, and pulling their sick, young and old.

He, full of compassion, healed as many as he could handle that evening.

Their enthusiasm grew at each blind one that saw, at each crippled one that walked, at each deaf one that heard, at each possessed one that got free, at each leg that was stretched or lengthened.

It got dark, the healed ones went home, and the sick ones, too, hoping for tomorrow.

During the night, he got restless. He came out from under his blanket. He went outside. He walked away from it all. He disappeared into the desert, and there he must have been asking himself: "Is this healing? Are those cups of coffee what I came to do? Is this my mission? Is this all?"

By morning, he knew his answer.

I think we all can understand what happened to him that night. I think we do because all of us have been in that same situation. You had a friend, a friend with a problem, a very serious problem. Maybe it was a drinking problem, and you said to yourself: "I have to do something about it. He or she is going to blazes. You can't drink the amount of bourbon he is drinking, or the amount of sherry she is drinking, without serious harm. I have to talk to him, I have to talk to her."

First you delayed, postponed, and procrastinated, but finally you had sufficient courage to go to your friend and talk. You sat down.

You drank a cup of coffee, and you talked about that coffee, about the weather, and about some other trivial things, and when it was time to leave, you had not spoken one word about the mission you had been on.

When the others discovered that he had disappeared, they went looking for him. They needed him because the sick were filling up the yard in front of the house where he had slept.

They asked him to come, but he had made up his mind. He had understood, and he told them: "No, I have to move on. I have to go on preaching the Kingdom of God, because that is why I came! Let us go!" And they left.

What he made clear to them, he wanted to make clear to us.

We, too, often think that he only came to heal, to get rid of our toothache, our stomachache, to save us from danger, or something like that. He definitely did, but that was not all. He came to change the whole world. He came to introduce the Kingdom of God, and that is more than healing a sickness or two.

When you look at television on Sunday morning with a cup of coffee in your hands, your TV screen is full of all kinds of healing. Blind see. Deaf hear. Livers and kidneys are restored. Legs are stretched and lengthened in miraculous ways. Even the dumb suddenly start to speak.

If all that is true and authentic (and haven't you sometimes had your doubts?) it certainly belongs to his Kingdom, but it definitely is not all.

That is what he understood that night in the desert after his spate of healing.

The Kingdom of God is a complete overhaul, a totally new creation: The new world and humanity that the prophets—including Jesus—dreamed and spoke about.

Let us not drown the Kingdom of God in cups of coffee. Let us not restrict it to a sick tooth here or a sick stomach there. Let us live in the fullness of its expectations: a new world, a new heaven, a new universe—God all in all.

SIXTH SUNDAY OF THE YEAR

71. Don't Tell Anyone

Mark 1:40–45

A leper came to him. He fell on his knee in front of him. He pleaded with his right hand over his mouth: "If you want to, you can heal me!"

Jesus looked at him, that creature of his, his brother, and once again he was touched with pity. He said: "Of course, I want to. Be healed!"

Having learned from what had happened to him before, he added: "Please, don't tell anyone except the priests you need to tell to get your health certificate."

The man not only went to those priests, he told the story left, right, and center.

And they came again, the hundreds and the thousands, looking for the easy thing—his touch—while remaining unchanged. They wanted to be healed like that leper, only on the surface.

It's a bit like those patients doctors sometimes speak of. Sick people who are looking for an injection, an ointment, a powder, or a pill, but who are not willing to change the eating and drinking habits, the smoking, the life style that is really the cause of their sickness.

They were a bit like those sufferers from VD who are quite ready to undergo all kinds of treatment but are not prepared to stop their promiscuity. Like all of us who are willing to discuss all the ills of society and how they should be overcome—how the goods should be redivided, how the poor should be helped, how the drunkards should be healed, how the prostitutes should be saved, how the orphans should be fed, how the wars should be stopped—in meeting after meeting after meeting, minuting everything carefully in writing. Yet nothing ever happens, because nothing goes deeper than our skins.

Jesus said: "I will heal your skin. I will heal the surface, but don't tell anyone. Keep it a secret. Because it is not all. If you tell, they will never understand what I really came for."

The ex-leper did tell. He was not really changed. And Jesus was proved right. They came. We came, and we come, looking for the easy thing—his touch—while remaining unchanged. We are willing to pray for a healing, but less willing to listen to what bishops write about the changes to be made in this world in view of justice for all and peace in this world in his—Jesus'—name.

SEVENTH SUNDAY OF THE YEAR

72. Jesus the Menace

Mark 2:1–12

Jesus had come back from Capernaum. People came from all over to see him. This time, he was preaching to them. He was explaining to them what he thought and felt about the world, about God, about humankind.

It is obvious from the gospel report that not all of them had come just to sit at his feet and listen to all he said.

There were some sitting there, some scribes and others, who were listening to him very critically and making objections every time he seemed to contradict their own set traditions.

He was doing that. If he had not done that, they would not have come to listen. If he had talked as they talked their god and man language, he would not have been a danger to them.

Here was one who was speaking in a way different from them, with a new type of authority, something he had done since the very first time he opened his mouth in the synagogue.

He questioned and criticized what they were accustomed to saying. He foresaw something new, an alternative, a possibility they could and would not admit.

So they had come to question him, to heckle him, to harass him, trying to get him to contradict himself while they defended their own position. They hoped to kill his influence and the hope he gave his listeners that maybe it all might change.

While he was talking with them, he was not healing. He was indoors, and the theological discussion about doctrine seemed endless, especially to those who had come with their sick.

They got impatient outside. They were not interested in talk about the possibility of a new world and a new order. They were interested in that new world here and now, not there and then. They were interested in instant healing.

Their impatience grew and, as they saw no chance of getting near him through the door or windows, they climbed on the roof. They uncovered it and, without any learned preamble, they lowered in front of him the most urgent and concrete item that exists in this world: a human being in pain.

Suddenly the dispute about the possibility of the end of the old and the beginning of the new between him and his opponents fell silent.

In that silence they all looked at the stretcher with the man dressed in a few rags, his body falling apart and its two piercing eyes asking for help, asking to be rid of the sick present and to start anew. Asking to fulfill the possibility they had said he was not even allowed to talk about.

Jesus looked at him, and then he said in the continuing silence: "My son, your past is done with, your sins are forgiven!"

A murmur went around. Their anger flared up. He had *done* what they did not even allow him to talk about. He had changed it all. All bonds fell away. The established order—the order established by them—broke up under their eyes.

Did it really? Was what he said a bluff? Unforgivable and blasphemous bluff, words in the air, threatening, but for the rest meaningless?

He looked at them, they looked at him. Did he smile? I do not know. He had guessed their reaction. No, he did not guess, he *knew*, and he said: "Why do you have those thoughts in your hearts? Which of these is easier to say to a paralytic, your sins are forgiven or get up, pick up your stretcher, and walk? To prove to you that the son of man has authority on earth to forgive sins"— and now he turned to the man on the stretcher—"I order you, get up, pick up your stretcher and walk, go home!"

To the horror of those scribes and the joy of all the others, the old world folded up and a new one was born: The man stood up from his stretcher and walked into the light of a totally new day.

EIGHTH SUNDAY OF THE YEAR

73. We Are the Bride

Mark 2:18–22

The occasion was simple. Some people came to him and said: "The followers of John and the Pharisees do fast, but your friends don't. Why not?"

In his answer, which was not simple at all, Jesus compared himself to a bridegroom preparing for marriage and those friends of his to the marriage attendants. He said: "I, Jesus, am going to take you, humankind, as my bride.

My disciples will be my witnesses in this. They cannot very well fast while preparing that feast.''

All this might seem very strange to us. Maybe it didn't sound so strange to the Hebrews, because they must have known that theme from the prophet Hosea: "Thus says the Lord: I am going to get her [humankind], I will bring her out into the wilderness, to a very lonely place, I will talk to her, I will praise her, I will tempt her, and everything will be all right.''

It is very difficult for us to understand that theme. It is so mystical, so romantic, so deep, so very poetical and daring. It almost embarrasses us.

One thing seems obvious: Jesus did not see this world and humanity as most of us do.

For most of us, this world in which we live is all there is. Whatever you are studying at a university, it is always *this world* in arts and architecture, in commerce and law, in engineering and medicine, in agriculture and science, in veterinary medicine, even in economics or journalism.

We analyze, measure, describe, plan, and develop it. We have been so successful doing all this that we got more and more involved in this world, up to the point where we almost became one-dimensional, believing only our eyes, ears, noses, fingers, and tongues.

Even if we pray, we only think of this world. We want to be healed here. We want to be successful here. We want to live as long as possible here. Just as the people around Jesus only thought of this world. "Stop my bleedings, and let me have children," whispered a woman. "Heal my son, he gets convulsions," said a father. "Take my skin disease away," said the leper. "Bring your friend Lazarus back to this life," asked his sisters.

It was and is always about this life and this world. It is so much about this life and this world that many Christians believe the resurrection means that we are going to live on as we are living now, forever and ever, after our death. They forget that Jesus did not rise from the dead the way Lazarus did, or that boy in Nain, or that other girl. He rose to a different life, a glorified life.

Would you always like to continue to live as you are living now?

There's a story about a monastery in Brittany about twelve hundred years ago. In that convent, nobody died. All the monks remained living, and they were very upset about that. They got older and older, but there was no end in sight. They decided to pray to be allowed to die. The prayer was not heard. They lived on and on, until the abbot had a dream. In that dream, he noticed that the gate of heaven through which the angels went up and down to and from this world was exactly above their convent. Those ascending and descending angels used the convent's compound as their earthly airstrip. The convent was a kind of illegal extension of the heavenly court, and that was why the monks did not die. Next morning, after matins, he told his story to the other monks. They decided, then and there, to break down their monastery. And they did. They shifted it to another place a few hundred yards beyond. Immediately, they started to die, the oldest ones first. And they were very, very happy.

We should not be bound to the *here*, we should not be limited to the *now*. Our possibilities extend wider, into a Kingdom to come: a marriage to be celebrated by us and by *him*.

74. Unhealthy Rites

Mark 2:23–3:6

It is already late in the evening. Suddenly the telephone rings in the presbytery; an anxious voice at the other side asks: "Father, is your Mass still free tomorrow?" "No, I am sorry, there is an intention already." "But, Father," the voice at the other side pleads, "Can't you do something about it? It is the anniversary of the death of my father, and we have been having a Mass all the years after his death on the day of his passing away. It is just this time that we forgot. Please, Father. It would be terrible if there would be no Mass this year, terrible. . . ."

You can hear the fear and even the terror in that voice at the other side. It is as if the deceased father is going to do something awful if that Mass were not said, as if he would come out of his tomb and spook around or cast a spell over the whole family.

You might laugh at this, and if you do, it means that such a thing would never happen to you, but would you be able to say in all honesty that similar fears never overcome you? Would you never be in such a situation? Are you trying to tell me that you don't have rites and rituals, gestures and words you use to try to control your life and destiny?

Do you never feel that you have to mumble a prayer, touch an object, swallow a bitter herb, walk over a grave, sprinkle some water, throw some salt over your shoulder, knock wood, spread some ashes, grind some bone, kill a chicken, because otherwise, terrible things will happen to you? All of us feel like that, because all of us would like to control and check our neighbors, nature, and even God.

That is what the Pharisees tried to do. By washing their hands, sprinkling their heads, dressing in a special way, wearing their hair in threshes, avoiding some and speaking to others, saying some prayers, laying on hands, not picking any ears of wheat from the field on a Sabbath day, sticking to hundreds and hundreds of small little rules, they tried to get a grip on themselves, their neighbors, their lives, and on nature. *What they really tried was to get a grip on God.*

They thought they had caught him. They thought they knew what she would do. They thought they felt how he would react, what she would reward, what he would punish. They had cut him to their own image. They were sure that

God was with them. Didn't they fulfill all the conditions *they had set them-selves?*

Jesus disagreed. That is too mild a word. Jesus threw out all their pretenses. Jesus was not against law, rituals, rites, or the words of sacred scripture. He was against any use of the law or the Bible, any rite or ritual that tried to control, check, and limit God's love, mercy, and grace, and consequently human love, grace, and mercy.

That controlling, checking, and limiting of God and God's power is what we all do too often through our rituals and rites.

"God is with us, not with our enemy." Weapons are blessed, and have been blessed, at the beginning of each crusade to crush, plunder, and rape the infidels in Syria, Israel, Iraq, Iran, South and Central America, Europe, Southeast Asia, South Africa, and the United States.

"God is with us, not with the others." The Bible was read and quoted by Hitler and his company in view of the *Endlösung der Judenfrage,* and the Bible is read quoted to separate the whites from the blacks, and the coloreds from the rest.

"God is with us, not with sinners and devils," and witches are burned, prostitutes despised, dissidents tortured, opponents put in prison, and capital punishment inflicted.

"God is with us," and the Bible is used to formulate doctrines that hinder our Christian inter-communion; that oblige all priests to live like monks, even at the cost of being unable to provide the Eucharist to all; that absolutize impossible human marriage relations and keep half of humankind away from the sharing of his bread.

In the gospel of today, Jesus turns against all those human laws and restrictions that make us fearful and afraid, that restrict God's love, mercy, and grace, and overlook the real command God gave us all: to love one another unreservedly, to share our bread unrestrictedly.

So don't be afraid: God's love and mercy and grace is greater than any of our rites. Don't use your rites, rituals, theology, Bible, your personal or societal values to limit God's love and mercy and grace to anyone. Never. Amen.

TENTH SUNDAY OF THE YEAR

75. They Brought Him a Man

Mark 3:20–35

His family got very upset. They had heard about his healing a leper on a Sabbath day. They had heard about his forgiving sins as if he were Yahweh. They had heard about his eating with sinners, a thing they themselves would never do. They had heard about him being surrounded by strangers, so he did not even have time to take his regular meals.

They had come to take charge of him, something he obviously was not able to do for himself anymore.

When they arrived in Capernaum, their worst expectations and all those weird rumors proved to be true.

They could not even get hold of him. The house he was in, Simon's house, was not only full, it was surrounded by so many people that they could not even get to the door.

They said: "We are his brothers, we are his sisters, this is his mother! Do you hear that: his mother! Please let us through. We are his family. We want to see him. We have a right to see him!"

No one listened. Nobody gave way. It was as if they had lost him forever.

Now and then they could hear some words from inside. That is how they heard that others considered him mad, possessed by a devil.

They tried to push, to no avail. The people around simply would not let them through. The only thing they could do was send a message in from mouth to mouth, saying: "Your mother, your brothers, and your sisters are outside at the door. They are asking for you."

Even before that message reached him, they heard him say: "A household that is divided against itself cannot stand." Was he speaking about them? They only wanted the very best for him. He should come back in their circle. He should not mix with those others. Who was this Simon, anyway? He should stick to their customs. He should be faithful to their rules. He should respect their taboos. He should understand his place in society. He should take into account the divine order of things.

Finally the message seemed to have arrived, because they heard him raise his voice and say: "Who is my mother? Who are my brothers? Who are my sisters?"

They could not believe their ears. Had he forgotten all about them? Then they heard him add—obviously while he was looking around himself: "All those here are my mother, my brothers, and my sisters. Anyone who does the will of God is my brother and sister and mother."

He had broken the circle of physical human relationships. He had broken through the circle of blood, race, and earth. He spoke about a new family, the family of God, his family. The family of those who are brothers and sisters because they are all born of God: a Parent to all, a Brother Christ to everyone, a Sister the Spirit with all of us.

P.S. Did his mother understand? Was she again wondering deep in her heart? Later she definitely did understand, and so did James, the "brother" of Jesus, when he became the leader of the first community in Jerusalem, where the rest of his family belonged to the one and the same community with very many others after his return to the Father.

76. The Good News

Mark 1:12–15

He must have sat down often to consider the state of the nation. He must have worried often about the leadership he saw around him. He must have talked often about the temple and its services.

He must have done all that very often, since he was like us in all things but sin.

Doing this, we compare the world in which we live with the vision of a world to come. Speaking about injustice, we know about justice. Complaining about dishonesty, we imply honesty. Worrying about wars and violence, we dream about peace. Protesting discrimination and violence, we suggest a more equitable world.

We all do this. We are all charged with vision; we are all full of hope. But we don't go any further, we don't move. We see as if blind. We hear as if deaf. We move as if paralyzed.

So did he, up to the moment he entered that desert for those forty long, very long, days.

Full of Spirit, he was challenging his spirit. Full of vision, he was facing his blindness. His ears ringing with the message, he was fighting his deafness. Asked to move, he had to overcome his lameness.

Mark says he was tempted, shocked, and shaken, fighting with all that held him back, struggling with everything that kept him small, restricted, paralyzed, and fruitless, fighting the devil himself.

He was going to ask us to do the same. He was going to invite us to follow him. He was going to show us what we would be able to do.

But before turning to us, before inviting others, he first fought and overcame the indolence and immobility he wants us to overcome.

We can no longer just complain about others, forgetting about ourselves. We can no longer think that the world will change and our vision will be fulfilled without ourselves being changed and moved.

That is what he learned in the desert, and that is why he came out of it—himself changed—to shout to us: "The time is ripe, the days are fulfilled, I overcame what holds you down. I could do it, you can do it. Change and believe this good news."

SECOND SUNDAY OF LENT

77. Human Glory to Come

Mark 9:2–10

One of the reasons they followed him must have been their sense of power-lessness. They knew that by themselves, they would not be able to do anything about the world in which they lived and the lives they were living.

They were like that soldier in the old Asian story who had looted a town. He was trying to sell an exquisite rug, one of the spoils. ''Who will give me a hundred dollars for this carpet?'' he shouted through town, once he was home from his venture. In no time he found an eager buyer. After the sale, a by-stander, aware of the value of the rug, approached the seller and asked him: ''Why did you not ask more for that priceless rug?''

''Is there a number higher than one hundred?'' asked the seller. His conception limited his awareness and his action.

Their conception of themselves limited their awareness and their actions. It even restricted their awareness of what Jesus might be able to do.

They had some hope in him, that's true. But they had no idea what they were really in for.

Maybe that's the reason he took them out of this world, out of the world they knew so very well, out of the relationships they were accustomed to, away from the water most of them had practically been living in as fishermen.

He took them with him to the top of a mountain. Once up there, he started to change.

First his clothing, then he himself, transparent and yet opaque, white and yet full of color, while heavenly beings appeared: Elijah and Moses. They heard him discuss with those two the coming change, the passover, a transformed, shining world.

They did not know what to say; they were taken by surprise. They mumbled something about staying there and about a tent for three.

Then, to top it all, a cloud came down, a shadow fell, a voice was heard: ''This is my son, the beloved one, listen to him!''

Suddenly, everything seemed over. He was standing there again, just like they had seen him so often before. One like them.

Now they knew what he was in for. They understood what the future would be, not only for him, but for themselves, too. Hadn't he always been like them? Hadn't they always been like him? Hadn't he told them that anything he would do, they would do even better?

He ordered them not to tell anyone what had happened to him, or what would happen to them, before that new life had risen from the tomb of the old. Though they did not yet fully understand, they looked at their hands and their feet. They looked at one another, and they knew that the power of change would be given to them. They knew that one day they, too, would shine. They understood that they would be able to do more than they ever expected to do.

So should we, seeing ourselves reflected in the image of his transformed self: Emmanuel, God with us!

THIRD SUNDAY OF LENT

78. The Sign Given

John 2:13–25

He had overcome the temptations so common and normal in the world. He had shown himself in the brightness of our real human possibilities, the possibility of a change, of a passover, of a new human life.

That morning, he entered the temple, the center of their religious life; the center of their *old* religious life. A temple of stones, gold, and silver, a temple of sacrificed animals, of dying bullocks, of butchered pigeons. A temple against which the prophets had been shouting in the name of God: "The Lord says: Do you think I like all those sacrifices you keep offering to me? I have more than enough of the sheep you burn as sacrifices. I am tired of the blood of bulls and sheep and goats. Who asked you to do all this when you come to worship me? Who asked you to do all this tramping about in my temple? It is useless to bring your offerings. I am disgusted with the smell of the incense you burn. I can't stand your new moon festivals, your sabbaths, and your religious gatherings. They are all corrupted by your sins. I hate your feast days. They are a burden that I am tired of carrying. When you lift your hands in prayer I won't look at you. No matter how much you pray, I will not listen, for your hands are covered with blood. Wash yourselves clean. Stop all evil that I see you doing. Yes, stop evil, and learn to do right. See that justice is done. Help those who are oppressed. Give orphans their right and defend widows."

He had told them that he had come to fulfill the prophecies. If so, didn't he have to stop the temple service?

That's what he did!

That morning, it was not only a question of chasing away the bankers and merchants. It was not only a question of letting those animals and birds loose. It was not only a question of silver and gold.

What he did went much deeper, was more fundamental. What he did was to stop the temple service that had outlived its aim and was no longer faithful to its vocation.

Those present must have known this. That's why they asked: "What sign can you show us authorizing *you* to do these things?"

It was as if they had expected this end any day, but who was *he* to terminate it all?

He did not give them the sign they asked for.

He had given them that sign already: The old temple service had been stopped by him and the new temple had been announced. The one in which God is with the orphans and the widows, with the sinners and the sick, forming through Christ one body: *God's temple with us*.

FOURTH SUNDAY OF LENT

79. Backed Up by Him

John 3:14–21

Being invited to speak about the hunger and famine in Africa, I have been giving lectures all over the country. While making that tour here in the United States, I gained, of course, some insight into the situation here, too.

I spoke mainly to groups that were, in one way or another, trying to do something about the disastrous situation in Africa. But after the talk, after the questions, after the input and the feedback, there was practically always that last question.

It's an unavoidable question: "Is there any hope? Isn't humanity so sick that it would be more realistic to just give up?"

When that question was asked, you could see people quickly look at one another, and at me, checking the reactions, and at the same time confirming that this issue had to be faced, that this question had to be answered.

All three of the readings of today are on this very question.

The first reading speaks about a situation where all hope seemed to be lost: the people scattered and disbanded, only vagrants on the wide face of this earth, powerless, sick, and dying.

The second reading explains how we were, or are, dead through our sins because of our faulty options, wrong decisions, and poor priorities.

And in the third reading, Jesus explains that there was no hope, that he would be crucified, lifted up on a cross, and murdered.

It is true that humanity is sick. It is true that humanity might be called dying.

But it is also true that another power is in this world. The *power* that brought us here together. The *power* that brings all the people organizing themselves in justice and peace groups together, again and again.

When we think about Jesus' redeeming work, we often think about his blood shed once and for all, about the pain suffered so long ago, about the death endured on the cross.

We have a vague impression that those events saved us.

In a way, that is true; in another way, it is not.

What saved us, and what saves us, is that in spite of his suffering and death, the movement he started in this world did not give up and never ended.

During his life, he formed a small group of hardly more than ten people. He had organized, inspired, and led them. Together they had started the struggle for a better world full of hope, because they believed themselves to be backed up by him and God.

That group did not disappear after his death. It remained, notwithstanding that death, because of the Easter phenomenon we call resurrection.

A movement, a process, a growth, a network, that even reaches us this very day and is our hope in this world.

If you effectively join that movement, you will dispel all gloom and doom together with him.

FIFTH SUNDAY OF LENT

80. The End of the Circle

John 12:20–33

It started very simply. There were some Greeks at the festival. They went to one of his followers, Philip, to ask him to introduce them to Jesus. In fact, they asked him for more. They wanted to *see* Jesus, and experts tell us that this meant, in the language of their time, that they wanted to be with him.

Philip must have looked at those strangers, exotically dressed, speaking with a different accent, eating other food, and consequently even smelling differently, with some apprehension.

He hesitated, and not wanting to make a decision alone, he went to explain to Andrew.

Would it be a good thing to hand on their message? Wouldn't it be a precedent? Wouldn't it be the end of their rather secure ethnic life together? What if all kinds of people were taken into their circle? Didn't those others do everything in different ways?

Finally they decided to go to Jesus and to explain to him the issue, their hesitations, and their doubts. Should the circle be broken up? Should their approach change?

It seems Jesus did not answer their question, because he said neither yes nor no. And yet he answered it, but at a much more profound level, at a level where everything, his whole life, was at stake.

He answered them by giving them insight into his own feelings, hesitations, and decisions. He answered them by making them share in the monologue, or dialogue, he had been having with himself for quite some time, especially during those last days at the festival.

Philip and Andrew came to ask him whether their circle and company should not remain unchanged, notwithstanding the request of those Greeks. He, himself, was struggling with the question of whether or not *all* should change.

Shouldn't the life he had been living be given up? Shouldn't the life they had been living together be broken up, so new life would be able to begin: a new era, a new perception, a new morality, a new everything? Shouldn't the grain that existed and lived—restricting that life to its narrow confinement—fall into the ground, break open and die, thus giving new life?

He was reasoning with himself when he said: *Now the hour has come*, and *how troubled is my heart*, and *shouldn't I ask my Father to excuse me* and *but didn't I come precisely because of this hour?*

Shouldn't he do what he had been tempted to do since the day he had known about himself, his Father, and his mission?

Shouldn't he turn the stones of this world into bread and gold to save himself? Shouldn't he use his extraordinary possibilities to realize the most fantastic religious one-man show ever performed, with guaranteed applause from all sides? Shouldn't he use his power to rule them all with the crack of the whip he had used in the temple, making them turn left, right, forward, and backward at his command? Shouldn't he live the life they were all living, the only life possibility they knew?

Would it be worth it, to change it all?

He thought of the cross, his death, his blood, the wounds, and the dirt. Would they understand? Would anyone ever understand? Would the new ever grow, the seed he was going to sow in the tomb of this earth? Philip and Andrew must have been wondering about his reaction. Probably they did not understand it at all.

Did he say yes, or did he say no?

Before he had finished his answer, his agony was over. The decision was made, the *yes* said.

And a voice from heaven sounded as the echo to that *yes*: glory, glory, alleluia.

Sentence was passed, the prince of the world was overthrown, life would start afresh for all, including the Greeks and you and me.

PASSION/PALM SUNDAY

81. The Jerusalem Journey

Mark 11:1–10

Today we commemorate how he changed his direction; how he started a new movement.

Up to then, he had been moving into his own inner being. In the desert for forty days; before that in Nazareth for almost thirty years; and even later, during those nights he was on a mountaintop, or hidden deep in the forest, alone with himself, alone with God, shining in his glory from within.

Up to then, he had moved from within that glorious center in him out to the others. Coming out of the desert; establishing himself in the most cosmopolitan town of his region (or was he just there, sleeping in a street? Who knows?); contacting Jews and aliens, Greeks and people from the diaspora. He had been traveling in an ever-widening circle, as far as his feet could carry him: to Samaria and Bethany, to the Decapolis, and in the direction of Syria. He had met and touched all kinds of people: the woman from Samaria, the Roman officer, the Greeks looking for him, Nicodemus the Jewish scholar, Simon the Pharisee, and even the Syro-Phoenician woman who asked his help.

Now he changed his direction. He was not entering into himself; he was not going out to others. Entering Jerusalem, he started that final movement foretold by so many prophets, the movement that would bring all and everything together.

There were the animals, the ass and her colt; the branches, leaves, and flowers thrown under the feet of those animals. There were the sun and the sky, the stones and the cobbles in the street, that threatened—according to his very own words to shout out loud.

There were, above all, the people, the young and the old, the rich and the poor, full of expectation, and yet not too sure of what was going on. They were pushing and pulling all around him, singing and dancing, shouting and ululating: "Glory to God, hail to the King, Son of God, Son of David, alleluia!"

There were also scribes, friends, and opponents, who understood better than anyone else what he started to do and where all this would lead.

The old prophecies tumbled and rumbled in their heads. Hadn't Zechariah prophesied that the Messiah would enter the town sitting on the young of an ass (Zechariah 9:9)? Hadn't he spoken about a final day that Yahweh would put his feet on the Mount of Olives in Jerusalem (Zechariah 14:4)? Didn't Jesus act like a king when he simply sequestered the animal he needed (1 Samuel 8:17)? Didn't the Book of Genesis tell that the Messiah would tie his young ass to the vine, to its stock the foal of the she-ass (Genesis 49:11)?

They were afraid, not only for him, but also of him.

And he, sitting on his donkey, surrounded by the shouts and the colors, the smells and the perfumes, the excitement and the enthusiasm of the people of old Jerusalem, must have been thinking of the new Jerusalem. He must have been dreaming about the great day he foresaw, the day that all people would come together with everything in creation, assembling on the mountaintop to be with their origin and their source, to be with God at table.

That enormous table where everyone will find a place, *her place, his place, your place, my place* in the house of our Mother, our Father, our Brother, our Sister: in the home of the Spirit of God.

EASTER SUNDAY

82. Alleluia

Mark 16:1–8

Easter is his dream come true. It is his desire fulfilled. It is his community formed. It is his love reigning.

We usually say that he overcame sin, that he conquered death, that he undid evil, that he crushed the devil.

There is much more to Easter than just that.

We act as if Jesus, who rose from the dead, came back to take up our type of life, the life we live.

He returned a different being, not only physically walking through doors and changing place with lightning speed, but also in another way.

The new life he had lived here on earth—the cause of his death—had now been certified, guaranteed, sealed, approved, confirmed, and established by God.

They had killed it.

To be sure of that, they even pierced his heart in a heartrending extra. They buried it deep in the rock, with a stone in front, some seals on top, and a couple of guards next to it.

That life had come back, still a bit strange in this world to begin with. Now nothing will ever be able to undo it anymore. It will grow, not as a threat, but as a fulfillment to the whole of humankind.

Alleluia.

SECOND SUNDAY OF EASTER

83. In His Absence

John 20:19–31

Jesus appeared to them over and over again. In one of today's readings, he does it twice.

Every time he appeared, he disappeared, and that is why he had to appear again.

Take the case of Thomas. First Jesus appeared to the other ten; Thomas was not there. Thomas did not believe them. Thomas had to see him first. Thomas had to see him in his presence before he would believe in his absence. So he had to appear again to convince Thomas. After his appearance to him, he promptly disappeared again.

Why didn't he stay with them? Why was he more absent than present? Once recognized, off he went.

The Easter story is more a story of his disappearances than of his appearances. The times he was away were considerably longer than the times he was with them.

It was as if he wanted to tell them something. It was as if he wanted to indicate to them: "All right, I am alive. Do not have any doubt about that, not even you, Thomas, dear. But I will be absent. I will be absent all the rest of your time. It will all be up to you!"

In the gospel of today, he not only tells them that. He also tells them what they should do, how they should react to his absence.

They should take up their responsibility. They should enter the process he had come to introduce in this world. They should no longer be mere victims. They should no longer be passive observers. They should no longer be only objects. They should be actors and activators entering human history.

He blew over them. He said: "Forgive, change the shadows of the past!"

And before he left them finally, disappearing as dramatically as possible, endlessly high up, straight into the sky, he told them from above: "Go out into the whole world and bring them all together: one Father, one Mother, one Brother, one Sister, one Spirit, one family, the life of all!"

Very many do not want to hear this news about him and themselves.

Very many act as if Jesus did not leave.

They are saying: "He is the answer! He is my savior! He is my personal savior! Everything will be all right. Maybe not now, maybe not here, but definitely then, and certainly there!"

Saying this, they do not really engage themselves in this world, as he asked and ordered them to do.

We should not forget the message he gave us after his resurrection: "It is all up to you!"

That is why he blew over them, giving them his Spirit before he left, leaving us in his absence, as long as we will be here in this world.

THIRD SUNDAY OF EASTER

84. Words Fail

Luke 24:35–48

Jesus was talking to the two companions. Did you know that the word *companion* means people who have their "panis," their bread, together?

He was talking and talking and talking. He explained to them the whole Old Testament. (He did not talk to them about the New Testament because it had not been written as yet.)

They got sufficient material for their bachelor's, their master's, and their doctoral in Bible Studies, and yet *they did not recognize him*. Maybe they understood, but they did not see.

They asked him to stay. He stayed, and he talked on. They remained blind until he took their bread and broke it, giving each one a piece of it. It was at that moment that they suddenly *saw*.

The talk had not helped. Words had failed. The sign worked. Immediately they rose to go to Jerusalem to take up the new life.

Signs are more significant than words. Words do not help. Verbosity is useless. Poetry falls flat. Prose betrays the issues.

The old prophets knew that. When they had talked their throats sore and their tongues out of their mouths, when they had been shouting for days and days at the tops of their voices—voices calling in the wilderness—they would finally refer to signs in silence.

In that silence they would crack pots to show the threatening end. They would let their vestments rot to show the rottenness of the situation. They would grow beards and nails; they would even—as Hosea did—marry a prostitute and start that difficult and almost impossible life to show that the nation had become a whore in its relations with God. Hosea had a son, and he called him *Break-the-bow*; he had a daughter, and he called her *Unloved*; he had a second son, and he called him *No-people-of-mine*. Isaiah, that venerable man, walked as a sign of the coming doom, naked and barefooted for three years—as the sacred text says, *his buttocks bared*—through the whole of the land.

Let us come back to Jesus in Emmaus. His words failed, his sign spoke. Do you think it will be different in our case? We are no better than our master.

Our words will fail. The words of all good men and women will fail. The words of the righteous will fall flat, as they have always done before. We do not even need the international conference racket to know that.

You might even go a step further. Our prayers failed, too. We spoke, and nothing changed. We prayed, and nothing happened.

Everybody is waiting, not for more words, but for a sign: the breaking of the bread.

That is what we should do in our politics, in our education, in our business, in our lives.

Jesus talked and talked and talked, and they did not see. They did not see a thing. They did not even see him.

Then he took his bread, he broke it, and they said: "IT IS HE!" They saw, and straightaway a new life started.

FOURTH SUNDAY OF EASTER

85. One Shepherd Only

John 10:11–18

Jesus said: "I am the good shepherd, the only one." He added: "I am the gate. I am the door. I am the only entrance, I am the only exit that will lead to anything."

Our reactions to those statements can be very different. They can be positive, even to the point that we say: "In that case, we should do what we can to spread that vital piece of information." They can be negative, especially when we think about all that has been done in his name during human history.

"I am the good shepherd. I am the way. I am the truth. I am life, if anyone rejects me he will die."

What did he mean? What did he want? Did he mean what Christians mean? Did he want what Christians want? Did he intend what Christians so often call their "Christian ethics"?

That is a good question.

In 1454, Pope Nicholas V wrote a decree *Romanus Pontifex* in which he blessed, in the name of Jesus, the slave trade. In 1668, a theologian at a university wrote that the justification of slavery is a matter of faith, and he quoted, in the name of Jesus, Leviticus, the first letter of Peter, the first letter to the Corinthians, and the letter to Philemon. In 1864, the Church still had slaves. In fact, the first *general* statement against slavery dates only from the Second Vatican Council.

Study Christian Church statements on the place and role of women in this world, even the most recent ones, and you will be reminded of what an old Church father wrote: "Women are the gateway of the devil."

We Christians know that those statements are wrong when we read them against Jesus' vision. It is that vision of Jesus we should test when we want to know what he meant, *not* the so-called Christian version of that outlook.

It is in his vision that he, seeing the crowds, had pity on them because they seemed to be scattered, to be like sheep without a shepherd.

He saw in a very special way how all human beings belong together. How we all hang together—or at least should—as one tree of life.

He expressed this in his idea about God: a Mother and a Father, and we all in the same family, brothers and sisters.

This he expressed when his family—his mother, his sisters, and his brothers—wanted to see him. He did not come, because, he said, everyone is my mother, my sister, and my brother.

He expressed this when he handed his bread around and said: "This is my body, eat it, all of you." When he handed his cup around and said: 'This is my blood, drink it, all of you.'' Just as we are doing now during this mass, being one without considering age or wealth, social groups, race, or the schools where we studied.

He expressed this when he was interested in all the people he met during his life: the young, the old, the sick, the healthy, the dead, the sinners, the crooks, the lost girls, the runaway boys, and the saints.

It is a vision in which slavery, discrimination, apartheid are out. It is an outlook in which the human family is really one family, in which peace will reign, conflicts will be solved, the economy will be interested in all, without a war that might destroy us.

His vision is the only one that saves us. That is why HE, living that vision through life, passion, and death into resurrection and glory, is the only way and the only door leading in and out.

Let us never forget that twice, prophets thought we Christians had lost that vision in the practice of our lives.

Mohammed, almost fourteen hundred years ago, started a new "jamaa," a new human family, because the Christians he lived with did not want to associate with him or his people. More than a hundred years ago, Karl Marx started his new "commune," because he doubted whether Christians, with their belief in God, could do it.

They both made a mistake: They thought Jesus was at fault. He is not; his followers were.

He remains the only good shepherd, the exclusive door leading in and leading out.

FIFTH SUNDAY OF EASTER

86. Interconnectedness

John 15:1–8

Today Jesus tells of some of his experiences in life.

He sees himself, he explains, as connected with us, with the whole of humankind, with all and everything.

I don't know whether you ever had the same type of experience. I don't think it's an experience unique to Jesus. So many people had it. I had it. I am sure that you have had it, too.

It is a feeling that has been described in many ways. It happened in all kinds of circumstances. I will tell you some. See if you recognize any of them.

It is a very nice summer evening. All is quiet. You are standing in front of a beautiful, limpid lake. The sun is just touching the horizon, coloring everything a golden red. You look out over the water. A gentle breeze blows in your face. Suddenly everything seems to fall away—the trees, the sun, the lake, the water. It is as if everything is streaming into you (or is it out of you?) and you feel one with it all. One with everything. One with everybody.

You are listening to music. It could be the *Messiah* by Handel. It could be a beautiful piece of jazz. Suddenly you are taken up, you become one with the music. The choir, the trumpet, the saxophone (or is it the clarinet?) takes you out of yourself, and there is the feeling that you belong to the whole of the universe, and the universe to you. You're looking at the one you love. You get nearer and nearer. . . .

You are sitting in a train, in a bus, or in a plane with all those people around you. Suddenly you realize that all those people are as full of the wonder of the world as you are, all filled with potency, Spirit, and God-self.

You are sitting at home, knitting with the wool on your lap, or you are doing the washing-up, with the cat purring at your feet, and again it comes: a sense of great contentment, a great sense of belonging to the earth, the water, the sky, the sun, the moon, the plants and the animals, your family, all those you know and even those you don't.

Don't you carry in you all human feelings? Isn't that why you like to read books, watch a good film, go to a concert, a disco, or sing a song? Today Jesus tells us that he had those experiences, too. Today he tells us how he feels connected with us, as a vine is connected with the branches, leaves, flowers, and fruits.

Today he tells us that we have our home in him, as he should have his home in us.

The difference is that for him, all this was no vision that passed after some moments of insight and enlightenment. For him, it was not only a vision that passed. It was and is the life he lived, and lives, always. It is the life he wants us to realize and live all the time, forever and ever.

Our experiences of those moments are right. We belong together! He is with us, and we are with him.

SIXTH SUNDAY OF EASTER

87. Can Love Be Commanded?

John 15:9–17

You know the story. It's told so very often and known so well that we sometimes overlook its force.

She said:

I was a child in a large family. I was in the middle somewhere. I am sure that my father loved me, that my mother loved me, and sisters and brothers loved me, too. We were not rich. We were barely surviving.

The school fees for me and the others were really a burden to my parents. My father worked the whole day. So did my mother. There wasn't much time left to talk with one another; everyone was so busy.

I had accepted myself, and the others had accepted me. Nevertheless, I thought myself rather plain and very common—nothing special. When I looked at myself in the mirror, I didn't exactly like what I saw: too pale, too flat.

Then I met him. He looked at me. I saw him looking, and I wondered what he saw. Then he said to me: "You are very pretty." And he said to me: "You are very beautiful." He asked me: "May I be your friend? I like what I hear from you." Later on, he added: "You are my all and everything." And then he said to me: "I think of you all the time!"

I looked at myself with other eyes when standing in front of my mirror. I looked with other eyes at everything around me: the sun and the moon, the flowers and the birds, the water and the air. I was loved. I was loved, and I loved. I could have danced all day and all night. I sometimes did, with him.

You also know the reverse of that story: The feeling that no one loves you. How often I have heard people say, with tears in their eyes, with fists hopelessly clenched: "Nobody loves me. Nobody in the whole wide world loves me."

It's only in the context of that love—the warp and woof of all our novels, plays, and films, the substance of our lives—that we can understand the readings of today, in which Jesus says: "I love you, you are my friends. I am willing to give my life for you. Don't think that it is only you who decided to love me, but I love you because *I* love you."

He went further when commanding us to love him and one another. *"This is my commandment that you love each other."*

It is that word *commandment* that sounds strange when speaking about love. Can love be commanded? Can I tell you: "You have to love me"? Can you tell another: "You have to love me"?

That's the reason some translate the word *commandment* as "prescription"; the type of prescription you find in a cookbook. The kind of prescription the doctor gives you, indicating the type of medicine you have to use in order to become healthy.

You cannot cook chicken and rice without rice. You cannot cook pea soup without peas. You cannot make raisin bread without raisins. Those raisins are prescribed; they are a condition, a commandment.

In the same way, Jesus says: You cannot have human life without love. You can't; we exist because we are loved. It is only through love's power that we live and can live; that we see and can see, taste and can taste, smell and can smell, touch and can touch.

Without that divine ingredient, human life is hell.

ASCENSION DAY

88. He Left It to Us

Mark 16:15–20

He had been with them for forty days. They had been very glad to see him again, but something had changed. There are no reports of miracles worked by him during that time. Nothing at all, except the way in which he appeared suddenly through ceilings and floors, unopened windows and locked doors.

He spoke to them, that's true. But when he spoke to them, he only spoke about *them*. He told them that he was giving *them* power. The power to forgive one another. The power to cast out evil. The power to handle snakes with their bare hands, animals that had always been the symbol of sin. He told them that they would drink the deadly poison of this corrupt world without harm. He told them that he would send *them* his Holy Spirit.

As for the rest, no news. Nothing happened until the fortieth day, when they met on a mountaintop.

It seems to have started with their question, a question that had been burning on their lips and in their minds for such a long time: "Lord, has the time come? When are *you* going to restore this world?"

When they asked that question, *his feet left this earth a little bit.*

"When are *you* bringing us the salvation and redemption [he got a bit higher], the emancipation and the justice, the goodness and integrity [he got a bit higher again], the health and the life, the development and the Kingdom of God you have promised and we are waiting for?" *He was very high, now.*

The more they insisted, the higher he rose. Then, from above, he said: "Let us not discuss times and dates. Let us not discuss when it all will be finalized. Let us discuss how you—yes, you—will receive the Spirit. How you will have to go out proclaiming the good news from here till the end of the earth, baptizing those who believe, casting out devils, picking up snakes, using your gift of tongues, laying your hands on the sick. Start moving. *You*, not me. I am leaving; it is up to you now."

While he was saying this, he left this earth, getting higher and higher, until they could not see him anymore.

They went to Jerusalem to wait for his Spirit.

Many of us claim to be Christians, to be the followers of Jesus Christ. How many of us take the task he left us seriously?

We are quite willing to pray, to spend some time in church, but how many of us carry our tasks out of that church and into our daily lives?

We live in a world that is far from good. We all know about the snakes, the sins, the corruption, the hunger, the bribes asked for and given, the neglect, the deception, the widows, and the orphans.

Don't we often use Jesus as an excuse for sitting comfortably in this rubble and rubbish? We say: "After all, he redeemed us. We are washed in his blood. We are safe. We are saved. We look up to the Father, we fold our hands, we bend our knees, we distribute Bibles, we contribute to the church collections, we close our eyes, we close our ears, we close our noses, we close our hands, we close our mouths, and we bless the world. We even bless its bombs and its fighter jets, and we sing: 'Amazing Grace' and 'We Are Not of This World' and 'Alleluia, Praise the Lord.' ''

Insofar as we are concerned, insofar as it depends on us, nothing is going to change in this world. Nothing is going to change because we glorify him who sits at the right hand of God the Father.

Sister or brother, do you know what Jesus Christ is doing there at that right hand? It's explained to us in the letter to the Hebrews, chapter ten, verse thirteen. The letter reads: "He took his seat at the right hand of God *where he is waiting*, until his enemies are overcome by us!''

His disciples were left behind on earth because of that.

That is why he said to them: "I leave you as salt. I leave you as yeast. I leave you as light.''

We often piously think that we should be waiting for him.

In actual fact, he is waiting for us!

SEVENTH SUNDAY OF EASTER

89. Your Nearest One Is Naked

John 17:11–19

In February 1979, a very famous and infamous German-American philosopher, Herbert Marcuse, became eighty. He had been the leader of the 1968 student revolutions all over the world. He has been struggling his whole life with the idea of changing this world, of getting rid of the actually existing structures, of its capitalistic tendencies, and of its alienation. When other philosophers went to congratulate and interview him on his eightieth birthday, he was still thinking in those terms, but he said he had begun to see that the doctrine of Sigmund Freud is probably worth more attention than the one of Karl Marx.

Karl Marx said that we should change the world and its structures by changing its economic system, by abolishing practically the whole existing situation: our salary and wage system, our competitive educational system, our marriage customs, the division into national states, and so on.

Sigmund Freud had also been thinking about a radical change. He, however, had situated the difficulty—the snake that poisons us—not only outside, in the world around us, but in the human being.

He had said—and I am obviously simplifying—that we have two tendencies in our hearts and minds: one to make life and one to destroy. One to be with others, and one to assert ourselves at their cost. One in which we love, and one in which we kill. We have a life wish and a death desire.

The old Habermas said, without any reference to Jesus: "If only we would be able to change the human person, so that its forceful destructive power would be put at the service of its life-giving tendencies."

That is exactly what Jesus proposes: that we change in that way. He wishes us to change internally, psychically, psychologically, and spiritually.

He used the powers he had to build and construct, not to destroy.

Once when they were not well received in a village on their way, his disciples told him: "Destroy it and its people!" He said: "No, let it live," because he loved them.

When they arrested him, he showed them his power by letting them fall on their faces, but he did not destroy them. He let them live, because he loved them.

He told his disciples, who wanted to defend him with power and force, and later Pilate, that he could have mobilized all the heavenly armies of the world of spirits, but he did not do it, because he loved them all.

He did not react as the others, or as we ourselves would have reacted. He was a new human being, a transmutation.

It is a pity that Habermas never seems to have met him.

We should acquire that same changeover by practicing that new humanity, by loving one another. We should show our love in our relationships with the ones nearest to us.

The nearest to us is the one to whom we promised to give ourselves fully and totally, free and naked, for always and always. That promise made in marriage is something terrific. It is something almost unbelievable. It is also something very delicate. It puts the two of you in an extremely vulnerable position toward each other.

You are so near to each other. You can make the other grow, if you use your life-giving power. You can murder the other, if you use your destructive tendencies.

Giving life in marriage is not only a question of genes or bodily cells. It is not only a connection between sperm and ova. It is an issue of giving life to each other, woman and man, spiritually and psychologically.

If a husband always tells his wife: "You are good for nothing, you uneducated clown, you useless creature, you blot on my name," she is not going to survive. If she has that kind of attitude toward her husband, he will not survive, either. They might together fill her womb with children and new life, but she and he will dry up in that harsh, dry climate.

You can make many mistakes when you marry and try to live together. Some mistakes are very simple, and therefore so easily and often made. There is the mistake of not organizing your finances well before you marry. You might not have built in an emotional outlet. There might be many other mistakes. The main mistake always seems to be that you don't build your lives by affirming each other, that you destroy your love by negating each other.

If I say yes to you, you grow (and so do I). If I say no to you, you die (and I, too).

Habermas, at the age of eighty said: "Find me a new human person."

Jesus said, "Love one another." He sent his Spirit of love to work out that change. By sending that Spirit to us, he said yes to you and me, working in us the possibility of building a new world, the new humanity everyone is dreaming about—starting with that naked one next to you.

PENTECOST

90. They All Spoke of the Great Things God Had Done

John 20:19–23

It is Pentecost, the fiftieth day after Easter, the day of the Holy Spirit.

The readings abound in their description of that Spirit. There is the powerful wind, the noise that filled the whole house. There is the bundle of tongues of fire that separated itself over them. There is the gift of languages and the thousands believing in the streets.

There is a second scenario, the contrasting picture of him standing among them on the evening of that very same day, Easter day, with the doors closed, saying: "Peace be with you! As the Father sent me so I am sending you." Breathing, just breathing—not even blowing—breathing over them, saying: "Receive the Holy Spirit, for those whose sins you forgive they will be forgiven."

In a third approach, Paul is speaking about the influence of the Holy Spirit in our lives. No one can say, he wrote, Jesus is the Lord except in the Spirit. All the services rendered to each other, all the works we work, all the gifts and talents we use, it is all from the same Spirit.

The Jerusalem wind and fire are over. Jesus does not appear anymore. But the Spirit remained. As Paul wrote, it remains in the humdrum of our daily lives, hidden and mostly unnoticed by us.

Being unnoticed does not mean not being there!

Some weeks ago, we had three sessions in our community on how to pray. In order to pray, one first has to concentrate, to become quiet and peaceful. Three methods were given for that concentration, and all three methods came down to the same thing: *to become aware of the unnoticed experiences we have.*

Our breathing goes on all the time, so become aware of your breathing. Sit down comfortably, close your eyes, and pay attention to your breath. Is it very fast? Slow it down. Is it superficial? Make it deep; control it. Become aware.

Our hearing never leaves us, so become aware of your hearing. Sit down comfortably. Close your eyes. Listen to every noise you hear. Let those noises penetrate you, deeply and freely. Become aware.

We feel bodily sensations all the time. Become aware of those feelings. Close your eyes. Sit down comfortably. Feel the touch of your clothes on your shoulders. Feel the touch of your clothes on your back. Feel your back touching your chair. Feel the touch of your hands resting on each other. Become aware, and peace will set in.

Without some concentration, the presence of the Holy Spirit, the fruits of Pentecost, will remain as unnoticed to us as our breathing, hearing, and bodily sensations.

Some days ago I asked some schoolchildren to tell me about the Holy Spirit. They told me about the fire, the storm, Peter on the balcony, the languages, and the baptisms in the street. When I asked them: "Did you ever notice the work of the Holy Spirit in yourselves and in others around you?" no one knew what to answer. They looked at me with their large, querying eyes. I changed the question. I asked them: "Did you ever do anything really good?" Again they had no answer. I asked: "Did your parents, your father and mother, ever do anything really good?" No answer.

So I said: "Sit down comfortably. Close your eyes and ask yourself, what good did I do?"

They sat down as comfortably as they could. They closed their eyes. And then suddenly the answers came. One had saved a small child from a river. One had forgiven her sisters. One said: "My mother takes care of me. That is good." Another said: "My father is helping a poor man." Slowly, slowly, they became aware of the good, the love, the care in their daily lives: the work of the Holy Spirit.

Today is Pentecost. The wind passed over, though it sometimes still blows among us, thank God. The fire went out, though it still sometimes heats our hearts, thank God. The gift of languages disappeared, though some of us still speak in tongues now and then, thank God.

Jesus even left us, leaving his breath in us.

It is with that breath that we live, a breath we too often do not notice. What a pity! A breath we do not often speak about. What a shame! But a breath that is still in us.

So close your eyes, sit down quietly, and become aware of her work in you.

If you do that today, this Pentecost will bring you nearer to the Spirit and yourself.

91. Trinity Traces

Matthew 28:16–20

It must be obvious to anyone that we touch, in the feast of the Blessed Trinity, on a mystery, a secret, a riddle, a drama, God's inner life.

As soon as you start to understand a person—any person, even yourself— you bump into that very same type of mystery.

Do you understand yourself? Can you explain yourself to someone else? Is there any mother or father who really understands his or her daughter or son?

Who can fathom the human heart? Who can understand the human mind? Who can measure the complexities of his emotions? *No one.*

Who would be able to know God? Not one human being in this world. *No one.*

That is, if you think about it, terrible. It's frightening, especially in this case, where the unknown other one, God, has power over life and death. Power over the standing of the trees and their falling down; power over thunder and lightning; power over storms and rains; power over the moon and the stars; power over the animals and all that lives.

It's not good, it's frightening, not to know anything about a person who has power over you. What kind of woman is she; what kind of man?

Students who have to sit for an oral examination will always try to find out— sometimes desperately—about their examiners. What do they look like? What are their preferences? What are their hobbies? Are they married? Do they have children? Are they believers? Should I shake hands? How should I dress, very nicely or a bit slovenly, very rich or rather poor? What color would they like? Do they drink? Do they smoke?

A student who has been arrested because of some stupid mishap will also try to find out certain things. What court do I have to go to—one, two, or three? Who is going to be the magistrate? What kind of person is she or he? How should I approach him? Does she like people to wear ties? Should I put on my jeans, or should I wear a solemn suit? Should I plead guilty like a butchered lamb, or should I proclaim my innocence like a roaring lion?

All those authorities are only human beings, made of flesh and blood. Their power is great, but always restricted. *But what about God?*

We depend totally and integrally on God in our lives and our deaths. We will have to appear before God, our final examiner, our last judge, at our transition from this life to that other life. At the moment we are born from this world, our common Mother, into God's lap, on the knees of our common Father, he will inspect and test us, giving us our final eternal name.

Who is God? How is God?

In a way, Jesus of Nazareth, the person many of us call the anointed one, Christ, did not reveal anything else but that. He revealed to us who God is and how God is.

He revealed to us that God is community, that God is not alone, though one. He told us that God is family, not isolated, not aloof, haughty, or unsociable. God relates. God loves, God is *one*, but also *many*.

God is not sitting on a throne as hard as a diamond, blinding as the sun, cold as crystal, majestic as a dictatorial ruler. God is a life process. God is parent and offspring and their love. Loving, loved lover, *doubly loving, doubly loved lovers*. That is what *Trinity* means.

Theologians were not content, even knowing all this. They tried to find out more about this life from which we all are born and from which we all are carrying the *seed* and the *Spirit*. They asked, "What do those three in one do?"

They found the answer, and they used a Greek word, a beautiful word: *epichoresis*. That means a dance. They are dancing hand in hand, three in one, enjoying one another, enjoying their lives.

If that is true, and if we are their children, it should be true of us, too. If that is true, that dance must be the core of their divine culture.

Here in Kenya, this intuition has special significance. Didn't the late president of this country, Mzee Jomo Kenyatta, say that the core of African culture is the dance?

Not the dance around something. Not a dance around a golden calf, but the dance in which men and women, the old ones and the young ones, enjoy and dance and celebrate their lives together in peace and community without fear, not thinking of themselves alone. To be able to live that life, to be able to dance that song, we must be like them, those three in one, without fear of one another.

The seed and the Spirit are planted in all of us as *traces of Trinity*, and one day they will break through and off we will go, citizens of God's Kingdom, participants in God's family life, companions, sisters and brothers, born to dance together.

ELEVENTH SUNDAY OF THE YEAR

92. While He Is Asleep

Mark 4:26–34

There was a farmer—there are millions of them—who went into his field, sowed his seeds left, right, and center, and went back home.

He never returned to that field, neither during the day nor during night, before harvesting time. He trusted that in his absence, *even while asleep*, the seed would grow. It did.

In the Greek text of the gospel for today, a very modern word is used to tell us of that growing process. The word is *automate*, automatically!

Jesus sowed his seed in our hearts, then off he went, like the farmer in the story, like farmers all over the world.

Of course, he knew things would not be ideal. There were the birds and the droughts, the weeds and the insects, the parasites and the blights. But there was also the power of the seed itself, maturing and growing in humanity. A divine power showing its force all the time.

Sometimes we say things are worse than before. We know that's not true. They are better, though not yet for all.

Think about the past: the trading in slaves, the horrors of child labor, the nonrecognition of human rights, the privileged few, and the miserable many.

Things are not worse, but our expectations are greater, for the very good reason that the seed has been growing among us, and it is still growing. There are plenty of examples. There have been many famines in Africa, but there has never before been so much goodwill to solve that calamity. There have been many industrial injustices since the beginning of the industrial revolution, but never has there been a greater willingness to protect the poor. Land has been stolen in South America and elsewhere in the world, but the outcry against it has never before been so loud.

Don't tell me that the seed is not growing. It is. And if you seriously don't think so, isn't it because you yourself are old and fruitless, a barren part of the human field, a dry spot in the human earth, a stone where others flower, a dried-up yellow stick where others bloom, a moody grumbler where others sing?

Are you involved in the work of peace? Are you engaged in the work of justice? Are you a peacemaker in your community? Are you actively taking part in political life? Did you vote in the last election? Did you opt for the poor at the last referendum? Are you networking to stop the possibility of an all-ending nuclear blast?

If you are not, you must be asleep. His seed did not grow in you as it did in his community. It did not keep abreast with what is happening all around you. You are out of tune, underdeveloped.

Maybe you don't even know the latest letters from your bishops about justice and peace, about the mission of the Church in these days.

No wonder you complain. You are asleep while the seed is growing all around you.

It is not you who should be asleep. He sowed his seed in us and went away, knowing that one day we (and you, too) would find that seed growing in us through all the weeds, all the droughts, all the dangers, and all the blights. We would be *like a tree that is planted by water streams, yielding its fruit in season, its leaves never fading* (see Psalm 1:3).

The outcome is sure. Whether or not you will be part of it depends on the growth of the seed in you while he is away and asleep, to wake up at harvesting time.

Grow with the rest, grow with the best!

TWELFTH SUNDAY OF THE YEAR

93. With His Head on a Pillow

Mark 4:35–41

That evening they had set out at his word. It was he who had said: "Let us cross over to the other side."

The other side always promises to be better than this side.

They had taken him on board, notwithstanding the darkness of the sky, the threatening clouds, and the wind coming from the wrong direction. Everything was forecasting disaster.

Their experience told them it would be wiser not to venture onto the lake, but after all, they were going with him whom angels and devils seemed to obey.

Even when the storm broke loose, as they expected it would, they were not immediately alarmed. They pointed at him, in the stern of the boat with his head peacefully on a pillow, a cushion one of his many admirers had made for him.

It was only when the water started to fill the boat with so much might and power that they threatened to be swamped, that they woke him up and shouted: "Master, don't you care? We are going down!"

He woke up. He looked around himself. He stood up, leaving his pillow behind. He raised his hand and ordered the wind to be still, calming the sea. All was quiet again. Then he looked at them and he said: "Why were you so afraid? How is it that you have no faith?"

Their fear turned into awe, a reverential fear, and they said to one another: "How can this be, how can this be?"

They took their oars—because he had not left them even a gust of wind—and they rowed the boat the rest of the way to the other side, while he again laid his head on that pillow made for him.

That awe never left their lives, as long as they were accompanying him.

Every step he made seemed to be so new, every word made such a difference, that they felt their old securities fall away again and again.

The old situation crumbled under their eyes. It was as if he always said: "Let us go away from here, let us go to the other side!"

And he seemed to be so confident about the possibility of the final outcome that he simply put his head on that pillow made for him.

THIRTEENTH SUNDAY OF THE YEAR

94. He and Women

Mark 5:21–43

The gospel reading of today contains two totally different reports. One is about that embarrassing woman who had been bleeding for twelve years. She had gone to doctors and spent all her money making that endless circuit over and over, again and again.

The second report is about a younger woman, in fact a child, the daughter of Jairus, whom Jesus recalled from what they had called her death and from what Jesus had called her sleep.

The preacher can choose between the two stories. It is, of course, very tempting to leave the bleeding lady a bleeding lady, to avoid all the embarrassment involved, and to speak on the faith and love of Jairus, or about Jesus' love for children, or about those famous words: "*Talitha kum!*" meaning: "Little girl, I tell you, get up!"

If we do that, we miss the chance to say something about an issue that seemed to be very near to Jesus' heart: The place of women in human society.

I don't know whether you, male or female, are well-informed about the place of women in the society and time of Jesus. I don't even know whether you have ever reflected about the place of women today.

I do know that the women who are described in the gospels give very clear indications of their place and role.

Most of the women speaking to Jesus excused themselves for doing so. In that society, women were not allowed to speak to him just like that. A woman was not supposed to approach a "rabbi" at all.

Then there was the case of the other woman who, by praising his mother, Mary, reduced her—with the best of intentions—to the way people saw women in that time. She hailed her, seeing him: "Happy the WOMB that carried you! Happy the BREASTS that suckled you!"

Immediately he turned around to her and said: "Don't speak like that about my mother: happy her womb, happy her breasts. Stop reducing her to her reproductive functions! No, happy any PERSON who listens to the word of God!"

In 1879, Henrik Ibsen wrote a play that became famous all over the world: *A Doll's House*. In that play, two persons are talking, a man and a woman.

Helmer says to Nora: "Before anything else you are a woman and a mother." Nora answers: "I don't believe that any more. I believe that I am in the very first place a human being, just like you." He: "You are talking like a child, you don't understand anything of the society in which you live." She: "That is true, I don't understand it. But from now on I will go on to try to discover who is right, society or I.''

The woman in the gospel of today excused herself for having touched him, not only because she considered herself unclean, but because she knew that, according to the rules of that time, after her touch Jesus, too, would be unclean for a week.

Being a woman was not a good thing in those days. Women were unclean for seven days after their period. They were unclean for seven days after giving birth to a son, and for fourteen days after giving birth to a daughter.

They were not allowed to enter any place of worship for another thirty-three days after the birth of a boy, and for another sixty-six days after the birth of a daughter. The day a girl was born meant bad news to the mother, because she would be restricted for eighty days, after which she had to bring a sacrifice to be ''purified.''

The woman of today's gospel was *always restricted* because of her bleeding. She was desperate about it, and in her desperation, she did the forbidden thing: She touched him. She was healed.

Instead of whooping and shouting with joy, she tried to get away as quickly as possible. He called her back. She approached him in fear and trembling: ''Forgive me for wanting to be healed; forgive me for being a woman; forgive me for having touched you; forgive me for bothering you; forgive me for having made you unclean; forgive me; forgive me!''

He only said: ''My daughter, *your* faith has restored you to health. Go in peace.''

Not a word was heard about that old law. No step was taken because of his legal defilement. Not a word, not one word!

The impact reached much further than just this healing. It meant a total changeover, a miracle in the moral and legal order. Even today, we are afraid to go this far, afraid to admit that in all we do, and in all we don't do, we are equal in everything, notwithstanding the difference that makes our equality fruitful. Even in most of our churches nowadays, women are still seen as unclean. They are not allowed to touch Jesus, like men do. They can't be priests. Oh no, not that! It seems that to his church, the bleedings are not yet over.

FOURTEENTH SUNDAY OF THE YEAR

95. Too Much for Them

Mark 6:1–6

The rumor arrived before he did: He is coming, he is coming!

They had all heard about his miracles. They had all heard about his powers. They had all heard about his parables. They had all heard about his extraordinary ideas. And now, finally, at last, he was coming. He was coming home.

He did not come alone. What his family had told them proved to be true. They could see it now for themselves: He was in the company of followers, young and old, rich and poor, men and women, as if he were a rabbi.

Sabbath came. They all went to the synagogue. And just as all had expected, some had hoped, and others had feared, he started to speak.

He taught in a way that really amazed them. That is why they did not even let him finish. Where did *he*, that man she knew so very well, get that power? Where did *he*, that one they had been working, praying, talking, dancing, quarreling, and walking with, get those words from? Wasn't he a carpenter? Wasn't he the son of Mary? Didn't they know his sisters and brothers?

There was something strange about it.

Didn't some scribes say that he was bewitched, that he was possessed by the evil one? Hadn't his own family gone after him because they thought that he was out of his mind?

How could a human being like him, an ordinary man like themselves, be like that? Confronted with his power, listening to the marvel of his words, enjoying his stories, seeing him there in the semidarkness of their not-too-well-lit synagogue, full of majesty, dignity, divinity, humanity, and Spirit, they did not accept him. They did not believe their eyes. They did not believe their ears. It could not be. He was just like themselves, and they were not like that. They were just ordinary, unimportant, insignificant, small provincial townspeople. So was he, wasn't he?

He was just too much for them.

They did not accept him. By not accepting him, *they did not accept themselves*, either—their own possibilities, their own potentialities, their own humanity, their own divine origin.

They were the victims of an orchestration, an indoctrination that had been going on and on. They were tied by chains they would never be able to break. They had been too often labeled as useless, mean, low, as nobodies by those who ruled business, state, and temple. They could not believe that they or he could be liberated like that. He had to be as they saw themselves—practically useless, passive objects in the history of humanity. He could not be what he pretended to be.

If he could, shouldn't they, too?

Who could ask a thing like that of them?

So they threw him out, preferring the status quo. He was really too much, much too much for them.

It must have saddened his heart. Only some let him heal, having faith in him. And for the rest. . . . He made his tours in the villages nearby, preaching the *good news* of our liberation that was too much for them in his own home.

96. He Sent Them Out

Mark 6:7–13

Something is changing in the church. It is a change that is affecting all regions in the world. It is not even necessary to quote statistics to prove the existence of that change. Everyone knows about it. You can see it very easily.

For some time the church has been accustomed to having priests, Sisters, and Brothers, plenty of them. They were well taken care of, having a security that others, especially poorer people, only could dream of. Each village had its own priests and Sisters. Young men and women went to seminaries and scholasticates to be trained in an educational network that spanned the whole of the world and that no multinational would even be able to match.

The number of priests is going down. Their average age is going up. If no miracle happens soon, a priest will be as rare as a cardinal. The story of the gospel of today might not be repeated any more. There is nobody to be sent even though the call to preach change and repentance, to chase away evil spirits, to anoint and heal the sick, seems to be sounded more than ever before.

Some people say it is the fault of the church leadership. Why doesn't the pope change his attitude regarding obligatory celibacy for priests? Why does he restrict the priesthood to men only? Why do they give future priests a training that is much more academic than pastoral? And so on.

As long as we talk like that we might overlook another development taking place in that very same church we are members of. Because of the declining number of the older, formal staff, others are taking over.

We all know stories about the small Christian communities, as they are called here in east Africa. In those small Christian communities, many tasks of preaching and teaching, of chasing away evil spirits and healing are being taken up by the members of those communities themselves.

We all must have heard about the basic Christian communities in South America; how women and men are organizing themselves in grass roots parish communities all over Europe; how in the United States more and more parishes are run under lay leadership.

We all can easily witness how those communities are insisting on change regarding the ownership of land and energy, money spent on armaments, health care, the treatment of prisoners, and the abolition of capital punishment.

They are members of no-nuke movements. They sympathize with Amnesty International. They struggle in favor of justice. They combat racism, tribalism, genocide, and geocide. They are teaching and preaching change and repentance. They are actively chasing away evil spirits, they are anointing and healing.

Although I told you at the beginning of this reflection that there is no need to give any statistics, let me give you one. Did you know that according to research done in the United States in 1975, the United Nations' "Year of the Woman," it was shown that 25 percent of all Catholic women in the United States were involved in one or another church activity, and that 95 percent of that 25 percent were laywomen? A very high number, indeed, but they were involved in tasks officially considered as informal church activities.

Didn't Jesus send out *all his disciples*, 100 percent of them, to chase and heal?

What about you? Do you know yourself to be sent? Do you feel yourself to be sent into the world to cause it to be changed and repentant, purified and exorcised, anointed and healed?

SIXTEENTH SUNDAY OF THE YEAR

97. His Compassion

Mark 6:30–34

The gospel text of today is very short, not even 130 words. In that very short text, Mark, the author, mentions Jesus' compassion *twice*, in a way, even *thrice*.

First he took pity on his disciples. They were coming back from their first apostolic trip. They had been preaching, teaching, and chasing evil spirits away. They had even been healing. Power had gone out of them all the time, a power they had never expected in themselves.

They were very excited about it. They told one another, and him, story after story. They were sure the world was going to change. It had cost them a lot. They dropped their sandals, they brushed their hair, they massaged their tired legs and arms. While they were giving their reports, they were constantly interrupted by dozens and dozens of people who wanted to see him and them, who wanted to be touched, who wanted to draw their attention to their sick children.

They did not even have the time for a bite. They did not have a second for a drink. They were eaten alive by all those others.

He took *pity* on them. He said: "Let us go out of here. You need rest. You need some time for yourselves alone." He organized a boat and a skipper, and off they went.

They left the others—the dozens, the scores, the hundreds, and the thousands—behind.

It was so obvious where they were going that the crowd first started to walk and then to run around the lake so they were all there when they arrived, waiting again, hoping again to be touched.

He took *pity* on them, and sent his disciples off to have a rest, a drink, and a meal, while he began to attend to that crowd himself.

We might think that *compassion* of his was not very important in the total richness of his life. Since it is a sentiment that is so often mentioned as the *moving force* in his work, we have to be careful about underrating it in his personality. It was such a moving force in his life that it is not an exaggeration to say he came into this world because of his *pity*, because of his compassion. Every one of us knows what Jesus must have felt when he experienced compassion. Every one of us has felt *pity* from time to time: when seeing the smashed-up victim of a road accident; hearing about an old mother or father left behind; looking at the photo of some executed robbers; hearing about arrests and disappearances; smelling the odor of unwashed children who stink like the contents of trash cans they have been eating from.

We know pity, we feel pity, but that does not mean we really understand where pity comes from or what pity's significance is.

More than three hundred years ago, a mystic in Wales, Henry Vaughan, wrote this:

> Charity is a relic from paradise,
> and pity is a strange argument
> that we are all descended
> from one human being.

It sounds rather mysterious and very mystical, yet he was right: Our compassion for others derives from the fact *that we are one*. We all participate in the same human, God-given life. Though many, we are one. We form one communion, or at least *we should*.

That is what we *know*, that is what we *feel*, when we see one another smashed up, hungry, thirsty, frustrated, or miserable.

There is something new going around our world these days. More and more communities of laypeople and priests, more and more congregations and societies of sisters and brothers, are becoming aware of the necessity of doing something about justice and peace. Our pity is growing, due to a development by which we feel more and more united.

It is that pity, that awareness of our oneness, that is at the heart of the growing concern for justice and peace.

Henry Vaughan foresaw this very long ago, when he added that he believed words like *alien* and *stranger* would disappear. He believed that those words—often indicating a total lack of pity—*were notions received from Cain and his posterity among us. They feature in the vocabulary of the killers and murderers among us.*

We are many, though one. We are one, though many!

Doesn't that sound like the echo of the divine Trinity: One though three, three though one? Weren't we made in their divine image?

Let us pray that Jesus' compassion may grow in all of us.

SEVENTEENTH SUNDAY OF THE YEAR

98. One Small Boy

John 6:1–15

The report on the miracle of the bread and the fish is about what happened to somebody who gave all he had.

It is, of course, a story about Jesus multiplying all that bread and fish. But whose bread did he multiply? Whose fish did he divide?

It all started with the real hero of that story—a small boy. Let's have a look at the eyewitness report.

There were all those people: five thousand men and, most probably, at least double that number of women and children.

It is Jesus who says: "What are we going to do? How are we going to feed them?" Philip knows what to do to feed them. He says: "You just buy the food." Then he added: "One piece of bread for each one in this crowd would most probably cost you thousands of dollars. How are you going to manage that?"

Andrew gets another bright idea. He asks the crowd: "Has anybody any food?"

There is a big hush and a great silence. People look at one another. There must have been quite a few in that crowd with some food, but they kept their mouths shut. Nobody admitted to having a crumb of bread or a bit of fish. They were afraid they were going to lose it.

And then there is that small boy. He had been looking at Jesus with an open mouth and a wet nose. He patted his pockets, he felt under his shirt, and he shouted: "Yes, Sir, over here!" Out he came with five slices of bread and two fishes, small ones, very small ones, the ones small boys catch.

The whole crowd laughed. Jesus did not. He took those slices of bread, he took those two fishes, and he told the people to sit down.

There was a great deal of noise and everyone sat down. Only that small boy was still standing there, looking with eyes full of wonder at his fish and bread. Jesus gave his fish and his bread to those big apostles of his and said: "Divide it among them!" They said: "Divide what?" He said again: "Just start, will you?" They started to break and to break and to break, until everybody had enough, even more than enough. So much so that they still had pieces in their hands when their stomachs were full.

Jesus said: "Can you please collect the leftovers?" They collected twelve basketfuls, and Jesus must have given them to that small boy; after all, it was his bread, his fish. The people praised Jesus. They even wanted to make him king. I think Jesus praised the small boy who had given all he had. It is that attitude that should be king, and, in Jesus, was.

Those who give will receive, and will receive in abundance.

When you are asked for something you think you are unable to give, think of that small boy, of his story, and think of the twelve baskets full of food given to him because he gave all he had.

EIGHTEENTH SUNDAY OF THE YEAR

99. Taking Him as Our Bread

John 6:24–35

They had come back. Again they surrounded him with eager eyes and ready stomachs. He looked around and said: "I know why you come to me again, not because of me but because of the bread I gave you. You want more bread. You want more fish. You want more food." They watched him with even more eager eyes, and the most hungry of them must have already felt the water gush into their mouths.

Once more he looked around and said: "I am not going to give you that bread anymore. *I am the bread of life, take me as your bread.*"

They must have been unable to understand what he meant, and I wonder whether we really understand after the two thousand years that separate us from those words.

All the same, the very language we use might still have something from the bread he spoke about. In English we sometimes say that an attitude or a skill is like *bread and butter* to someone. We mean that he or she is so accustomed to it that it has become a second (or even a first) nature to her or him.

That is what he must have meant when he told them: Take *me*, take *me*, as your bread in your life. Take *me*, take *me* as the bread the Father is sending from heaven. Take me as the fountain in your life. Take me as the principle for your life from day to day, from hour to hour.

If we take him as our bread and butter in life, we always choose what is good for the world, what is good for humanity, for all of us.

It would mean that our work for peace in the world and in our lives would no longer be a mere pious desire or the subject of a clever workshop, but a task that asks our effort. It would mean that the hunger in the world would no longer be an incident at the margin of our lives or the topic of a naive social analysis, but a challenge to provide the bread they are looking for every day.

It would mean that we would enter the mercy and sadness he had because of our situation in this world.

To enter into that mercy, to enter into that sadness, would make us like him, voices for the voiceless, sufferers for peace, organizers of justice, chasers of evil, healers of wounds. We, who without too much hesitation call ourselves by his name, would be like that: making *him* our bread in life.

NINETEENTH SUNDAY OF THE YEAR

100. Drawing Power

John 6:41–51

According to the gospel of today, there is something mysterious here in the world, in the Church, in all of us. We don't see it. We don't smell it. We can't touch it. We can't hear it. It escapes our taste. It does not leave a physical trace.

It is there; that is what Jesus said.

There are many more of those mysterious powers and energies all around, even through and within us. At the moment, it seems to be very quiet in this church, at least when I don't speak. Just listen. What do you hear? Nothing. Silence. Yet you know, as well as I do, that all this space around us is full of waves, energies, and powers. Were I to switch on a radio, music would burst forth out of this audible silence: hard rock, country music, monks singing plainchant in a convent, a symphony orchestra from Montreal, and voices from all over the world. That power is there, those vibrations are present, all that energy is hovering around.

The gospel of today is about another type of mysterious energy: a divine one, a terrific one, a mighty, powerful, all-explaining, all-unifying one. It is here even if it does not seem to be here at all. Jesus calls it a *drawing power*. It is a power, an energy coming from God, attracting all of us, the whole of creation, through Jesus to God.

It's clear there is a drawing power in nature. Things are born. Trees grow up toward the light of the sun. Plants flower, fish swim. Insects are crawling, birds are flying. Animals of all kinds are roaming around, looking for an equal, searching for a mate, getting offspring. Adam embraced Eve, and Eve embraced Adam. Boys kiss girls, and the clouds are perpetually chasing one another.

Jesus speaks about a power that draws all of us to him and, at the same time, to one another. Protestants and Catholics, Christians and Hindus, Muslims and Jews, Americans and Russians, Asians and Europeans—aren't we all communicating and dialoguing more than ever before? There is a power all around us, and it is changing the face of the earth. Jesus not only revealed its nature, but even what its outcome would be: It is the *drawing power* of our origin, our Father and Mother, attracting us to their home, to his table, to the table and the home we are all coming from. We are surrounded by that power. It is all in and through us. It explains why you, why I, why we, have that deep, deep feeling that the world in which we live is not all there is. That the colors we see are not all the colors there are. That the sounds we hear are not all the music and all the language there is. That there are other recipes for the food we eat. And, even more important, that the relations we have, the ways we touch one another, do not fulfill all our desires and hope. The love we meet— and that love can be so great, so fulfilling and consoling—is a mere beginning, giving us an inkling of the time when God's drawing power will have brought us together, feasting and celebrating the Kingdom of God, the fullness of life, the power and the glory given to us. Jesus gave the lead, so let us plug in, becoming all we really are.

TWENTIETH SUNDAY OF THE YEAR

101. Eating His Flesh

John 6:51–58

He repeated again and again: "I am the flesh, I am the bread, I am the life. I come from the Father, I have seen the Father, I was sent by the Father," and so on and on. It seems a mysterious, deep, difficult, and endless discussion.

It is a type of discussion we have all experienced, though at another level, from time to time in our lives.

There is your son, standing in front of you. He doesn't smoke tobacco, but something he calls *weed*. You talk and talk. You want to make him participate and share in what you know, in what you have experienced, in your wisdom. He remains aloof and unapproachable. He stays unresponsive. And you say: "If only I could creep into your head. If you could only look through my eyes."

You are standing in front of your daughter, the beautiful one who comes home very late from discos and parties at which there are all kinds of people you do not know, that you have no relations with. You talk and talk. You weep, and you implore. You tap all your experience, you fall on your knees, and you say: "If I could only let you know what I know. If only I could let you experience what I experienced. If only I could let you feel the bitterness I have felt. If you only could drink the water I drank."

You are laying next to your lover. There is a very delicate point. It is very important to you. He does not see, she does not understand, he does not feel. You take her hands, you kiss his eyes. You stroke his back, you put your head in her lap, and you say: "If only I could be you. If only I could let you see with my eyes. If only I could make you hear with my ears. If only I could make you touch with my hands. If you only could eat the bread I ate. If you only could be my flesh. If only you could have my blood!"

That is how Jesus talked that afternoon to them. He knew that only his type of life—loving, forgiving, community building, taking children as your first issue, simple, nonviolent, always ready to dialogue, never hardened, God-fearing, and human life respecting—could save this world and humankind from disaster.

He pleaded: "Please, see my point. I do know. Please, hear me out, I am sure. Please feel my feeling. I come from on high. Eat my bread, drink my water; eat my flesh, drink my blood."

He pleaded with them. He pleads with us to change, to see the need for conversion.

To give an example of that need: Did you know that in 1973, in a country like Nigeria, $9 per person was spent on arms, $1 per person on health, and $3 per person on education? And in "God's own country," the U.S.A., the numbers were respectively $373, $171, and $348 that year?

Think about Jesus pleading in his time, but more relevant still, try to understand how he would plead now in this world, in Uganda, southeast Asia, Nicaragua, Lebanon, Ireland, and everywhere.

We should eat him. We should drink him.

That is, of course, what we do during this Mass. But it is as if we are not serious about him at all. We fragment him to nothing, to a paper-thin wafer, and we reduce his drink to a drop of wine.

When eating his bread, we should feel what we do. We should be obliged to eat a whole loaf here on the spot eucharistically, so it becomes an arduous, difficult, and *felt* task, in order that we might really turn into him. That is what we need, and this world needs, too. It is what he knew so very well.

TWENTY-FIRST SUNDAY OF THE YEAR

102. Science, Technology, and He

John 6:60–69

Jesus spoke about the flesh and the spirit. He seems to separate two things in us. He appears to put them apart.

That is strange, because we are not two, but only one.

He spoke about the flesh that has nothing to offer and the spirit that gives life.

In the past, many people came to strange conclusions about this text. They reasoned: "What is my flesh? My flesh is my body. What is my spirit? My spirit is my mind. As my flesh is useless and my spirit is all, I had better try to turn into spirit alone."

They called their body a donkey and kicked it. They called it a prison and tried to escape from it. They called it the cause of their sins and they mortified it, beat it, starved it, tortured it, did not use it, and regretted its existence very much.

Could that be what Jesus meant when he said the flesh on its own has nothing to offer?

Jesus, who was accused of not fasting, of not even teaching his disciples how to fast? Jesus, who was condemned because he was seen with women and enjoyed being with children? Jesus, who produced that wine in Cana, and the bread and fish at other occasions? Jesus, who obviously loved the hustle and bustle of a good party?

He must have meant something else. He could not have meant to say that our bodies are only occasions of sin.

Most probably he meant exactly the opposite of what these strange and dated saints thought.

He did not mean to say that we should separate spirit and flesh, body and mind. He intended to say that we should *never*, ever, do that.

He wanted to say that if we separate those two, we are heading for trouble, we are doomed. He said that flesh *on its own is dead*: The body of a man in a coffin is flesh alone. The body of a woman in a coffin is flesh alone. The body of a dead girl is flesh alone. The body of a dead boy is flesh alone.

As long as we live, flesh and spirit should be together.

But isn't that always the case, as long as we live?

In our body, maybe, *yes*; but in what we do, very often *no*.

Let me give you some examples. In 1634, some scientists met in France; in 1646, a similar group met in London; in 1660, some experts met in Florence. In all three cases, they started scientific societies. They wanted to invent, to improve, to develop, to progress, and to be useful scientifically. They all stated in their constitutions that they were not going "to meddle with divinity, metaphysics, morals," and issues like that. They wanted to study science, physics, and chemicals, techniques and skills, atoms and their explosions, biology and ballistics, aerodynamics and medicine, and all kinds of other things, without taking the spirit into consideration.

That is what Jesus warned against. We, living under the threat of all those scientific developments, might understand better than anyone before, how right he was and is.

What should this text about the useless flesh mean to us? It has been said so often: "Scientific research is useless and dangerous when we don't at the same time do research on the moral, ethical, and religious implications."

Insofar as we ourselves are concerned it means that you are wrong when you admit into your life items of flesh that are separated from the spirit. That wild growth exists in you whenever you say: Business is business, procedure is procedure, research is research, administration is administration, and, in the final instance, war is war.

It is the spirit that gives life. The flesh has nothing to offer. Its only offer is death, a body in a coffin, a corpse.

TWENTY-SECOND SUNDAY OF THE YEAR

103. Killing Laws

Mark 7:1–8, 14–15, 21–23

They had come all the way from Jerusalem to catch him. Not out of love for God, not out of love for God's law, but because of their hatred for him, because he threatened to undermine their power over the crowd.

They had been watching him all day, but they had not been able to find anything wrong in him. Obviously he was an observer of the law in dress, words, and behavior.

They stopped looking at him; they gave up on him. Instead, they started to observe his followers, that ignorant bunch who were no longer listening to them but were following him as if they had found a new leader, as if they did not exist anymore.

They looked and they watched, and finally they caught some who were picking corn as they walked along on a Sabbath day.

Why hadn't he warned them? Why hadn't he reproached them? Why did he let this pass without a word?

They attacked in the name of their law, in the name of their prestige and power.

They did not appeal to that law to create space and freedom. They did not appeal to that law to guarantee or improve the human lot. They did not appeal to that law to enable life and joy. They did not appeal to that law to enhance or celebrate. They did not appeal to that law out of love of God. They appealed to it to litigate and win, to profit and to gloat, to catch and to kill.

He looked at them, at their faked pious faces full of hatred and greed, and he said: "You hypocrites, how far are God's intentions from your hearts; how false is the reverence you seem to pay. Is that God's command, to catch and to kill, to hunger and to lust, to rule and to reign, to exploit and to plunder? You say that you stand for justice. You say that you defend God's will; but you only intend to profit yourselves at whatever the cost."

He did not say that the law is no good. He did not say that the law should be abolished. He did imply that law can be used in such a way that it kills, that it stinks, that it makes human life impossible. And it does.

It does in the most literal sense of the word. Haven't you heard how difficult it is to get help and assistance for a birth in certain states?

Haven't you heard that doctors and midwives, obstetricians and gynecologists are so afraid of a natural happening like a birth that they do not dare take the risk of assisting at it anymore? They might be sued if anything went wrong, and they cannot afford the insurance against that anymore.

Haven't you heard how fewer and fewer people will stop at an accident along the road these days because if you make a wrong move, you might be sued?

Jesus' words are a warning to us. If we do what those people from Jerusalem did—watch to be sure everything is done according to the letter of the law in order to catch and fleece—we are not sincere. We are hypocrites, making human life impossible.

Even a good thing like the law, even an excellent thing like God's law, can be turned into something that kills, as it did in the case of Jesus, when they nailed him on the cross in the name—so they said—of God's law.

TWENTY-THIRD SUNDAY OF THE YEAR

104. He Took His Time

Mark 7:31–37

Jesus had definitely come to heal all. He did not heal them all, at all.

That day he was surrounded by people, people from Tyre, from the Decapolis region, from his own country, and in a sense from the whole world.

Yet he took one man, who was deaf and consequently mute, aside in private, behind a bush. He put his fingers in his ears. He touched his tongue with a wet finger, and he said: "*Ephphatha,* be opened."

He took his time for that one man, while all the others were milling around. He took his time to put his fingers in his ears. He took his time wetting his own finger. He took his time speaking to him. He took his time asking him not to tell anyone what had happened.

He did not want to attract the whole world. He did not want to take up that kind of responsibility.

He definitely wanted to heal them all.

That is why he showed us what *we* should do and what *we* can do in the world in which *we* live: the world of our family, our work; the world of those who depend on us, of those we meet; the world of those we live with.

If each one of us would take that world as seriously as he took the world in which he lived, everything would change.

He knew that he could not do it alone. He did not want to do it alone, either. He knew that he would only be able to reach them all in the community he wants to form with us.

When he put his finger in the ears of that man, he showed us what he expects us to do in the world in which we live, saying: "*Ephphatha,* be opened!"

TWENTY-FOURTH SUNDAY OF THE YEAR

105. He Started To Teach Them

Mark 8:27–35

That morning they set out again with him, as they were now accustomed to doing. It had become a regular pattern in their lives; they had become quite settled in his company. It was nice, it was pleasant: sufficient to eat, plenty to drink, taxes paid, respect, and a good reception almost everywhere. A miracle here, a wonder there, signs of greater things to come, basking in his glory, interesting conversation, beautiful stories, thrilling discussions, plenty of self-expression. They never had been so contented during all their lives; they never had had it so good.

As far as they were concerned, it might last forever and ever. They seriously started to consider making following him a second career.

When he turned to them, asking: "Who do people say I am?" there was no hesitation. They gave him an honest answer—though they ought to have known better—they answered: "Some say John the Baptizer, others Elijah, and again others one of the prophets."

When he asked them again: "And who do you say I am?" they looked at one another, looked at Peter, then gave Peter a wink to say he should tell him, and Peter said: "You are the Messiah!"

That is what he said. That is what they thought he was.

"The promised one, who will march the whole of the people toward glory and victory, and we will be there in front with you, you bet!" Peter did not say that, but it's what they thought.

He now turned to them and told them they were right, but that the people were right, too.

He was the Messiah, as they thought. He was also a prophet, as the people intuited. He would be treated as a prophet, though Messiah. And he told them how he would be rejected by the elders, chief priests, scribes, and finally by his own people, as all the prophets and prophetesses had been in the past. He explained how he would suffer, be tortured and beaten, humiliated and spat at, naked and raw, crucified and murdered. Though, he added, he would rise three days later.

Again they looked at one another, at Peter, they gave him a wink, and this time Peter took him apart to tell him that they did not agree, that this should not happen, neither to him, nor to them.

Peter said: "Forget about those prophets. Forget about what the people say. Forget those ideas; be glorious, be victorious, be the Messiah, be the one we think you are!"

He turned against Peter, he turned against them, and he said: "Satan, get behind me, follow me!"

Then he called all the people together. He told them that they were right.

He told them they couldn't be his followers without understanding that they would have to take up their crosses, as all the prophets had done and he was going to do, going to Jerusalem. He told them they would have to forget about their own lives, if they wanted to save them. He told them: "If a person wishes to come after me, he must disown himself, carry the cross, and walk in my footsteps. Whoever tries to save his life, will lose it, while he who loses his life for me and the gospel, will save it."

He asked them to be prophets. He asked us to be like him.

TWENTY-FIFTH SUNDAY OF THE YEAR

106. He Took a Child

Mark 9:30–37

They could not have been walking with him. They must have been walking behind him, or maybe in front of him. They were discussing their relationships with him. They were discussing their importance according to him. We don't know what they said, but we can guess what it was all about.

Peter said: "Of course, without any doubt, I am the most important! Didn't he call me the *rock* on which that community of his is going to be built?"

John said: "I am sorry for you. What you say might be true, but that is only a question of administrative bureaucracy. The fact that you might be a good administrator does not make you the most important one. You should look for something else. You should be attentive to something more important. You should look for his love, and if you do that, well, he loves me most."

Then Judas spoke. He said: "The most important fellow is the man with the money. You don't need to be a Marxist or a capitalist to know that. The world is ruled by money, and to whom did he entrust *his money*? To me, and that is why. . . ."

Philip spoke: "All that is very nice. Do you remember when he had that catering problem in the desert with all those thousands, when nobody knew what to do, himself included? He turned to *me* for advice. I am sorry for you, but he asked me!"

Jesus must have walked ahead of them or behind them during that conversation, having his own thoughts, his own sentiments, while they had theirs.

He spoke about being delivered into the hands of men; they spoke about how others would be delivered to them. He spoke about saving others, carrying their plight; they spoke about themselves in the small circles of their personal lives. He spoke about being a servant: they spoke about being a master.

At first sight, of course, their conversation seemed to be very pious. They spoke about their relationship with him. They spoke about their relationship with God. Peter spoke about Jesus' trust in him, while beating his enormous chest. John spoke about Jesus' love, and he pointed at his heart. Judas spoke about Jesus' purse, indicating that it was the thing that counted. Philip spoke about Jesus' appreciation for his judgment and flair.

They were, in fact, all speaking about themselves. They were not only speaking, they were fighting, they were quarreling, there was tension, there was war. I'm not even sure their hands didn't feel for the knives and swords under their clothing. He must have walked ahead of them or behind them during that conversation. He could not have walked with them that time.

When I came to the United States for the very first time, I could not sleep very well because of jet lag. I woke up at odd hours in the middle of the night. I switched the television on in the room where I stayed. I was amazed to find people preaching about Jesus in the middle of the night. I was even more amazed at their message. That message seemed to be a continuation of the competitive fight those disciples of his had so very long ago.

It was all about "I." I, standing in front of my savior. I, being anointed, being in a holy place, with my loins girded, with my breastplate of faith and my sword of truth. I, feeling so fine, very pious, and very scriptural. And, in the very end, even Judas's purse and money were not forgotten!

They arrived at Capernaum. They arrived at his house. They went inside, they washed their feet, sat down. He asked them: "What were you speaking about? What were you quarreling about? What was all the noise about when I walked behind you, when I walked in front of you?"

There was no answer. They looked at one another. They felt ashamed. They felt stupid. They realized he knew.

When there had been silence for quite some time, he stood up, went to the door, and disappeared, leaving them behind, speechless. They did not even dare to look at one another.

He came back, holding a child by the hand, one he had found in the street. A small girl with a running nose and pitch-black eyes.

He put the girl in the middle of their circle and said: "Do you see her?" Of course, they did.

He put his hands on her, he greeted her, he kissed her, and said: "Whoever received a child like this one, breaking open the circle in which she or he lives, is receiving *me*, and not only me, but the one who sent me, too."

He looked at them and sent the girl around their circle.

I don't know what they did.

Maybe Peter gave her a pat on her shoulders. Maybe John kissed her on both her cheeks. Maybe Judas gave her a coin, and Philip put her on his knee while he dried her nose.

If they received that small girl in all sincerity that evening, they must have been filled—according to his word—with God self, and a question like, "Who is the most important?" did not make any sense anymore.

TWENTY-SIXTH SUNDAY OF THE YEAR

107. The Rubbish Dump of the Kingdom

Mark 9:38–43, 45, 47–48

Everyone seems to know what hell is. It is a place with eternal fire, stinking sulphurous smoke, and the constant grinding of teeth. There are fireproof worms that crawl through your flesh, and a clock that ticks as a constant contrast: *always, never, always, never, always, never; always in, never out.*

In the gospel of today, Jesus speaks about hell. When he does that, he uses a word that you did not hear in the text because it was translated into English. He uses the word *Gehenna*, one of the words for hell.

Because Jesus used that word, the Jews and others in Jerusalem who listened to him knew exactly what he was talking about.

When we think about hell, we think about something we never saw, smelled, heard, or felt. When Jesus spoke about hell, his listeners knew what he was talking about. They had seen that place, they had smelled it, maybe they were even standing in its smoke while he talked. They had seen the worms crawling through that part of the place where the fire had not yet reached.

Gehenna was the ever-burning *rubbish dump* of Jerusalem, where the city-council workers emptied all the trash cans of the town.

Knowing this, we might find Jesus' message.

You know what ends up in trash cans: food that is not eaten, meat that is spoiled, wrappings and paper, dust and dirt, empty bottles and waste. The things we could not use, the things that broke down, all those things that do not function anymore and are, therefore, thrown away.

That is what Jesus said: "If you are not useful in the building of the Kingdom—*human life, the human family, the human community*—you are going to be thrown away by me on the rubbish dump of my Kingdom called Gehenna."

He does not seem to say that you will burn there eternally. He does say that the fire is eternal, and he suggests that in that fire, all the useless items are going to be burned to ashes.

Jesus is very close to an African idea where everyone tries to destroy and wipe out even the memory of an evil person who dies, to forever end his or her influence.

So, we should be useful. We should be a help. We should be well-functioning cells or organs in his Kingdom-to-come, in whatever we do or decide not to do. Amen.

TWENTY-SEVENTH SUNDAY OF THE YEAR

108. On Married Love

Mark 10:2–16

The Pharisees came to test him. Was it to put him in difficulty on an issue that had caused the execution of John the Baptist? Or was it to catch him on a cause that was then, as it is now, very delicate?

We don't know. We only know that Jesus, in his turn, put them to the test. We also know that they failed it.

When he asked them: "What command did Moses give you?" they answered: "Moses permitted divorce, and the writing of a divorce letter." He did not agree. He did not agree at all.

He told them: "That is not what Moses did. He *obliged* you to write such a letter because of the hardness of your hearts."

Moses had a very good reason to prescribe—*in God's name*—that obligation. An obligation that in a time when hardly anyone could write, was a rather complicated affair, almost equal to a legal procedure nowadays.

Before that law, and even after it, men had been accustomed to sending their wives away for the smallest and strangest of reasons: a badly cooked meal, sickness, age, boredom, having fallen in love with someone else, and things like that.

That is why Moses put them under the obligation of a formal dismissal letter, to at least somewhat protect the rights of the women.

Jesus insisted: "He did not *allow* you to write such a letter, he *obliged* you."

Then he added his own reason why this cannot be done.

A woman cannot be disposed of as if she is something you can throw away when you have used it for lust or to perpetuate your name!

He says: "This relation between husband and wife is such that the two become one flesh. Therefore let no one separate what God has united."

Isn't this what all couples hope at the moment they stand in front of the altar, surrounded by their communities, saying: "Yes, I will!" "Yes, I will!"

That hope is sincere, it is their promise, it is their prayer, it is their blessing. Yet, seven out of every twenty couples who stood next to each other promising it, hoping for this grace, will be divorced within ten years here in the United States. In some regions, the proportion is as high as twelve out of twenty.

Hopes not fulfilled, prayers not heard, efforts in vain, promises unrealized, frustration, disaster, a curse instead of a blessing; death instead of life.

Does this mean that in those cases the two really became one flesh?

Should those couples remain together? Did he really want situations to continue like that? Jesus said: "They shall *become* as one," but does it always happen like that?

Let us pray, and let us hope, that it will happen to our children, in view of themselves, in view of our grandchildren.

Let us hope and pray that it will happen to all those we love.

Let us pray, and let us hope that we ourselves—married or unmarried—will never find ourselves in a case where a letter of dismissal would be the only way out.

Because it is true, it is God's divine ordinance, it is the way we are created: every woman, every man, needs someone with whom to be whole and to become one in human flesh.

TWENTY-EIGHTH SUNDAY OF THE YEAR

109. On Self-Love

Mark 10:17–30

He came jogging. He came jogging for his life, as joggers do.

It does not say where he came from. It does not say where he went to; he ran like joggers do.

He stopped for a moment, he fell on his knees before him, and he said: "Sir, what should I do to share eternal life? What should I do to find it all? What should I do to love completely?"

Jesus looked at him and gave him the common answer, the normal way out, the road most traveled, though anyone knows that it is neither the final answer nor the final solution.

He said: "Do not kill, do not commit adultery, do not steal, do not testify falsely, do not deceive, honor your father and your mother. . . ."

Before he even finished, the young man replied: "I did all that, I did it from my youth, but I know that it is not sufficient, that it is not all! What more should I do?"

Again he looked at him and said: "If you really want to share in eternal life; if you really want to share in it all; if you really desire to love completely; if you really feel the urge of the Kingdom of God, loosen yourself from all you have, sell it, give it away, and once free, totally free, come to me and be as I am."

That man looked up; no, it was I who looked up; no, it was you who looked up. His face fell, my face fell, your face fell. And he, and I, and you went away sad, knowing that what he asked was something we could not do yet. We were not ready to come, not ready to grow, not ready to enter, and we ran on. We are jogging still, constantly having with us that same question, that same desire, that same urge.

We should never forget what that young man never forgot, or those who were witnesses to the scene, or the one who informed Mark about it. That witness noted carefully that Jesus remained looking after him with love and a smile.

Just as he is looking after you and me, saying to his amazed disciples: "For a human being, it is impossible, but not for God! With God all things are possible."

I trust it is that love, that promise, we will find when our running is over, when our jogging for greater health is done.

TWENTY-NINTH SUNDAY OF THE YEAR

110. Authority and His Community

Mark 10:35–45

All around us in this competitive world, people are continuously trying to get elected, get promoted, get to the very top.

This pushing and pulling goes on every week, every day, every hour. Who will be first, who will be second, who will be third, who will be the boss?

This isn't bad; someone should be at the top. It's even good, with one condition: the condition Jesus seems to talk about when confronted with James and John in their drive to the top.

James and John came to Jesus; they had a favor to ask. Jesus asked them: "What favor?" and they answered: "Would you please allow one of us to sit at your right side and one at your left in your Kingdom?"

Jesus did not even really answer their question. He only said: "It is not up to me to make a decision like that." Then he added: "But why do you want those places? What for?" Not only the two of them, he suggested, but even the other ten who were later indignant that James and John had asked for the places they had been hoping for.

He answered his own question by saying: "I know why. I will tell you. You want to have power. Power in the old way. You want to make your authority felt. You want to profit from your position. You belong to the old pagan world, a world not yet influenced by me! In my Kingdom, in my community, it is *not* like that.

"There, those with power serve. They make the others grow. They protect the frail ones. They think more about others than about themselves. Look at me. Look at what I do!"

Politicians fighting for power do this in order to serve, they *say*; in order to profit, they *hope*.

Let us not blame them. That kind of power dynamics doesn't play a role only on the political level. It's found everywhere power is involved, even in our own lives.

Are we living a pagan life, or are we serving with Jesus?

THIRTIETH SUNDAY OF THE YEAR

111. On Seeing and Following

Mark 10:46–52

Bartimaeus was sitting in the street, blind, useless, and not counted. In fact, he was almost nameless. People never used his name; they called him *son of*, the son of Bartimaeus.

He had given up. He had been sitting there for years, pulling his cloak around him as shelter against the cold, the sun, the rain, the dogs, and the crowd. It was the only protection he had for himself and his bag.

He did not move. He moved as little as possible. He had learned that, too.

Now and then, his hand would appear from under the cloak to receive a penny, a nickel, or a piece of bread.

Suddenly there was a noise at the entrance of the street. It grew louder and louder; it came nearer and nearer. He quickly crept away from his gutter into a corner, pulling his cloak even tighter around himself. He had been in crowds before, and it's not good to be blind in the midst of an excited crowd.

He heard the name Jesus and people singing "Alleluia!"

This was no riot, no lynching party; it was Jesus who passed.

Bartimaeus opened his cloak and shouted: "Jesus!"

They told him to stop that, but he shouted even louder and louder: "Son of David, have pity on me!"

Suddenly he felt that all around him, things were changing.

He heard a voice calling him forward. He heard other voices telling him to get up.

Finally he understood. He threw his cloak away, stood up, and was guided to Jesus, who said: "What do you want me to do for you?"

"Master," the nameless Bartimaeus answered: "Master, I would like to see!"

And Jesus said: "Be on your way! Your faith has healed you."

His faith had healed him. His *own* faith. Did you hear that? Did you really hear that?

This miracle is the last one related by the gospels.

It is the last one because it is different. After the other healings, the people healed go home to their family, their work, their jobs, their chores, their fields, their boats, their money, taking up the lives that had been interrupted by their ailments.

Bartimaeus did not do that. Bartimaeus never even looked back at his cloak. He started to follow Jesus from that day.

Hadn't he told him: "Be on your way," even before he saw?

His faith had healed him; his faith would heal others. He was going to do the things Jesus did, and even greater things, following him, as we should in our turn.

So many of us seem to be nameless, too, still being blind in the shadow of the big cloak we throw around ourselves to hide—from what, we don't exactly know.

THIRTY-FIRST SUNDAY OF THE YEAR

112. About the Good Life

Mark 12:28–34

That man asked the deepest possible question, the final one, the determining one, the one all of us have asked at one time or another: Which is the first of the commandments? What is the most important thing in life? What should we do to live well? What is the good life?

The answer to that question seems to be *legio*, a thousand, a thousand different answers.

You might even meet those differences in your own family. You are a Catholic, your father is a Muslim, your mother Episcopalian, your sister a Seventh-Day Adventist, your son a Quaker, and your daughter . . . who knows what your daughter is?

The question was asked by one of the scribes, one of the learned ones of his time. If he was sincere in saying that he did not know anymore, he must have been confused, as so many of us are confused.

He asked Jesus, and Jesus answered by saying one word only!

Jesus said: "Listen!" He said : "Hear! Open your ears!"

Listen. With that word, he said it all.

That one word indicated all the rest that followed. That one word summed up *the love for God, the love for the other*, and *the love for self.*

You don't believe me? Just think of your everyday experience. Isn't the one who loves you the one who listens to you?

You have a problem. You go to a doctor, a priest, a lawyer, a psychiatrist, your father, your mother, or someone you thought was your friend. Your problem is serious, your anxiety great. But they say they have no time, they are too busy, that you don't have the money. Even when they listen, you see their eyes turn away from you in other directions. You feel their minds turn away; *they do not love you.*

Think of yourself when someone you don't like comes to make you a participant in her worries, his anguish, her sickness.

Do you ever listen, really listen, when you don't love her, when you don't love him?

Think of the times you found one who listened—really listened—to you.

Isn't it true that all of us complain that nobody seems to listen to us?

That learned man, that professor, went to Jesus and asked: "*What is the most important thing in life?*" And Jesus said: "*Listen*. Listen to God, listen to your neighbor, listen to the source of life, listen to human life. There is no commandment greater than this one: *Listen*. If you listen, life will be loved and the consequences drawn. All will be well."

You don't need much imagination to know and feel that this is true. If we listen to God, we will not fight in God's name. If we listen to God, things will be shared. If we listen to God, others will also be heard. If we listen to God, others will hear us, too.

Listening to God, God will be loved with all our heart, soul, mind, and our strength, and we will love our neighbor as ourselves.

Translate the word *love* as "listen," and you know what *love* and the "good life" are both about.

THIRTY-SECOND SUNDAY OF THE YEAR

113. The Real Thing

Mark 12:38–44

He was sitting in the temple, the place he called the house of my Abba. He had spoken about its discontinuation on several occasions. He had spoken about its closure. He had even spoken about its destruction, but it was still the old house of Abba.

He sat somewhere on the foot of a column, to take in more easily the things happening around him. The scene he saw must have been fantastic, as far as we can judge from the reconstructions made.

Very important people would suddenly appear on the scene, enormously rich merchants who made their annual pilgrimage to Jerusalem from far-off countries. They were lavishly dressed, full of money. They were very willing to deposit large sums of clanking silver and gold in the offering boxes in view of their further business interests before starting their deals. The priests in that time had quite a bit of influence.

Jesus looked at them, listening to the noise the money made. *He was not impressed.*

Priests would appear dressed in a way that singled them out from the common people as much as possible. When they appeared, the Jewish commoners immediately gave way. The best places were evacuated, pillows and cushions were brought in to allow them to pray after their servants cleaned the seats to avoid any kind of impurity.

Jesus looked at them. He listened to the noise of their prayers from the foot of the pillar on which he sat. *He was not impressed.*

Scribes came in, people who knew the law. They knew it so well because, for the greater part, they had made it up themselves. They would sit down to listen to the legal difficulties of those who were willing to pay and were defenseless against the hypocritical defenders and protectors of their rights. They would listen up to the moment that the last penny of their victims—often poor widows and disinherited orphans—had been paid to them, after having sold the last things they had in this world. Jesus looked at them, he listened to the noise of their voices and the scratching of their pens. *He was not impressed.*

Others were very impressed. They had come from all over the world to the temple, to see that spectacle. It was there, they thought, that you could see life, the real thing. It was there, they said, that human life was decided. It was there, they supposed, that the future was made.

Up-country people, a little shy because they felt badly dressed and not at all at ease, gaped at those merchants, priests, and scribes.

Jesus, too, looked at it all from the foot of the pillar on which he sat, *and he was not impressed in the slightest.*

Then she came in—old, wrinkled, sickly, and very thin. In her hands she carried a handkerchief. She was hiding something. She went to the offering block.

Jesus looked at her. He did not say a word. He just looked.

At the offering block, she opened her handkerchief. Now he could see what she had been hiding: two small copper coins, all the money she had.

She could have divided those two coins between herself and the temple, one coin for each, but she did not do that. She took both her coins and dropped them in the opening of the offering block, already being pushed aside by others with bags and bags of gold and silver.

Jesus stood up. He called his disciples together. In between all that pomp and circumstance, the silver and the gold, the cassocks and the copes, the mitres and the croziers, the books and the dusty papers, he pointed *her* out to them and said: "She gave all she had." She was pure in her intentions. Look at what she did, and forget about all the rest.

Many of us often wonder about the things we do in life. "Was I really born," a housewife might sigh, "to change the diapers of my children? Shouldn't I do something more important?" "Did I really come into this world," a never-promoted clerk might say, "to push papers all my life? Is that all there is to my existence?"

When we worry like that—and who doesn't?—we should remember that scene in the temple, where a simple act of love was considered greater than anything else in this world: the real and decisive thing. Amen.

114. The End of This World

Mark 13:24–32

The sun will be darkened. The moon will fade. It will be a time of distress.

At first hearing the gospel of today sounds very threatening. There will be wars, famines, earthquakes, families will be ripped apart. There will be conflicts, persecutions, horrible phenomena. Those among us thirsting for justice and peace will stand before judges.

Many people in our world are full of *doom thinking*. People still ask: Don't you think the end is near? Don't you think that Jesus will return soon?

Some lose all courage. They are not open to the future. They are not willing to continue life in view of that imminent end.

In certain countries in the north—where the fog is always thicker than here in the south, and where the darkness lasts for weeks—young people even decided not to have children anymore. Why have children, they say. To be roasted alive in an atomic conflagration?

Yet, sisters and brothers, when you read the gospel, even the short excerpt of today, more carefully, you will notice that a gospel like today's is *not* a gospel of doom. It is a gospel about distress, about pain, about dying.

That distress, however, is not the important thing. That pain is not the end. The dying is not the real sign.

Jesus made this clear in the parable he adds. In that story, he brings us before a tree that lost all its leaves during a drought or during wintertime.

He tells us: Look well, and you will see all over the tree small brown buds. You look at Jesus and you say: "So what?"

He says: "Keep looking, and you will see." And you do see some movement, change, life. The small buds open. The surrounding brown leaves give way. They crack, they bend, they break, they die. To them, this means disaster, the end, distress; yet new life is born, a pale green shoot. The old protecting leaves fall on the earth. They dry up in a sun that is darkening to them, fading away, while bringing new life to the shoot. Life and growth.

You might even use the more salient image in John, which is not bound to seasons like today's parable. It is the image in which Jesus compares the whole of creation to a woman giving birth. She is in pain, terrible pain. But it would be nonsense to only look at her pain, saying, how horrible, what distress, what drama. That pain is not the important thing. That distress is not the end. The pain is the sign of a new life being born. Once it is born, all that pain will be forgotten because of that new life.

Jesus teaches us how to look at the crumbling of the old world around us, at the falling away of so many things we are accustomed to. Jesus tells us how to interpret conflicts, wars, and starvation. He explains: "Be careful. Don't get confused. Don't let them frighten you! Don't worry! Keep going. In the end, all will be fine!"

He even added that because of us and our work, God will take care that the transitional time, the labor, misery, and distress, will be shortened.

Robert Muller is an undersecretary of the United Nations. He wrote, using practically the same kind of image: "We are witnessing a unique moment of evolution, the birth of collective organs in the human species. For the first time humankind is emerging as a global organism with a common blood stream, a central nervous system, a shared heart, a corporate brain, and a common destiny."

He said it in a secular way.

The gospel uses more mystical terms: "And then they will see the son of man, coming in the clouds with great power and glory, then he will send angels to gather together his chosen from the four winds, from the ends of the world to the ends of heaven."

Let us live with this vision: humanity in labor to give birth—through distress and pain—to that human and divine organism of whom he is head. Alleluia. Amen.

THIRTY-FOURTH SUNDAY OF THE YEAR

115. Royal People

John 18:33–37

Kings do not exist anymore; queens don't, either. The ones we still have are only remnants from the past, impositions, antiquities, well-kept but no longer functional.

Kings and queens do still exist in the world of fairy tales, where children young and old tell their stories of people who ruled in such a way that there was peace and prosperity, justice and equity, and a prince for each princess all over the land.

When people were in need, badly off, starving, frustrated, and enslaved, they always started to tell stories of a king or queen who would rule and reign in such a way that the seasons would follow one another harmoniously. The sun would shine during the day and the moon during the night. The plants would grow, and the herds increase. The fruits would swell. Fish would be caught in every crystal-clear stream.

Everybody would be happy and find a place, a husband, a wife, and plenty of children, in the world.

The Hebrews often had that dream and desire during their history. When they were in difficulties, they would pray: "Yahweh, give us a king!" And when they had one who was more part of the problem than part of the solution, they would pray again: "Yahweh, give us a king, a new one, a *real* one. The one we have is fake!"

That is why they even tried to make Jesus their king. He refused, walking away from them. Now Pilate asks: "Are you King?" His answer was: "Yes, I am a King, but not like the one you are thinking of. Subjects I have not in this world! Yes, a King, I am!" Hadn't he come into this world to fulfill that old dream, to get rid of evil and sin, to redeem and liberate us? Hadn't he come to bring us justice and peace, to ban wars and all want? Wasn't that the reason God sent him into this world?

"Yes, I am a King, but not like the one you are thinking of. Subjects I have not in this world!"

And then he speaks about all those who are listening to him, who are hearing his voice, who believe in his truth.

Is he suggesting that we are or should be queens and kings, too?

Queens and kings in the way humanity has always dreamed about kings and queens: those who establish justice and peace, prosperity and health for all.

I think that is what he was thinking about.

King he was and is, but shouldn't we be kings and queens like him? Aren't we of his royal stock?

Are you willing to be king or queen like he?

You should. That is what he is all about.

LITURGICAL CYCLE C

116. The End at the Beginning

Luke 21:25–28, 34–36

Today we start to tell again the story of Jesus of Nazareth, that wonderful human being, that Son of God, called by so many of us Christ, the anointed one. The chosen one.

This story has been told again and again, year after year, for almost two thousand years. That is one of the reasons he remained with us and lives with us. It is not the only reason.

It might sound strange that we begin his story with his announcement of the end of this world.

He speaks about a sun that is fading away, about stars losing their shine. He speaks about an end that will unavoidably come. He speaks about women and men at a total and final loss.

Why do we start by telling about that end?

But, brother or sister, is not every story that's about an end also a story about a beginning? Isn't the last day always the dawn of a new day to come? Isn't a last look at the past, at the house you leave, at the dead you bury, always followed by a look into the future, at the things to come?

When Jesus speaks about that end, he is thinking of a world that is going to disappear. The world of corruption and sin, hatred, jealousy, greed, apartheid, war, and murder we all know so very well, as it surrounds us like a second skin.

When Jesus speaks about the end of this world, he is foretelling the new world to come, a better one, a different one: The Kingdom of God, in which we will be changed.

Some call this only a dream, and they are wrong. They have no hope. Others hold that he only meant the new heaven to come. They, too, neutralize what he really said and meant by adding things like: "That end will come in four years' time, in five years maybe, but surely by the year 2000." Those prophets of doom say that God will finish this world in all-ending wrath, burning it away.

Is that what he meant when he said: "The new Kingdom is among you"?

Is that what he meant when said: "Go out into the world and preach, baptizing it in the name of the Father, and the Son, and Holy Spirit"?

Is that what he meant when he broke his bread and shared his wine in that hall there and then, to share like that all through this world remembering him here and now?

He not only spoke of a new heaven to come. He also spoke about a new world to be formed: A world recreated in his Spirit and given to us by his Spirit.

Come, let us break up. The dark is almost over; the dawn is very near.

SECOND SUNDAY OF ADVENT

117. A Voice in the Wilderness

Luke 3:1–6

John was the name of the voice sent to shout in a world that had been described by so many prophets before John as a wilderness, a jungle.

He was the voice of the Lord.

A voice heard no longer in a world where the original goodness of the sky and the earth, the water and the air, the fire and the light, the oils and the minerals, the flowers and the trees, the animals and their young, and men and women had been practically lost.

At the moment that things came out of the hands of God, at the moment she and he came out of those hands, the Lord had said: "How good is all this as conceived, ordered, and made by us."

But they, he and she, responded by saying: "Let us determine by ourselves what is good and what is bad. We don't need a god for that."

Eating from that tree of knowledge reserved for God alone, the whole tree of life grew awry in junglelike fashion, with offshoots and undergrowths, with wild growths and overgrowths in dissolution, sickness, and death.

They themselves, she and he, decided they were naked, and so they were.

Now the voice of the Lord was heard again, speaking about an ax lying at the roots of that sick tree, speaking about restoration and the filling of holes, about straightening and leveling, sifting and sorting out, pruning and weeding, liberation and salvation, a new life and a new spirit.

And the sky and the earth, the water and the air, the fire and the light, the oils and the minerals, the flowers and the trees, the animals and their young, its men and women—the whole of creation—were bathed in hope and joy.

A radiant light was and is on its way in that darkness of ours.

THIRD SUNDAY OF ADVENT

118. With Water Only

Luke 3:10–18

The story of John the Baptist had been spreading all through the country. Consequently more and more people started to turn up. They came from all sides in the morning, in the afternoon, in the evening, and sometimes even during the night.

They wanted to be cleansed, to be healed, to be touched, to be washed; they wanted to be baptized.

He was baptizing, baptizing, baptizing until he got a stiff arm, like someone who did not stop playing tennis in time.

He had become fashionable. Ladies in Jerusalem talked about him in their parlors: "Have you been there? Did you see him? Did he talk to you? Did he baptize you?" And men, gentlemen from Jerusalem walked in the sun for hours in order to see and hear him.

John was definitely a man who corresponded to a need. People had been hoping so much and so long for a change, a real change. And when they saw him at work baptizing in the river Jordan, they started to hope again.

As the gospel says: *"The people were full of anticipation."*

John gave himself completely to his task and mission. He was there day and night washing people of sins he knew he could *not* wash off. He worked with a symbol, with a prophetic sign, and they thought it was the real thing. John knew that what he was doing was like washing wounds due to poisoned blood. He was washing them externally, without being able to do anything about the internal poisoning.

His task was only to prepare and announce. His mission was very external. He could not reach the cause. He couldn't really touch sin, the poisoning, and the human disorientation itself.

They asked him: "What should we do?" The gentlemen from Jerusalem asked. The ones who had parked their chariots and horses outside, under the trees along the river. The ladies from town asked him, too.

He said: "If you have two pairs of trousers, you must share with the one who has none; and if you have something left to eat, share with the one who is hungry."

The local city-council administrators came, along with some officials from the customhouse. They, too, asked: "What should we do?"

He said: "Ask no more than the rate, and don't put it in your own pockets. No bribes, no nonsense."

The soldiers and the police who were sent to keep order also came to him: "What about us? What should we do?"

He said: "No intimidation, no extortion, no violence. Be satisfied with your regular pay."

Yet it seemed he said all this without too much conviction. He could give advice; he could wash, purify, and clean. He could amend, patch up, and repair. He could warn, advise, recommend, and urge, but it was like pouring oil and spices over rotten food.

He was not the Christ. He could not change humanity. He could only baptize with water. That is why he started to insist: "Don't think that it is me. Don't think that I will be able to change you. I baptize only with water. Someone else is going to come after me. He really will change your mind, your heart, your soul, and your body." He insisted: "Please, forget about me. Let me get smaller and smaller. Let me be forgotten. It is *he* who is going to change you."

In the end, they came to arrest him. They chopped off his head and put it on a silver tray carried by a beautiful girl who, up to then, had never seemed to use any head at all. He lost his head because of the sin he had not been able to eradicate.

Saint John was right: This world can change only if people change their minds and their ways. Saint John was right. It is only fire and Spirit that are going to do it.

Fire and Spirit; let us be willing to receive them. Let a feeling of expectancy and anticipation grow among us during these days of the coming of the Lord.

FOURTH SUNDAY OF ADVENT

119. Full of Grace

Luke 1:39–45

The beginning had been that angel coming to Mary. Considering the date of Jesus' birth on December 25, it must have been around March 25.

The angel greeted her, saying: "Hail Mary, *full of grace!*"

That's how it started: full of grace. That grace was not some *thing*. That grace did not fill her like water fills a bottle, or salt a bag, or books a box.

That grace was her being taken up in God's plan. It was her mission. That grace was what she was going to mean to all of us.

The angel not only told her the role she was asked to play. It also said: Listen, your Aunt Elizabeth conceived in her old age, too, and though old, she is already in her sixth month.

Mary, who had already said yes to her Lord, got up, packed her things (she was still free; Joseph had not taken her into his house), and hastened over the mountains and through the valleys to her aunt.

When I was a child, I remember I always wondered about the heroes in the books I read. The cowboys and Indians, the supermen and superwomen of that time. They did marvelous things, great things, but they never did the things that hold human life together and make it possible.

You could read a whole book without them ever drinking one cup of coffee or tea. They never needed their mother or their father. They never had to go to a washroom. They never brushed their teeth or polished their shoes. They never ate breakfast.

Even now, I am sometimes struck with this thought when I hear about the heroes of today, both the good ones and the bad ones. Do they ever live a normal life? Do they ever do an ordinary thing?

In the case of Mary, I never felt those difficulties. She had just been made into a mother of the whole of human future, but when she, full of grace, heard about her old aunt, she veered up, as only a girl of sixteen can do, and ran off to help.

Elizabeth was in her sixth month, and she was very old. She was so old that John began to tell on her in her womb. She was alone. She felt shy about her condition. Zechariah, her husband, was a dead loss, since he had come back totally dumb from the temple the very day she conceived.

The water jugs she had to fill at the well seemed heavier and heavier every day. She had difficulty getting things washed on the rocks in the river. She sometimes had terrible pains in her back because her old frame had difficulty accommodating that young, jumpy, prophetic new life in her. And there was no one to massage her back from time to time. Then one day she looked out her window and saw Mary coming around the corner, her bouncy, healthy, young, robust cousin. She knew her trouble was over, and she burst out in joy. Joy not only because she recognized in Mary the mother of her savior, but joy also because she knew that Mary, full of grace, would be a grace to her in her difficult days.

Mary's extraordinary mission translated itself into ordinary action.

Isn't the ordinary the test of the reality and relevance of the extraordinary? Isn't it the ordinary by which we live? Isn't it the ordinary *he* came to save?

Let us translate the extraordinary in our lives: the Holy Spirit and all that in the ordinary grace we should be to each other from day to day.

CHRISTMAS

120. The Christmas Story

Luke 2:1–14

Christmas is the time that we tell our children stories—Christmas stories. Even parents who normally do not tell stories at all will sit down, gather their children around their knees, and start a story.

Children love stories. Stories are essential to children. Children know what all kinds of learned people discovered after much research and study: The only way you can help a child with moral issues and finding its way in life is through stories. Don't think you can replace those stories by putting a child in front of television. Television is different. It does not really tell stories. It shows too many images and doesn't leave you time to build your own images with your very own imagination. A story does!

Children are often lost. They feel threatened. They don't know how to escape, how to relate, and what to value.

We have always known that, and it has always been through stories that confusions were cleared up, monsters killed, threats eliminated, relationships and values learned.

Of course, we have to tell the right stories, the helpful ones. And now, I'll tell you a story. Very, very long ago, somewhere in West Africa, a very wise man, Ananse the Spiderman, said to himself: "If we only knew the stories God tells about us." He spun a thread straight up into the sky and, climbing along that thread, he arrived one day in front of the throne of Nyame, the sky god. That god kept all the stories about us in a golden box next to his throne. When Ananse asked for those stories, he did not get them immediately. First he had to do three difficult things. But that is not the point. The point is that he knew we need those stories. We need those stories God tells about us very badly.

Tonight we heard one of them: How God sent a new human start, the prince of peace, his only offspring, into our midst. The one who is going to bring us all together. God-with-us, Emmanuel, the one whose life we are destined to pick up.

It is a beautiful story. It is a story full of stars and angels, about shepherds, a lively mother, and wise men and women. It is a story with good kings and bad, about murder and escape. A story about goodness galore.

Yet there is a difference between this story and all those other stories in which heroes overcome darkness and evil. The Christmas story is a tale based on reality, on a historic person, on facts.

That is why we came here together tonight. Not only to hear that story once more, but to celebrate it as the start of a new life among, and even with, us. A Merry Christmas to you!

Note Jesus relation to his mother — she sent to bring him home — he asks — who are my mother & brothers.

FIRST SUNDAY AFTER CHRISTMAS

121. Holy Family: The Will of My Father

Luke 2:41–52

It's strange, but when speaking about the Holy Family today, we are confronted in the gospel with a conflict. A conflict in the Holy Family.

You know what happened. Jesus was twelve by then, not yet a man, but no longer a child. A rather confusing period for the person in question and his parents.

Leaving Jerusalem for home, Mary noticed that Jesus did not walk with her. She thought: *Twelve. He considers himself to be a man, so he is walking with Joseph.* Joseph, noticing that Jesus was not walking with him, thought: *Twelve. He is still a child. He is walking with his mother.*

It was only in the evening of that first day on their trip home that they discovered he had not been walking with them at all.

They were frightened. They said: "How is this possible?" Next morning, they rushed back to Jerusalem, and it was only at the end of the third day that they found him in the temple.

The text says that they were "overcome" when they saw him. I don't know what that word *overcome* exactly means. Did they weep? Did they jump up? Were they angry?

Mary told him off, it seems. She said: "How could you do a thing like that? Didn't you know that your father and I were worried to death? Did you not think of us at all?"

He looked at her with his very clear eyes and answered: "But didn't you know that I had to do my Father's will? Didn't you know that I must be busy at my Father's affairs?"

He told Mary: "I am quite willing to listen to you. I am quite willing to think of you. I am quite ready to love you, but it is my Father, God, to whom I have to listen, of whom I am thinking, whom I am loving in the very first place!"—often hard for parents who may be possessive. *Impl. Does the child ever truly separate + leave home? Measure of health?*

Mary did not understand. Neither did Joseph, for that matter. She kept it all in her heart; she only understood later, while standing under his cross.

In the life of her son, something prevailed over all his earthly bonds. When we speak about the difficulties in our families, we have a lot to talk about: quarrels, unfaithfulness, disobedience, lack of respect, the misuse of money, and so many other things. But do we meet, in our families, the difficulty they were facing that day in Jerusalem? Do we ever ask ourselves whether we, as a

Many Adults never escaped from home —
but if they do — what who becomes the new
director — should be God. — the only adequate
direction

family, are realistically and concretely interested in the will of the Father, in the Kingdom of God here on earth?

I wonder.

Don't we lock ourselves up too much in our family affairs? Are we sufficiently open, as a family, to the larger issues in the world, to the issues of the Father: peace, justice, unity, and love? Wouldn't such an openness help us better overcome the internal and petty conflicts in our families?

Jesus went home with them. He obeyed them, the text reads. Nevertheless, everything had changed. They knew now what his first allegiance was going to be. From then on, he was doing the work of his Father first, as he would all the rest of his life. So did Mary, so did Joseph, as they, too, would do all the rest of their lives. In that way, they taught all of us what "holiness" in a family, in a community, means.

EPIPHANY

122. Packing Up

Matthew 2:1–12

It must have been dark when those wise men saw that star. It's possible to see a star by daylight, but then you have to allow for all kinds of gadgets. It was in the dark of the night that they saw the light. It was in the dark of their night that they saw that star at its rising.

Notwithstanding all their difficulties, notwithstanding the unbelievable troubles of their days, they had sufficient faith in God and humanity to pack up immediately and follow it. It was not the star itself that caused them to follow it. It was not its beckoning tail—come, come, come—that made them follow it. It was their faith in the possibilities of a new world, a new humanity, that made them follow.

During an interview for a special Christmas feature, theologian Dorothee Sölle was asked: "What does faith mean to you?" She answered: "It means that you believe that the Kingdom of God is possible. It means that you are confident that this world can be changed in the direction of that Kingdom. It means that you are convinced that it is not a dream, an illusion or a figment of an overexcited religious or ethical mind.

"That belief, or that faith," she added, "should be so firm and so strong that you are willing to work in order to help it grow, that you are ready to cooperate in its growth, and that you don't sit down waiting for God to clear the situation."

It is that kind of faith that must have been the moving force when those wise people packed their luggage, kissed their wives and children good-bye, and, facing the unbelief and ridicule of their friends, set off on a journey with a destination both known and unknown at the same time.

Even to us so many years later, notwithstanding our belief, faith, and hope, that destination remains unknown. And yet we know. There are hints where it all will lead us. There are indications, signals, and signs.

In the second reading of today, Paul gives us such a hint when he writes about a mystery, a secret he was given knowledge of. A mystery, a secret, he writes, unknown and hidden to anyone in generations past.

The mystery is that all human beings share in the same inheritance. The secret is that we all live under the same promise. The mystery is that in Jesus Christ we are all parts of the same being, the same body. We are one. We belong together. We are created in him. We should strive toward the realization and a further awareness of that fact. That was the reason those wise men (were there only three?) packed up and traveled toward him, and toward themselves.

SUNDAY AFTER EPIPHANY

123. The Baptism of Jesus

Luke 3:15–16, 21–22

There was something strange about the baptisms given by John. They were incomplete. They were without much effect. John baptized. He believed in his baptism. At the same time, it was John himself who said: "I am not the one. I only baptize with water. Wait till a stronger one comes; he will baptize you with Spirit and Fire."

In a way, John depreciated his baptisms. He probably did so because he knew that once his newly baptized disciples were back home, his baptism would quickly be forgotten. In fact, we don't hear very much—nothing at all—about the effect of those baptisms. It seems as if everything went on as before.

John knew his baptism needed a complement. And, though in another way, maybe, it is rather obvious that the baptism of many Christians seems to need a complement, too. Isn't it true that many Christians remain as cool as the water that once streamed over their heads? Isn't it true that many Christians are no different from the others around them?

When you read the gospel story of today carefully, you can see what happened to Jesus. He must have lined up in front of John along with the others. He must have stepped in the water when his turn came. According to Matthew, there was a short exchange of words between them, but then Jesus was baptized. And nothing else seemed to have happened to Jesus at that moment. Nothing at all. He just stepped out of the water like all the others. Then Luke's report continues:

> Now when all the people had been baptized,
> and while Jesus after his own baptism was at prayer,
> heaven opened.

All the others went home after their baptism, and nothing much seems to have happened to them. Jesus remained behind, and as he started to pray near the river, perhaps behind a bush, heaven opened and the Spirit came down. Could that prayer have been the reason the Spirit came down on him? Could lack of prayer be the reason the Spirit never seems to come down on us?

Weren't his disciples at prayer when the Spirit descended on them in the upper room in Jerusalem at Pentecost?

Luke mentions something else in his report of the event. The Spirit descended on Jesus in the bodily shape of a dove. In other words, the Spirit was visible, just as that Spirit would be visible in all Jesus said, did, and omitted to do afterwards.

Sisters and brothers, the story is so simple. The man from Nazareth, Jesus, went to John to be baptized. He was baptized; the water flowed over his head. After that baptism, he sat down somewhere, or maybe he knelt, he prayed . . . God's Spirit came over him in the shape of a visible dove, and a voice was heard, a voice that did *not* say: "Jesus is *the Son of God*," but that said: "*Jesus* is the Son of God."

What would happen if we prayed as he did?

SECOND SUNDAY OF THE YEAR

124. I Have a Dream

John 2:1–12

This week we commemorated the birthday of Martin Luther King, Jr. While turning on the radio yesterday, I switched on while he was speaking. Those words were taped, of course, because Martin Luther King was killed by a sniper in 1969.

In the speech I heard, his most famous one, he said to an enormously enthusiastic crowd: "I have a dream. . . . I have a dream . . . that one day. . . ." I am sure many of you would be able to fill in what Martin Luther King dreamed about.

I have a dream that one day all people will sit at one table, eating and drinking together, I have a dream . . . !

Mary had that same dream in the gospel of today when she saw her son coming to that wedding feast. It was the same dream, that old and ever-new human dream.

When she saw her son arrive, she thought: *Maybe, this is the beginning of* it all. *Maybe it is today, that from here, from this feast, from this house, from this table, from this kitchen all will start. Maybe after today I will no longer have to say: "I have a dream." Maybe today all is going to change. The final wine is going to flow.*

But her son sat with some people Mary had never seen before, and he took a glass, and he started to drink like all the others, happy and relaxed.

Mary thought: *Should I try? Should I provoke? Should I suggest? Should I stimulate?*

While thinking like that, she heard in the kitchen (that is where such news is always heard first) "No wine! This is the last jug. What are we going to do?" Too many guests, no wine, and no money, either, no solvency.

It was as if the sign had already been given: The old was over, the new should start. She decided and went to him and said: "They have no wine!"

He looked at her and said: "Not yet, not yet!" But she went to the kitchen and ordered: "Do whatever he tells you!"

That is what they did when, after some time, he stood up, went to the kitchen, and told them to fill all available pots and pans with water. They filled them up to the brim, and all that water was changed into wine.

John says that this was the first of the signs that would lead to his final work.

Mary was right. She knew that the final banquet would start, but she did not know when. Her timing was bad, but she knew it would come: The time when the dream would no longer be a dream. The sign was given. He intervened in the work she told those others to do. *And his disciples believed in him.*

One of those disciples, very many years later, was Martin Luther King, and again he said: "I have a dream. . . ."

That was not all he had. That was not all he did. He worked and sweated filling the empty jugs of this world with water, sure that once again *he* would come to change all that water, the bitter water of this world, into wine—sweet, nice, grade A, heavenly wine—preparing for the final banquet to come.

Let us work like him in the kitchen of this world, getting prepared for him who will do it with us. Amen.

THIRD SUNDAY OF THE YEAR

125. Are We Good News to the Poor?

Luke 4:1–4, 14–21

He had been baptized. The Holy Spirit, the Spirit of God, had descended on him. He fled into the desert, tempted to think of himself, to give up, or not even to start. He did not give in. He came out of the desert. He picked some company and went to that wedding feast in Cana to indicate where the foundation of human life lies.

When passing through Cana, he must, according to Luke, have been on his way to his hometown, Nazareth.

His fame had been spreading, and on that first Sabbath day in Nazareth, everyone who could move in that town went to the synagogue. They were curious, and they definitely expected him there, because—as Luke wrote—"It had been his custom to be there on the Sabbath day." When the leader of the service asked for a reader, they all remained very determinedly seated. No one stood up. They wanted him to stand up and take the reading.

That is what he did.

He stood up. They handed him the scroll of the prophet Isaiah. He accepted their choice. He took the scroll. He rolled it down—a hush went through all the building, all eyes were now on him—and he read: *"The Spirit of the Lord had been given to me, for he has anointed me. He had sent me to bring the good news to the poor, to proclaim liberty to captives and to the blind new sight, to set the downtrodden free, to proclaim the Lord's year of favor."* He then rolled up the scroll, gave it back to the assistant, and sat down. Another hush went through the building. Only teachers with authority sat down while speaking.

He said: "This text is being fulfilled today, even as you listen. The time has come!"

When we hear this text, we Christians might get up enthusiastically and go off to form networks and peace and justice groups. We'd march through the streets to the White House, to the treasury, to the offices of the *New York Times* and the *Washington Post*, to Capitol Hill, shouting that others should do justice to others, protesting that others should be of the Spirit of God, just and fair, charitable and loving.

That is true; they really should.

Let us not forget that it is *we*, too, who are baptized in him, washed and converted, filled with the Spirit of God, the Spirit of Jesus Christ.

It is clear from the text read by Jesus in Nazareth what the Spirit should do in us. She should do in us what she did in Jesus: bring good news to the poor, liberate captives, give sight to the blind, uplift the exploited, and proclaim God's grace.

It means that wherever we find any human being not fully living up to her or his human dignity, that wherever we find a fellow human being dehumanized, we should help that sister or brother be fulfilled, whatever the reason for the dehumanization might have been: psychological, spiritual, physical, medical, economic, or cultural.

We should be like him, as far as we can, helping, enlightening, and uplifting. According to Jesus, we will be judged on what we did. In the end he will say: "There was a human being who was hungry. You could easily have helped. What did you do? There were those others in prison physically, psychologically, spiritually, economically, and so on. What did you do?"

In the end he will say: "You met me, Jesus, dehumanized, disabled, exploited, wounded, hungry, handicapped, unemployed, a school dropout, a refugee, and what did you, what did your community do?''

Are we really *good news* to the poor? To him?

126. His Unforgivable Inclusiveness

Luke 4:21–30

While he spoke in that synagogue in Nazareth, his own townspeople were astonished by his words, and they said: "How right he is," and they added: "What a blessing to us over here in Nazareth. Isn't he the son of Joseph and Mary, people who live in this town? What a blessing to us. What an honor. How greatly our community will profit."

That's what they said, but in their hearts, in the local bars, in the kitchens and the workshops, they were already blaming him. They were gossiping about him all over the place.

He could work miracles; so far so good. But why had he given them that wine in Cana, of all places? What about their own thirst in Nazareth? Why those healings in that far-off harbor of Capernaum? What about the sick on the street where he had lived for so long? Why all those spectacular things among strangers and foreigners? Why hadn't he come home immediately after that baptism, where it all started? Wasn't he Joseph's son? Didn't he belong to them? Wasn't he of their flesh and blood?

He should be ashamed of himself. He should change his attitude. He should change himself. He should heal himself. He should stay with them. First things first.

He knew them very well. He guessed their thoughts exactly, so he said: "No doubt, you want to tell me: Heal yourself, do here the things you did up to this moment elsewhere. Stay with us. Restrict yourself to your own circle. Don't betray us!

"No doubt, you want to tell me: When you gave them that wine in Cana, we over here in Nazareth were very thirsty. How could you think of them and forget about us? Didn't we drink with you while you were here with us? Shame on you! Shame!

"No doubt, you want to tell me: While you were healing in Capernaum, there were sick people over here in your own town, in your own family. What do you think they thought when they heard that you were healing elsewhere, wasting your time in far-off places? Shame on you! Shame!"

They wanted to restrict him exclusively to themselves. They wanted to bind him only to his blood relatives. They wanted him to take the attitude that causes almost all the trouble in this world: apartheid, nationalism, fascism, racism, tribalism, nepotism, and elitism.

He told them: "That time is over. That sin should have been overcome by now. Even the prophets of old showed this was of the past. Didn't your ancestors tell one another that all humanity is created by God? And what about Elijah? In his day, there were many widows starving with their children in the land of Israel. He didn't help them; he helped a foreign widow in Zareptah. What about Elisha? In his day, there were many lepers suffering bitterly in the land of Israel. He did not help them; he helped an alien one, Naaman, a Syrian."

They got so furious that they sprang to their feet. He had hit them at their hearts. God was their God, not the God of any other people.

Many people are very good within their own families, excellent fathers, perfect mothers, wonderful children. But when facing others from outside that family circle, they are hopeless. Southerners facing Northerners; Northerners facing Southerners; whites facing blacks; blacks facing whites; Americans confronting Russians; Russians confronting Americans; Christians despising Muslims; Muslims despising Christians; settlers struggling with nomads; nomads struggling with settlers.

Yet there will be no peace, justice, liberation, and no end to exploitation until those groups and circles, those clans and classes are broken through. It is often very difficult to accept that truth. It is often very hard to humanize our relations to that point, which is Jesus' point.

In Nazareth they said: "If you don't want us exclusively, then we don't want you: fall dead, perish, get lost, disappear!"

They marched him to the brow of the hill, ready to throw him off the cliff. That time he escaped by walking through them.

FIFTH SUNDAY OF THE YEAR

127. Touch and Go

Luke 5:1–11

Up to that morning, Peter had not been overcome. He had been surprised, but no more than that. He had not really been touched, and he had not really decided on what to do, either. He drank the wine in Cana, but he was not impressed. He always bought his wine when he wanted some, and it had always been there in a bottle or a leather sack when he needed it. He had never thought about all the work that goes into the making of wine. To Peter, wine seemed easy; you just fill barrels with grape juice, you add certain things, you store it, and you wait. That's all there is to it.

He had never been overcome by the fact that Jesus had thrown a devil out of a demoniac. He had been astonished, and he had said with the others: "What a teaching and what a teacher. He gives orders to unclean spirits and they obey him just like that!'' That was all. Nothing really struck home.

This fish was different.

They had been fishing all night. They had caught only a few dead crabs, an old sandal, a broken pot, and some pieces of firewood. Hopeless. They had already started cleaning their nets when he came along, the man of the wine in Cana, the man of those healing incidents.

And he said: ''Throw out your nets!'' They answered: ''Now listen, you might be able to turn water into wine, but a vineyard owner can do the same. You might have healed some people, but a doctor does the same. You want us to throw our nets out after this night? No. Do you want us to make fools of ourselves in front of all those people? We are fishermen, you know, and you are not!''

They looked at Jesus and saw that he insisted, so Peter said: ''Okay, we will do it! Let's make fools of ourselves.'' Looking at Jesus, he added: ''We are in good company!''

They threw out their nets. They splashed into the water, and suddenly there was a kind of rush in the lake. It moved all over, the boats were almost pulled down, and the nets were filled with fish—all kinds of fish, an onrush of fish— tilapia, eel, pike, and whitefish.

Peter almost automatically evaluated the contents of the nets: tilapia at six dollars a pound, eel at seven, and whitefish at five.

And then, suddenly, he was touched. Oh boy, he really was touched! It suddenly struck him: He was standing in the company of God! He shouted: ''Get away from me. I am a sinful man. Go away!''

Just as Isaiah, in the first reading of today, shouted at the moment he saw God: ''See how wretched I am. I, a man with unclean eyes, I saw God. I, a man with unclean ears, I heard God. I, a man with dirty sinful hands, I touched God. I am lost, let me go, let me die!''

As the African proverb says: ''It is not good to be too near to a chief.'' It is not good to be too near to a king, except when you are called, and even such a call is a bad sign.

It is not good to be too near to God: God wants too much. God knows too much. God is too single-minded. It is not good to touch God. It is too danger- ous. You are going to lose your *life*, you are going to lose *your* life.

They did.

An angel came to Isaiah from behind God. Isaiah was trembling and shaking all over, like a small boy before he is beaten by his father. The angel took a burning coal, a live burning coal, and he burned the evil out of Isaiah. A voice was heard, he was sent, and off he went. He lost *his* life and won it back in God and his new mission.

Peter fell on his knees. James fell on his knees, too, and John as well, just like men condemned to death pleading for their lives. Jesus said: ''Be not afraid, follow me, and you will catch men and women together with me, just as I am catching you now.''

They brought their boats to the shore. They arranged for the fish to be sold by their friends, and they left everything and followed him.

They lost their lives and won new ones.

That is the risk we, too, live under when we live with Jesus. That is why it is so hard for us to really be with him. It's the reason we have so much difficulty with our prayers. We do not need the devil to tell us not to pray. Our own nature tells us not to do it. It is too dangerous, you are going to be caught, you are going to be sent.

Who wants to be with him? Who wants to open her or his heart to God? Who wants to be touched? Because to be touched means to be sent, to be sent by him, who in his single-mindedness is thinking of only one aim: his Kingdom to come.

SIXTH SUNDAY OF THE YEAR

128. Plain Talk

Luke 6:17, 20–26

When Jesus gives his Beatitudes in Matthew and Mark, he first climbs a mountain, as if to indicate that what he is going to say is as yet above us: an ideal, a promised outcome of the long climb ahead.

When he gives his Beatitudes in Luke, he comes down from the mountain into the plain, at the level where we live and where his listeners had assembled.

Those listeners had come from very far, from all parts of Judea, from Jerusalem, Tyre, and Sidon. They had come, the gospel explains, to hear him and be cured. The people assembled were men and women who had left their homes, jobs, work, worries, and opportunities behind. They had gone a long way to hear him and to be helped by him.

Then, looking *at them*, fixing his eyes *on his disciples*, Jesus says: "How happy are you who are poor! How happy are you who are hungry! How happy are you who weep now!"

What did he mean?

Was he insinuating that poverty—with its squalor, bedbugs, lice, and fleas, its unavoidable rats, prostitution, child death, hunger, starvation, lack of education, sanitation, security, and vitamins, with its tuberculosis, kwashiorkor, rabies, scabies, and deformation—makes anyone happy?

Of course not! How could he? He was, on the contrary, speaking to people and about people who were hoping to have all that changed!

Take the incident as it stands: He came down from the mountain after a night of prayer. As he came down, he saw those hundreds, maybe thousands, waiting for him. What did they come for? They came because they hoped for a change. They came because they wanted to see. They wanted to hear. They wanted to know. They came because they considered themselves poor, hungry, thirsty, ignorant, frustrated, and sad. They came because they were eager for a change, greater integrity, greater human dignity, greater justice, and more joy.

That is why he praises them and blesses them. Those people, who considered themselves in danger and helpless, were (and are!) the hope of this world.

They are the ones willing to listen to him.

There is hope because of that willingness. A hope not present in those who remained home, thinking they already knew, that they already had their fill, that they already had their consolation, laughing at any change or its possibility.

Jesus praised those who had come because they were willing to listen.

He told them that if they would really listen, the whole world would change. A new human alternative would be realizable. He also told them that very many would be against those changes, that they would be hated, accused, exiled, abused, denounced, and arrested as criminals.

Yet, he added, be happy, as you are right: *The change will come.*

SEVENTH SUNDAY OF THE YEAR

129. Love Your Enemies

Luke 6:27–38

Some people say that the Bible is old, that it is irrelevant. Even people who believe in Jesus sometimes say this. Tired of all those stories, they are more interested in how the Christ we are talking about is living now.

That is what I would like to do. I would like to show you today how the Christ we talk about is living among us *now*.

How could we do that if we were not first informed about that Christ by the Bible? That is why it is good to start with a Bible text.

Let's use the one we just heard: "Love your enemies, do good to those who hate you, bless those who curse you, pray for those who treat you badly."

In the case of Jesus, this was not only a question of words. He prayed for his executioners while dying. He healed the ear of one of the people who came to arrest him, when Peter chopped around with his sword on that fatal night.

All that happened long ago, almost two thousand years ago. Where is that Christ now? When we start to think about his followers, we too often look to far-off regions, to far-off cultures, to ages ago. We think of saints and martyrs, confessors, virgins, and holy children *there and then*. What about *here and now*?

Some time ago a famous Ugandan author, Taban Lo Liong, gave a speech here in Nairobi at the German Goethe Institute.

He spoke about this country, but what he said might be applied to all countries. He said that one of the difficulties in modern African education is that there seem to be no valid African models. The models used are coming from other cultures, literatures, and times, from Shakespeare and from the Old West.

Is that true? Are there no African models? Are there no contemporary heroes? Are there no modern saints?

Did you read the diary of the Ugandan archbishop who was killed some time ago?

In the early morning of Saturday, February 5, 1977, soldiers climbed over the fence around his house in Kampala. They forced their way into the house.

They threatened Anglican archbishop Janani Luwum at gunpoint. They searched his house. They scared his children. He declared: "There are no arms in this house, we pray for the President, we pray for his security forces." After searching for two-and-a-half hours, they were ready to leave. They asked him to open the gate for them. His wife suggested to the archbishop: "Don't open the gates. Let them go out as they came in, over the fence!"

Archbishop Janani Luwum told her: "We are Christians, we have clean hearts, and as a witness we are going to open the gates for them." That is what he did.

"Love your enemies, do good to those who hate you, pray for those who treat you badly."

Ten days later, Archbishop Janani Luwum disappeared. He was shot. The Christ we talked about, living then, dead now.

Is he really dead? If he is dead, then why are we speaking about him? We say: "What a shame, what a terrible shame that he was killed." Archbishops and canons have been saying: "What a loss, what a terrible blow to the African church leadership." They are right, and they are not right.

He disappeared, that is true. Even his body is lost. It was burned and scattered in the wind, because his murderers were afraid of him, even after his death.

Is he lost?

Aren't we thinking about him today as an example, as a model? Don't examples and models lead and guide us?

Archbishop Janani Luwum decided to resist violence in a nonviolent way. He *won*, because of what we now think of him and because of what we now think of the violence he resisted.

In fact, he was sure to win, because he proved to be a son of the Most High. The spirit of the archbishop, the saint Janani Luwum, will triumph because it is *God's own Spirit*. God, the lover of all.

EIGHTH SUNDAY OF THE YEAR

130. The Treasure in You

Luke 6:39–45

When we speak about Jesus, we can think of the many roles he played. The one we know best is that he died for us on the cross, giving his life for our salvation. He played other roles, too. One of the things he always did was try to convince people of their own worth. When someone came to ask him a question such as: "What is the most important commandment?" he would answer: "What do you think?" referring them back to themselves. He continuously expressed his amazement at what he found in the ones who came to ask his help or advice. In the gospel of today, he speaks about the person who draws good from the store in her or his heart.

I would like to tell you a story to illustrate why Jesus does this. It's an old, well-known story. It's *your* story, it's *my* story—at least it might be. Maybe it should be. There was a man in the heart of Africa who had a dream one night. He dreamed that he left his house, his hearth, his cooking stones, his cooking pot, his children, and walked, walked, and walked. He passed one village after another, and he finally came to a place with a bridge in the road just before the entrance to the village. He dreamed that he started to dig under that bridge, and under that bridge, he found a real treasure. When he woke up, he did not pay any attention to his dream. He had had so many dreams before. But then a second, third, fourth, fifth, sixth, and a seventh night he had that same dream. So he said to himself: "This must be true. I must find that village. I must find that bridge. I must find that treasure."

He told his wife, who agreed, and he left her, his children, his cooking stones, his cooking pot, and his hearth, and started to walk. He passed village after village after village until he arrived at a place with a bridge in the road just before the entrance to the village. He recognized the place immediately. He was overjoyed. He left the road, went under the bridge, and started to dig. He dug, and he dug, but he found nothing.

An old woman came along. She stopped and asked him, "What are you doing there?" He asked her, "Why do you want to know?" She told him how she had a dream night after night, over the last seven nights, and in those dreams she had seen a man digging for treasure under the bridge. She dreamed that she had said to that man: "What you are looking for, you can only find at your own home. It is under your own hearth, under your own cooking pot, under your own three cooking stones."

When the man heard this, he stopped digging and went home, running as fast as he could. When he arrived at home, he started to dig under his own fireplace. His wife and children all helped him. And there, lo and behold, he found his treasure, and he was very happy ever after, together with them. In the gospel of today, Jesus invites us to look for the goodness hidden in our own hearts.

He told them so often that God's Spirit, that the Kingdom of God, can be found within us. We Catholics are so surrounded by sacramental signs, we are so accustomed to a pope, cardinals, bishops, priests, sisters, brothers, and long lists of female and male saints, that we are tempted to look outside ourselves to find holiness and goodness. I am sure that if we met Jesus, he would find it in us, just as he did in the people who surrounded him in Palestine.

May I ask you to look for the goodness within you and in the ones around you? Open your heart, open your mind, and you will be like that good person bringing out goodness, pure goodness, in all you decide to do!

NINTH SUNDAY OF THE YEAR

131. Hopeless Pessimists and Hopeless Optimists

Luke 7:1–10

Hope is important. You cannot hope without faith. Your faith is useless without hope. Hope is not only a virtue, it is also an abstraction, something that does not exist.

Soap exists. Sugar exists, salt exists, you exist, but hope does not exist. It only exists in a person. So we must start with a person when speaking about hope.

Take the officer of this morning's story. He had a sick servant, a favorite of his. He had heard about Jesus and his healing. The officer could have done different things. He might have said: "It is useless to go to him. He is not going to help me. Why should he? I am, in fact, his enemy." Speaking like that, the officer would have been a pessimist. He would have stayed at home, even when he heard Jesus was in the neighborhood. The gospels have no report on what happened to those pessimists who stayed at home when Jesus passed.

The officer might have reacted in another way. He might have said: "This sickness struck him before. I know what it is. It is going to pass, though he is very badly off now. It will be all right. I do not need any help." Speaking like that, the officer would have been an optimist. He would have stayed at home, even when he heard Jesus was passing his house.

The gospels have no report on what happened to those optimists who stayed at home when Jesus passed.

Optimists and pessimists are without hope, hopeless. They are self-centered. They remain alone, they do not go out. They do not need anybody else. There are no stories about them in the whole of the four gospels.

The gospels are full of stories about people in pain, about people worrying about others, about people with sore eyes, lame legs, internal bleedings, stiff tongues, deaf ears, stupid heads, and about people carrying their dead with them.

They left their homes. They came out of their hiding places. They were brought out of their homes by others because they hoped.

They were realistic and humble enough to do so. Most probably, they had done everything they could to escape their fate. They had bumped against the barriers of their impossibilities, and they had recognized that fact. They went out to find somebody else; they did not stay alone, they asked for help, like the centurion in the story of today.

They prayed for help. They prayed hopefully, they entered into communion with somebody else, they confided in someone.

That is what hope is about. Hope in a woman, hope in a man. No egocentric optimism, no egocentric pessimism, but a realistic, trustful relating to someone and communicating with that someone *hopefully*.

That is what makes hope so difficult for many of us. We are too sure of ourselves. We want to be self-reliant. We are optimists, and it is no help to be an optimist. Or we are pessimists, and it is no help to be a pessimist.

We are rarely really "hopeful," notwithstanding the possibilities we know of, the possibility of going to Jesus, the possibility of approaching the Son of God, the Maker of heaven and earth, like that Roman officer did. Didn't Jesus himself say that he only rarely met that type of hopeful faith?

TENTH SUNDAY OF THE YEAR

132. Are You a Savior?

Luke 7:11–17

A savior came to the world, a new light went up, God showed his love to the world: God, love, light, world, peace, savior, all people. I often get impatient when I try to listen to that type of religious talk during radio services, during "lift up your heart" programs, during religious epilogues, and the endless exhortations of evangelists over the television.

I hope you are not scandalized, but I do not believe Jesus is a savior, a light, a power, a liberator, or even useful in that most general of ways, in what a specialist would call a historical or abstract way.

It does not help anyone. It really does not help.

I believe that Jesus is a savior in another way.

I believe that Jesus was a savior to that mother in Nain who was walking behind the coffin of her only son. Being a widow, she was practically burying her own life. He told them to open the coffin and do it quickly. I believe Jesus was a savior when he returned that beautiful son—her hope and her pride, with his broad chest and his nice pitch-black hair—to her.

I believe that Jesus was a savior to that marrying couple in Cana that ran out of wine, when he provided, through the water of their kitchen, the necessary extra gallons of wine.

I believe he was a savior to the father of the mad boy who had fits three, six, nine, or twelve times a day. He healed the child, and the child suddenly said, without any fit and without any foam on his lips: "Thank you, Sir. Thank you," because his fits were over.

I believe he was savior to the blind he met; to the deaf he healed; to the lame he made jump with joy; and to the hungry and thirsty he fed.

I believe he was a savior to Zaccheus, who thought only of money and interest and capital growth of land, farms, and cows, and whose heart he opened to the others.

I believe he was a savior to that adulterous woman whom he told: "Okay, your sins are forgiven, the past is the past, no nonsense anymore. Think of your family, think of yourself," and she went away free and saved.

I believe he was savior to that coward called Peter, whom he promised his prayers and added: "You are going to be hopeless, you are going to betray, but you will never get lost, because I prayed for you."

I believe he was a savior to that murderer, the armed robber hanging next to him on a cross, to whom he said: "Do not bother, take it easy, you will be with me in a minute or two forever and ever."

I believe he was a savior—or should we say a liberator—because he helped, because he really and concretely saved those men and women, those girls and boys.

I believe he is my savior because he showed me, while doing all this, how I should live, and more importantly, how I am able to live with his help.

Those who believe in him and his power are not the ones who murmur: "Lord, have mercy. I am a wretched sinner," while beating their chests. Those who believe in him are not the ones who sing: "Alleluia, praise the Lord!" raising their voices and slamming their organs and their drums. Those who believe in him are not the ones who multiply their "I believes," in very orthodox ways, checking their catechisms, the latest World Council of Churches or papal statements.

Those who believe in him are those who try to live his type of life.

He lived as savior, and his believers also try to live as saviors with his help, with his Spirit, or, if you prefer that word, with his grace.

Are you a believer?

Do you try to live as a savior to the people around you? Are you a follower of Jesus? You, father, while educating your sons and your daughters. You, mother, while running your family. You, teacher, while teaching the hundreds and thousands of children entrusted to you. You, administrator, with all the powers of your papers and their clips, your pencils, files, drawers, and computers. You, policeman, with your stick, your pistol, your statements, and your dogs. You, politician, with your responsibility for your constituency, your promises, your election speeches, and your people. You, brother; you, sister; you, man, with all that money in your pocket.

Are we trying to be saviors to others?

Parents should be saviors to their children. Do you hear that? Children should be saviors to their parents. Do you get that? Saviors, especially when your parents are old; husbands to their wives, wives to their husbands, brothers to sisters, and sisters to brothers.

If this really happens, if this spreads, then this world will change, because all people would be saviors to all people, and at that moment all people would be Christ-like: the Kingdom has come.

Let us try, Alleluia. Amen.

FIRST SUNDAY OF LENT

133. His Respect for Us

Luke 4:1–13

Anyone can see what power can do and what it does. In a way, it's nice to see it. A mighty military parade with one man shouting "ah-eh-march," and then thousands, tens of thousands of soldiers marching in the same way, left-right, left-right, left-right. It's a nice sight, but at the cost of military obedience, which controls the minds, the wills, and the bodies of all those thousands.

Anyone can see what popularity can do and what popularity does. Tens of thousands or hundreds of thousands of fans come together to see their idol: a singer, a performer, a criminal, an entertainer, a leader, the pope. Every word the idol says makes their enthusiasm grow. They behave unusually, hysterically, ecstatically, but at a cost. Didn't all those fans lose themselves in that enormous hero-worshiping crowd?

Anyone can see what a miracle worker can do. They are advertised regularly on the walls of our cities, they are seen over television. Those people seem to have a grip on God. They seem to pray authoritatively, and God seems to bend to their prayers, for suddenly the deaf hear, the blind see, the thousands and tens of thousands under the influence of those signs are suddenly overcome, taken over. They pray and convert.

Marching along, but forced. Singing along, but infatuated. Praying along in a trance. It is all very good. It is all very fine. It is all very inspiring, and yet the danger is that nothing happened at all. The danger is that the inner being of those marching, singing, praying people is not touched in the slightest.

Today we hear, in an obviously symbolic story, how Jesus was tempted to make the people sing and shout because of the *bread* given, to make them pray and admire because of the *sign* shown, to make them march and obey because of the *power* exercised over them.

In his respect for us, and in his respect for the work of the Spirit in us, he refused. Instead he started to rely on what one sometimes calls the "tender forces" in us. Happy are those who are poor and willing to share; happy are the merciful; happy are those who weep; happy are those who hunger and thirst for justice and peace.

Let us believe in those forces found in him. Let us believe in those tender forces found in us. Let us believe in them because they were put in us by him: the power of the seed, the power of the yeast, the power of salt, the power of the light of his Kingdom. Amen.

SECOND SUNDAY OF LENT

134. He Started To Change

Luke 9:28–36

It's obvious from the gospels that the people around Jesus expected him to do all kinds of things. They hoped he would change their situation, that he would better the world. That was, in a way, even what the devil wanted him to do: change the stones of this world into bread; interrupt the laws of gravity and be famous; take over political power and rule as no one ever ruled before.

That is what his disciples expected him to do. That is what all his followers wanted him to do, and they brought him their sick, the crippled, the mentally deranged, their children, and their worries.

The expectancy that had been growing around John the Baptist was now concentrating around him to the extent that they expected miracles and wonders right, left, and center. In the gospel of today, he took Peter, James, and John aside. He told them: "Come with me, I will show you something." They followed him excitedly, proud to be chosen, sure of themselves. He brought them up that mountain and, again, heaven opened, Moses and Elijah were seen.

Their expectations grew almost wild. Was the change going to come? Weren't Moses and Elijah the great experts on change and development? Wasn't it Moses who had brought his people from Egypt into the new land? Wasn't it Elijah who had changed his people from an old-fashioned, sinful one into a glorious nation?

The three must have been sure it was about to start: A totally new world, with Israel at the top. A totally new era, with rich harvests everywhere. A totally new order, with food for all. A totally new environment, with more water than was needed. A totally new ecology, with plenty of power and energy. A totally new economy, with health opportunities and social security for everyone. A totally new cosmos, economically wealthy, technologically robust, and politically full of peace, love, and unity.

They looked at him while he was discussing this changeover, this passover with Moses and Elijah.

Suddenly the change did start, but the grass didn't grow more lush. The trees didn't grow bigger fruits. The maize did not increase the size of its cobs. The rain did not fall more abundantly. The sun did not get any brighter. It was not developments in the fields of communications and transport that changed human life. It was not all kinds of buildings changing the skylines. It was *he* who changed. It was *he* who started to shine, *he*, the son of humanity, the model of all.

In this way, he made it clear to them—those privileged three and we who read this report—what should happen to this world: *We, humankind, should change and start to shine.*

While he shone, everything around him picked up that shine: the grass, the mountains and their tops, the birds and the insects, Peter, James, and John.

A voice was heard. The voice said: "Listen to him," do what he suggests, change yourself according to his model, according to his Spirit, and all the rest will follow. But do not change this priority list. Never.

THIRD SUNDAY OF LENT

135. Where Does the Good Come From?

Luke 13:1–9

It is sometimes almost weird how gospel stories written so long ago fit into the world in which we live. Take the gospel of today. There had been a riot in town, and some people had been killed. They were building a tower in town, and some stones had come loose, and they, too, had killed. Didn't all this just happen in our world? Who forgot the violence at the beginning of this month? Who forgot about the people who were killed when that apartment building came down some weeks ago? All this has been accompanied by a question, a well-known question, a question we all ask: Why were those people killed, and why did others survive? In Jerusalem, that question was even more urgent, because the people killed during that riot had been doing good by bringing their sacrifices to the altar. Why do bad things happen to good people?

We have a solution. We think we have the answer, just as those who went to Jesus thought they had their answer ready.

It is the answer we often give when facing the same issue in our lives. I will tell you a story to explain what I mean.

An eleven-year-old boy was given an eye test at school. This eleven-year-old boy was just nearsighted enough to need glasses. No one was terribly surprised, because his father, his mother, and one of his sisters wore glasses. So what?

Nevertheless, the boy was very upset, and he did not want to tell anyone why. Then one evening, just before he went to bed, the story came out. Two days before the test, he had found some magazines on top of an overloaded trash can somewhere in the street, *Playboy* or something like that. Though thinking it very naughty and bad, he had looked at the pictures of naked men and women. When the doctor told him, only two days afterwards, that he had to wear glasses, he had thought: "There you are! God started to punish me already. God is going to make me blind because of what I did."

That's the kind of issue Jesus is confronted with in the gospel of today. He tells them very clearly that they were wrong. Those people were not killed because of their faults. If God acted like that, he said, all of you would be killed, because all of you are sinners. If God acted like that, all of us would be wearing glasses or be blind.

Then he told them the story of a fig tree planted in a garden. Through exhausting the soil, having its place in the sun, absorbing oxygen, consuming chemicals, and using lots of precious water, there were no fruits on the tree.

There were no fruits for the first year, the second year, and even the third year. The owner came to look for fruits, but he found none. He wanted to uproot the tree and plant another one, but the caretaker convinced him to have another try. While he told that story, he must have been looking around at them, at us—so dry, so dry.

Their question was not answered: Where does evil come from? Why do bad things happen to good people?

His story does, however, answer another question: Why is it that we find so much goodness and patience in this world?

Where would all the good come from, if God did not exist?

FOURTH SUNDAY OF LENT

136. Give Me My Money Now

Luke 15:1–3, 11–32

Jesus was surrounded by people seeking his company. They were the people who felt they needed him. Those people who felt they needed him were the tax collectors and the sinners.

There was a second group that kept away from him. They were the Pharisees and the scribes, who blamed Jesus for being surrounded by that first group of tax collectors and sinners.

When confronted with that clash, Jesus told both groups a story, a parable to explain himself.

You know the story. You have heard it dozens of times before. It is the story of the "prodigal" son. The story of that boy who went to his father and said: "I want my money. Give me my money now!" The story of the younger one who wanted all he could get to spend it freely, prodigally, in order to share in the "good life."

He went to town, and there he spent all he had—so the story goes—by profiting to the full from the corrupt situation of that time. He gambled, he bribed, he got drunk, he bought and paid for the bodies he wanted, he led a life of debauchery. Then something happened. There was a drought, a terrible one. It did not rain for weeks and weeks. It did not rain for months and months, and everyone was feeling the pinch. That son, too. He felt like dying, and because of that pinch, he came to his senses and said: "I am dying. Let me go back to my father." He went back.

This story always repeats itself. It is repeating itself at this moment in our world and in this country. All went well; there was plenty of everything. Prodigality and luxury were all over. Corruption set in and remained undetected because all went well: tax collectors and sinners, exploiters and profiteers, sugar daddies and sugar mammies, gambling and playing, bodies sold and bought, drinks and drugs. Then came the great drought: There was no rain, heaven remained closed; there was no oil, minerals drained away, the pinch was felt, and sickness struck.

We are slowly coming back to our senses. There are probing committees everywhere. In the civil service, the universities, the commercial boards, the post office, the hospitals, the banks, the insurance world, in imports and exports, the military and the foreign service, we are discovering prodigal sons (and daughters) all over. We are like a dying generation, a dying nation, a dying world.

In this time of probing, let's try to probe ourselves: How far are we guilty, coresponsible? Where did we cheat and lie, bribe and profit, waste and spoil, live dangerously and luxuriously? Where did we brotherize and favor?

Let us, like that prodigal son, change our ways, serving the Father and one another. If we do this, we will be received by God with open arms, and we will be brought back from death to life.

The question remains whether we can do this alone. Shouldn't we come together to do all this? We, the sinners, and those others—the older brother in Jesus' story—the just. That is the point of his story. What we need is a new family, a new community, brought together again around the table of the Father.

Preaching is not enough. Being filled with the Holy Spirit isn't, either. Service to the poor is not enough, neither is political action. Prophecy is not enough, or resistance to unjust structures. What we need is that new family, that new community, like the one in the story of today.

FIFTH SUNDAY OF LENT

137. On Not Drawing a Line

John 8:1–11

That morning, Jesus did not agree with the people around him.

They had been doing the simplest thing in the world. They had been doing something so simple that we do it all the time. They had been drawing a line, a very sharp, divisive line, between the good ones and the bad ones. They were good, and that woman was bad, very bad, no longer worthy of living.

You heard the story. She had been found early in the morning. She had been found in bed with a man. Maybe it was her husband who found her. He had raised the alarm. Neighbors had come out of their houses, more and more of them. They all liked a scandal like that. It made them feel good. They had taken her from her warm bed, thrown her out of her house, and hustled her to some Pharisees, to some scribes, the defenders of the law, to ask them what to do. They had been speaking about mob justice, about killing her. Then one of the Pharisees got an idea. He thought: "What if we confront Jesus with this woman? Let's ask him what we should do."

He did not want Jesus' advice. What he wanted was to catch Jesus. If Jesus said: "Yes, stone her, kill her," he would most probably lose his good name with the crowd. He would no longer be seen as the merciful miracle worker. He would lose his popularity, he would lose his appeal to the crowd. If he said: "No, don't kill her," he also would be caught, because then they would be able to accuse him of being against the law, of being against their most sacred traditions.

He talked to the others, they liked the idea, and so off they went to Jesus, who was teaching near the temple.

They arrived in front of him. They pushed the frightened woman in his direction, as if they did not even want to touch her. She was unclean, a sinner, dirt. Jesus did not even look up at them. He remained sitting, doodling some lines in the sand with his fingers—crosses, circles, triangles.

They told him: "This woman was caught in the act of adultery this morning. What should we do?"

He did not answer them. When they persisted, he finally looked up, and even then he did not answer *their question* at all. He gave them *his question*. How could they draw that line between themselves and her? Was she a sinner and they not sinners at all?

He told them: "All right; let the one of you who is without sin throw the first stone!"

They looked at him. They looked at her. They looked at the stones they had ready in their hands. They looked at one another and suddenly it must have dawned on them what he meant.

They had drawn a line around her. They had put her in a circle. They had declared her a sinner. They understood. They belonged in that circle, too. One after another—the eldest one first—they dropped their stones and disappeared as quickly and silently as possible.

Her husband must have been there, too. Otherwise, how would she have been able to go home safely after all this? He, too, dropped his stones and left.

Finally she was alone. Jesus looked at her and said: "Is there no one left to condemn you?" She answered: "No one, Sir." He said: "I am not going to do that, either. Go away," and then he added—not only for her, but for all those who had left and were in the same position as she: "Don't sin anymore."

A simple story, a story so simple that it repeats itself among us all the time. How often do we divide the people around us into the good ones and the bad ones?

The good ones *we* belong to, the bad ones *they* belong to.

How often do people frustrate, boycott, arrest, torture, and execute each other in their families, businesses, and national and international affairs?

Jesus said: "That line is a lie; no one is good. You are all sinners. You have to leave your ways and sin no more."

PASSION/PALM SUNDAY

138. From Alleluia to Crucify Him

Luke 22:14–23, 56

Within a few days the "Alleluias" of the beginning of the week changed into the "Crucify him!" of the end of the week. How come? We could know how come, since this changeover is also taking place around us in our times, in our days, in our lives.

In 1980 the new Archbishop of Canterbury was enthroned in a beautiful ceremony, in splendid splendor, in great solemnity, in grandeur and joy. He was wearing a mitre and a cope on which one of the last English professionals capable of working with gold thread had been working for months and months. The crowd was enthusiastic: *Alleluia* all over the place, combined with the hope that everything was going to change.

In the same week, Monsignor Oscar Romero, Archbishop of El Salvador, was shot with a silenced gun while saying Mass.

You could see a photo of his murder in all the papers. In that photo, you

[handwritten annotations at top: Parades - why do we have them? to celebrate what? Who p have you been too? 4 july. to day. what were the people celebrating? - Palm Sunday Jesus the King was coming.]

don't see the archbishop, you only see the soles of his feet. He is flat on the floor, and a sister is praying next to him, her mouth wide open with shock, like Mary under the cross.

In Canterbury, hope and ringing bells; in El Salvador, death and a blasting shot. In Canterbury, hope that the new archbishop will change his church, his country, his world. In El Salvador, an archbishop changing his church, his country, and his world.

Hope and realization; words and deeds.

We all hope, we say. *[handwritten: do away w/ hunger / are we willing to give]*

Do we really want our hopes to be realized in this world during our lives? We hope that misery will be taken away, that starvation will disappear, that thirst will be quenched, that all people may be happy and free. We hope we might live a simpler, more honest, purer human life. Do we really want all that? Isn't it at the point of the possible realization of our hope that we betray this hope ourselves?

[handwritten left margin: Kinder / gentler Nation. Are we willing. Gorbiachev]

[handwritten right margin: the Price of a men each week. Put a money when our mouth is.]

A political example from the past might help to clarify what I mean. In 1968 the whole of France was full of expectation. There was a student revolt, a very serious one, with manifestations and demonstrations all through Paris, day and night. The students alone could not change France. They had been in contact with the trade-union leaders who had also been speaking about the necessity of a change, a needed one, they said, a drastic one. Together with the unions, the students might have been successful. According to some, that was the hope; according to others, that was the danger.

When the students came to the trade-union headquarters to make the final arrangements and sign the final signatures, they not only found the doors closed, they found them welded together, with iron bars over them.

We should transpose this example from a political context to a religious one.

[handwritten left margin: Will Israel dare to speak to the PLO]

At the critical moment over there in Jerusalem—at the very moment that change seemed possible—it was suddenly seen as a *risk*.

You know what you have. You don't know what you are going to get.

The street emptied. The doors closed. The windows were shuttered. The alleluias lost their echoes. A new noise was heard: "Get away, crucify him, we don't want you!"

Isn't that what often happens when we face a change or the possibility of a conversion? It happened to them, and it became his undoing!

EASTER SUNDAY

139. God's Final Word

Luke 24:1–12

We met Jesus during these last days surrounded by human beings, men and women like you and me, shouting "Alleluia!" in the beginning of this week; having a last supper with him halfway through the week; and betraying him shouting "Crucify him!" by the end of that very same week.

Women and men like you and me surrounded him like a pack of wild wolves, trying to tear him to pieces. We succeeded: *He fell and did not come up again.*

Surrounded and trapped by all those people, Jesus fought valiantly. He tried to answer and to overcome. He washed their feet and kissed Judas. He healed the ear of Malchus and answered Pilate's questions. He looked silently at Herod and admonished the women on his way to the cross. He thanked Simon of Cyrene, a place somewhere in Africa. He forgave the soldiers and prayed for his murderers. He encouraged the robber on the cross next to him from here to there. Finally he bent his head and gave up his heart: *He fell and did not come up again.*

It was and is as if we human beings had the last word in the history of this man and, consequently, in the story of all of us. *Wasn't he our last and only hope?*

With him all possible goodness seemed to have died in this world.

Today we celebrate that it was God who rescued him, who brought him back to life. It was God who validated him, his life, and the life of us, his people.

The last word is not death, it is life. It is not *no,* it is *yes.* The last word is not, "We will overcome," it is "We did overcome!" We overcame in him.

God not only overcame the corruption around us when he raised Jesus from death. He also overcame it within us. God freed him, God freed us, alleluia, alleluia, alleluia.

The old came to an end; a new world started to live.

Do you reject Satan and all his works and his promises? With him, risen from the dead, we can answer: "YES, YES, YES, WE DO!" Amen.

SECOND SUNDAY OF EASTER

140. The Hesitation of the Ten

John 20:19–31

That evening of the first day of the week, the disciples were sitting together because Mary of Magdala had brought them her news: "I have seen him!"

They did not believe what she told them. They did not understand why they should not have been the first ones to whom he appeared.

Nevertheless, they came together to wait for him. Only Thomas had not turned up. They were waiting for Jesus, they were waiting for his knock at the door.

That knock never came.

He did.

Suddenly he stood in their midst. They were speechless. He spoke to them, giving them their mission. He said: "I am sending you into the world in the same way as I was sent into it by the Father."

The implications were obvious: Go into the world, even uninvited. It needs you. Enter it without knocking, without waiting to see if you are allowed or not. Just go.

They looked at him, full of doubt, afraid, unprepared, uncommitted. He breathed over them, and he continued: "Receive the Holy Spirit and undo sin."

He left.

They all started to speak at the same time.

They did not do what he said. They did not go out. They did not undo sin. They remained together and talked, though the Spirit had been breathed into them.

Finally Thomas came in, late. Too late. They told him that they had seen him, that he had eaten his favorite fried fish with them. How he had come straight through the door without knocking.

They also told him how he had sent them. They even added how they received the Spirit, his Spirit, when he breathed over them and told them to go out into the world and cancel sin.

It was then that Thomas started to doubt. If they had really seen him, if they had really been sent by him, if they really had received his Spirit and his power, why hadn't they gone? Why had they stayed on the spot? Why had the Spirit not worked?

Thomas told them so in as many words. He said: "I am sorry, but I cannot believe you. Let me first see him for myself. Let me see his wounds, let me touch his side. I don't believe you! How is it that you tell me all that and that you are still sitting here?"

The Lord did come again, and Thomas saw him. Thomas touched him. Thomas recognized him. Thomas got his mission. Thomas got the Spirit. Thomas said: "My Lord and my God!"

Thomas believed, and with a last look at his Lord and Master, he went on his way—all the way to India.

Let's not only compare ourselves to Thomas in this story. Let us compare ourselves to the other ten who believed when they saw, but who—notwithstanding that belief—did not move at all.

We should compare the people around us with Thomas, the people who ask the same question about us that Thomas asked about the ten: "If it is really true that they saw, if it is really true that he sent them, if it is really true that they got his Spirit to undo all sin, why didn't they go? Why didn't they move? How can we believe the story they tell?"

THIRD SUNDAY OF EASTER

141. Do You Love Me?

John 21:1–19

They had their mouths full of fish, his fish. He had caught (or bought) it for them, he had fried it, and he had asked: "Do you like it?" They had answered: "Yes, definitely yes!" and they patted *their* filled stomachs with that very nice glow of being satisfied inside, and they repeated once more: "Yes, we liked that fish."

They had their hands full of bread. He had baked (or bought) it for them. He had asked: "Do you like it?" They had looked at it, they had put it in their mouths, and while they were chewing it carefully to be sure of the taste, they had said: "Yes, certainly yes. It is exactly like bread should be so early in the morning, delicious." They had looked at him very happily. What a friend they had in Jesus.

Then he asked them that other question, that old, human, tricky, ambiguous, deceiving question: "Do you love me, Peter? Do you love me?"

Every time a woman asks a man that question and he answers: "Yes, I love you," what does he mean? Every time a man asks a woman that question and she answers: "Yes, I love you," what does she mean?

Does he mean that he likes to have *his* eyes filled with her? Does she mean that she would like to have *her* satisfaction with him? Or are they really, when answering that question, speaking about the other?

Peter said: "Yes, Sir, I love you." That is all he said, and the question Jesus asked had not been answered, at least not clearly. Peter might have meant: "I love you because *I* love to be with you, because *I* love to eat your fish, because *I* love your bread very much, because *I* love myself."

Jesus asked him a second time: "Do you love me?" Again Peter did not really answer his question. Again he said: "Yes, I love you," without making it clear what he really meant. So Jesus asked him a third time: "Do you love me?" And when Peter again did not answer the question, Jesus answered it himself. He said: "If you really love *me*, if you really love *my* approach, if you really love *my* style of life, if you really love *my* way, then be not interested in yourself, but in others."

In this country, we live in a community where we often blame one another. Isn't it true that we blame one another all the time for the same thing?

"Everybody seems only to care for himself or for herself." How often we hear that being said. How often we say it about the people around us.

I do not think that is the true picture of this society. It's not. So many of us who get in trouble in this country are surrounded by friends.

Yet, we continue to blame one another for so much carelessness, selfishness, for so much lack of care, interest, and love in all kinds of things: in education, medication, shops, transportation, counseling.

So many of us say that we love Jesus. So many of us regularly come together to witness to this. So many of us come together to sing about it, and nevertheless. . . .

There remains that question of Jesus: "Do you love *me*?" That is our vocation, the human vocation. It is a vocation and a call that we should take upon ourselves as a community. It is a vocation that is asking for leaders, doctors, lawyers, journalists, teachers, and also for people specializing in religious leadership like those apostles of his. It is a vocation that asks for dedicated people.

Let us pray. . . .

FOURTH SUNDAY OF EASTER

142. They Will Never Get Lost

John 10:27–30

About forty years ago, when this world was a very different place, I was a small and—according to the photos of that time—a very thin boy.

I was a Mass server and a choirboy. One day we had an outing to a forest with a kind of pond in the middle. While playing in that pond, I suddenly fell from a tree trunk on which I was sitting, right into the water. I bumped my head, and because of my fright, I forgot to swim. I went under once, and I saw all kinds of air bubbles. I came up and went under for a second time, again seeing all kinds of bubbles. I came up, and just as I was disappearing for the third time, the curate who was with us came running along. He jumped into the water and dragged me out. I was unconscious; everybody thought I was dead. After quite some time, I came back. Suddenly I was a hero.

One of my aunts did a thing she had never done before and would never do afterwards. She invited me for tea, and when I got my tea, she asked me: "What happened while you were drowning? What did you see?" I told her that I only saw water and air bubbles, and she was disappointed. She asked me whether I had said an act of contrition, and I told her that I forgot. Then she told me that people see all kinds of things as they die, that they see their whole lives in a kind of short film, and that there is a light and . . ..

What happens during and after our death?

Saint John gives his answer today, and so does Jesus. They say that God will spread his tent over us. We will never hunger and thirst again. The sun will not burn us. The wind will do us no harm. They say that we will never get lost, that we will never be rustled or stolen.

In other words, we will be understood, received, welcomed, and taken up. *We*, not only you and me, but *we* will be taken up by God.

At the moment there are many confirmations of what my aunt had heard about that quick film and the light that people experience while dying. Many people "died" and came back. There are some in the gospel: Lazarus, the boy from Nain, and the daughter of a Roman official.

Even nowadays that happens so often that recently a study was made of one hundred and fifty cases. In all the reports of those who came back—people who did not know one another's stories—you find more or less the same ingredients. They tell how they left their bodies. They then went through something like a dark tunnel with a growing light at its end. A light like the sun, but it did not blind or burn, and they saw their whole lives in short flashes, the good and the bad. Then the light proved to be something personal, a somebody. They report how that somebody looked at all those flashes with them, and how all was understood. The selfless acts were approved and the selfish ones disapproved. The reproachable ones, too, were seen as part of a learning process.

And after that . . . they came back, changed people.

They all say that the light—some call it Christ, some call it God, some call it light—was kind and protective, humorous and understanding, forgiving and fulfilling.

We do not need all those reports to know all this. The gospels tell us all there is to know. The shelter will be there: sun, rain, and wind will do no harm to us anymore. The tears will not only be wiped away; there will be no more tears.

The light will be there, and all whom we love now. Those we don't love so much will be there, as well, but changed. We all will be there, changed.

FIFTH SUNDAY OF EASTER

143. The Price of Love

John 13:31–35

The gospel of today brings us back to the Last Supper. Jesus is at the table with the twelve. In the beginning of the text, the number is reduced to eleven when Judas leaves in the dark of the night to make his last arrangements for having Jesus arrested, detained, and killed.

No wonder that many of us consider the numbers thirteen and eleven unlucky.

At the moment Judas left, Jesus started to speak about *glory* and *glorification*, about *love* and *loving one another*.

Those words: "*I love you*," are heard so often. What do they mean? What does it mean when a mother kisses her disabled child and says: "I love you"? What does it mean when a husband visits his sick wife in the hospital day after day, and says: "I love you"? What did it mean when Jesus told his disciples (and us): "I love you"?

You all know what it meant. You all know the price of love here on earth. You all know what it means to give life in a world that is dying: It means pain, tears, crying, and mourning. In our common language, we often reduce the meaning of that life-giving word *love* to a harmless, sweet, sometimes even sensual feeling of goodness. We didn't do that without reason, yet in the gospel, the word *love* is always cross shaped.

When Christ said: "I love you," the cross was included, the cross was meant.

When Christ says that we should love one another, as he loved us, that love, too, is cross shaped. The cross is meant.

Didn't he say that the proof of love is to be willing to lay down one's life for the other? Because of this, we often refuse to love. We do not help, because we do not want to be involved. We do not want to be hindered. We refuse the possible and unavoidable tears and pain. We say that if you are too good, you are crazy. We say there is a limit to everything. While rationalizing, we refuse the risks, the costs. We refuse to love as he did, taking those risks, paying those costs.

It is in that sense, too, that we say the love of a mother for her disabled child, the love of a husband for his sick wife, the love of Jesus on the cross, is something glorious and victorious.

It is in this way that Jesus' love for us is his glory. Jesus' love for us took all the risks involved. Its price was very dear: blood, sweat, tears, pain, and death.

Soon all the pain would be over, the price would be paid. It was his love that remained, just as our love will remain in the final outcome, in the Holy City, where there will be no tears, no pain, no death anymore.

All that will disappear, and we in our lives will remain, together with him, the one *glorified*.

SIXTH SUNDAY OF EASTER

144. We and the Spirit

John 14:23–29

According to the gospel of today, a Spirit will be sent, a Spirit that is going to renew the whole world. That means a change of the whole of humanity. In the second reading of today, that Spirit is present, because the disciples of Jesus write almost triumphantly after one of their meetings: "*The Spirit and we ourselves* have decided. . . ."

The new Spirit was there, the new Spirit is here, but that Spirit was sent into a world that was and still is old; into a world that has to be renewed, that has to be developed.

Most of the Christian students in this country [Kenya] who enter college are enthusiastic about being a follower of Jesus, which is often a new experience for them. They come to the Sunday services, they discuss all kinds of issues in a lively way. They are full of expectations. They are full of hope. They are looking for the poor. They try very hard to live up to their ideals, and as if the new world has started already they call each other sisters and brothers, and God their common Father. But after some time, they slip or fall away. When you ask them why, they will tell you that they started to understand how hard, how political, cruel and businesslike this world is, full of deceit, bribery, threats, *gambling* and competition. They will tell you how they began to understand that Christians who live up to their ideal have no chance of surviving, that Christians are not adapted to that type of life and how in the struggle for survival they will be eaten by the hyenas, the vultures, the wild dogs and the rats.

Those students do not want to be hypocrites or pretenders, as so many Christians are in this world, as they would not like to give the wrong impression about their hope in Jesus. They prefer in all honesty to opt out in time, calling themselves victims of their "realism." Though invited to new life, they choose the old one.

The world and humankind will never change and never come one step further this way. Though it is still unusual, it is nevertheless possible to see the person of Jesus, his life and his death, as a new step forward, a new evolutionary step forward in God's creative history.

In the beginning, matter developed slowly, under the influence of God's creative power, into life. Then under the same power of God, life slowly developed in all kinds of directions. One of those directions was human life, and that again was quite a change, a mutation, a tremendous changeover, a jump.

Then in the fullness of time, God introduced to us—in his offspring Jesus—a completely new version of humankind, a new creature, a new creation, a person totally new, of a different Spirit, with new possibilities, a new type of love, a new life code, an enormous change, a new jump, a new person.

Those students know that all too well. They realize Jesus is a jump and brings that newness. That is why they say: "*We* can't do it. The world is not yet ready for him!"

They hesitated, or they refused, as so many hesitated or refused before, leaving the world and humankind as it is, as it was, and as it has been for so very, very long.

Let us pray that we may be willing to receive, to accept, and to stick to the Spirit of God.

ASCENSION DAY

145. Handing Over

Luke 24:46–53

It must have been a very difficult day for them. A sad one, too.

He had told them they should be glad. "Because," he said, "if I don't go, the Spirit will never come to you. Now, I am sending you."

It was Chesterton who once wrote: "The really great man is the one who makes others feel great." Another English author, H. G. Wells, wrote: "The test of greatness is: what did the person leave to grow?" He added: "By this test Jesus stands first."

We don't need those British authors to tell us that; we know it from our own lives. We know it from those moments when others, who had been responsible for us, made us responsible for ourselves.

We know it from the joy we experienced when they allowed us to do something on our own for the first time: a commission, a message, a task, herding some sheep, driving a car, caring for a baby, or whatever it was.

From the beginning, God had done the same. God made man and woman king and queen, rulers and organizers of nature.

In Jesus, God did it again. Not only Christ is going to be the light of the world; not only Christ is going to be the salt of the earth; not only Christ is going to be the yeast of human life.

We are invited to be that light, that salt, and that yeast.

He said to them: "Go to the city and stay until you are clothed with the power from on high."

They went to wait for the Spirit to manifest herself in them.

SEVENTH SUNDAY OF EASTER

146. The Oneness He Wanted

John 17:20–26

Jesus is away. The Easter candle that reminded us of him is put aside. We are, like the apostles in those in-between days, waiting.

Those apostles must have been waiting with a certain amount of apprehension. They knew their waiting was a lull before the storm, a pause before their work, an intermission before their mission.

It is about that mission that Jesus speaks in the gospel reading of today.

The gospel of John speaks again and again about that mission left by him. In John's gospel, Jesus speaks twenty-one times about being sent by the Father into this world.

Today's mission is well-known: "That they may be one, as you, Father, and I, your offspring, are one."

We all know that text. We know it very well. We especially know it within an ecumenical context.

"*That they may be one*" seems to mean that Jesus prayed the Lutherans, Presbyterians, Roman Catholics, Quakers, Methodists, Baptists, and Reformed Churches might be one.

We might be wrong. Maybe Jesus did not pray for that unity, though that unity will be the outcome of his prayers.

He prayed for another unity among his apostles and those who would listen to those apostles.

Reducing the text to "ecumenism" may be one of our attempts to escape from our real mission in this world, if only because ecumenism is something that seems to concern church leadership, and therefore *others*. We always try to escape from our real mission.   .

Jesus said: "That they may be one as I am one with you, Father, who sent me: one in the intention to redeem, to save, to liberate, to serve, to assist, to deliver, to make grow. Father, let them be one in that redemptive purpose of ours."

It is at that very practical level that Jesus prays we should be one. It is at that level that Jesus hopes the world may start to believe in him, the Father, the Spirit, and us, his followers.

It is from that point of view that Jesus says, when they report to him that others are driving out the devils of this world in his name: "Don't bother, my name is preached, my mission is on its way."

Father, that they may be one, as you and I are one, you who sent me into this world. Amen.

PENTECOST

147. In Exchange for Their Religiosity

John 20:19–23

Up to that fiftieth day, the apostles had been very pious. The gospel tells us they went back to Jerusalem after his ascension, as Jesus had told them to do.

They were seen in the temple every day, praising God their Father in heaven with their alleluias and praise-the-Lords.

After that worship in temple, they came together in that upper room to commemorate Jesus, tell and retell their endless stories about him, and break their bread together in honor of him.

As for the rest, they did not seem to do very much. They prayed to the Father, they commemorated his offspring, but without any manifestation of the Spirit within them. Without that Spirit in them, nothing much happened. Jerusalem did not notice them. The country did not pay any attention. The corruption in town went on. The temple service continued. The town girls walked through the streets every evening. The street boys remained street boys, the hungry and the exploited remained hungry and exploited. The differences remained the differences, while *they* were praising the Lord and commemorating Jesus Christ.

It was only at the moment the Spirit descended on them that they and everything else started to change.

They caught fire, divine fire; they went off to preach, to heal, to prophesy, and to change the world.

That is what they did after having been changed.

What do we do after the same change?

Aren't we living anachronistically? Aren't we living as those apostles lived *before Pentecost*?

We adore God the Father, the first person; we commemorate Jesus Christ, the second person; we believe in the Blessed Trinity.

We pray: "Praise the Lord," while our conduct is no different from anyone else's. We hang a cross around our necks and put badges with: "Jesus loves me" on our T-shirts, coats, and cars, while we remain corrupt, sinful, overly lusty, and—insofar as Jesus' plans are concerned—totally reactionary.

We praise the Father, we love the Son, but are we really willing to receive their Spirit to change our lives, to spiritualize and purify our work in that fire?

Many of us proudly say: "Americans are notoriously religious." It is true that the Sunday practice in the United States is more prevalent than in any other Western country. Our religious leaders say so, but too gladly and too often. They are obviously proud of it.

Are we really willing to hand over our religiosity to the hand of the Holy Spirit of God in us?

Let us praise the Father; let us honor the Son; let us surrender to the Spirit.

This country, this continent, this world, needs our life in that Spirit desperately, in all ways of life!

TRINITY SUNDAY

148. We Are Not Alone

John 16:12–15

Today is Trinity Sunday. We commemorate the fact that God, though alone— because God is only one—is not alone, because God is in three.

That is very difficult to explain. In fact, I would not be able to explain it, because we really do not know that much about God. We only know about ourselves, about you and me. There is one thing I know about myself and also about you: That nobody likes to be completely alone. To eat alone, sleep alone, walk alone, work alone, live alone, talk alone—that means talking to yourself. To be alone, totally alone? It is impossible. The thought alone is unbearable.

Some days ago I read a story about a man who was so alone and lonely that nobody ever shook his hands, patted his shoulders, gave him a friendly push in the ribs, hugged, or even touched him. He felt so lonely that he spent the last of his money, but not on food. Food would not help; it does not make contact. He did not spend it on a bed; a bed does not help, either. He did not spend it on a drink. A drink alone is poison. He spent his last money on a hairdresser, so he would be touched and taken care of by someone for a few minutes.

Loneliness is one of the most frightening experiences in life. Did you ever lose your way in a forest? Have you ever been so lost you couldn't hear any human voices? No dog barked, no truck passed, and you were totally alone. Have you ever been alone in a prison cell for twenty-four or forty-eight hours? Locked up, you begin to wonder whether they have forgotten you, and you are not even allowed to warn anybody at home.

If you are alone like this, you change completely. You dry up. You hear noises outside and inside of yourself: bubbling noises, getting louder and louder. It is not good to be alone, not good at all.

It is terrible to be alone, terrible, even if you are with others.

I recently heard a report on a prison. The prisoners were rather well taken care of, as far as food went. But they were not allowed to speak. They were not allowed to work, since even working together creates contact. They had to sit on the floor a few yards from the wall, and they were not allowed to have any contact at all with the others. They were not even allowed to move. Terrible!

You might object: Doesn't everybody want his privacy? Doesn't everyone here at the college want a single room?

I don't think everybody wants that. Even those who want a single room, do they want it so they can be alone?

Nobody wants to be alone, and I hope and pray that none of us will ever be alone, imprisoned, or lost during our lives. I hope none of us will ever feel alone between the two walls that limit our existence here: the wall behind us, which is the womb of our mother, and the wall before us, which is the womb of the earth, in which we sometime will all, in one way or another, be buried.

One of these two wombs belongs to the past—the one of our mother. One of those two wombs belongs to the future—the one of the earth.

Will we be alone then, while in that earth?

That fellow student of ours, our friend Richard Amolo, who died this week on this campus, is he alone now? Completely alone in a world without hope, without fellow beings, in a world without God?

During his funeral Mass, the following text by Saint Paul was read: "We want you not to remain in ignorance, brothers and sisters, about those who sleep in death. You should not grieve like the rest of humanity, who have no hope. We believe that Jesus died and rose again, and so it will be for those who died.''

God will bring them to life. God will be there at the other side of that womb in the earth. God will not only be there, since mere presence is no help. Mere presence does not take loneliness away. God will be there to relate to us as a father, a parent, a brother, a friend, a loving, hugging motherly Spirit.

That is what we celebrate today. God is not alone, but we are not alone, either, and we will *never* be. Aren't we made in God's image?

ELEVENTH SUNDAY OF THE YEAR

149. The Good in You

Luke 7:36–8:3

Jesus was invited by a Pharisee. His host had surrounded himself with friends, professional religious people, the leaders of the religiosity in their country. Though invited, Jesus was not well-treated by his host, who had received his professional friends better than this prophet from the street. Their feet had been washed, his had not. They had been embraced when they entered; he had not been greeted at all. They had been welcomed. Jesus, that commoner from Nazareth, uneducated and very strange, with some extraordinary ideas about himself, had just been allowed to come in. When they were at the table, a woman came in. A woman with a bad name in town. They all knew about her bad name, they all knew about her. Did she recognize some of her customers lying around that table? Who knows?

She went to Jesus. She had a bottle of perfume with her. Had it been a gift from one of her clients? Had it been, maybe, a gift from someone who was present?

She touched him. She wept, dried the tears that had dripped on his feet, and then anointed those feet, expressing in that way her love, her respect, her faith.

Simon, seeing all this, thought to himself: *If this man were a prophet, he would know who this woman is. He would never allow her to express herself like that.*

In that same stream of thought, Simon, the religious professional, could not believe there was the possibility of anything of value in that woman. At the same time, he doubted there was anything of prophetic or religious value in Jesus, either.

That is why he said to himself, as the others did: *How would this Jesus be able to do anything in the name of God?*

Simon the Pharisee had a very low opinion of the spiritual content of his guests, both Jesus, the invited one, and that woman, the uninvited one.

We often have a low opinion of the spiritual possibilities of the people around us, and of ourselves, conditioned as we are, even today, by the professional religious leaders around us.

Some days ago we had a theological exchange here in our community. The topic was "The Holy Spirit." We asked one another whether we knew about the work of the Holy Spirit in our own experience. It was strange, but almost everybody spoke about *others* healing, making peace, speaking in tongues. Only after some time did someone say: "Why are we looking for the extraordinary things done by others?"

Slowly we began to remember events in our own lives: peacemaking, sharing, healing, forgiveness, communication.

Some months ago I was in a primary school. They also were speaking about the Holy Spirit in us. I asked the children in front of me: "Did you ever do anything good in your lives?"

They all looked at me with their enormous eyes and said, almost spontaneously in chorus: "No!"

Was this a reflection of the opinion of their professional leaders at home— their parents—saying all day: "You are no good"?

It was only after some time that one small girl remembered: "Oh yeah, I helped an old lady cross the street." And a boy said: "I had a piece of candy and broke it in half to give a piece to my friend. I think that was good."

I then asked: "Did your parents ever do anything really good?" Again they all said in chorus: "No, never!" I said: "Now, listen, think carefully." One boy looked up and said: "My father, do something really good? No, never."

After some minutes they remembered: My breakfast is always ready in the morning; my mother tells me a story every evening; my father brings me to bed; sometimes my mother sews for the poor. . . .

Simon the church leader thought: *Look at her sins.* Jesus told Simon: "No, look at her goodness. You did not greet me, she did. You did not wash my feet, she did. You did not kiss me, she did. You do not respect me, she does!"

Turning to the woman, he added: "Don't listen to him, forget about the evil in you, think of the good. I do."

Simon had a low opinion of that woman; Simon had a low opinion of Jesus. According to him and his friends, they were too common to have any good in them.

Because of their influence, many others must have had a very low opinion of their own spiritual possibilities. This was one of the reasons the temple flourished.

We often have a low opinion of our own spiritual content, too.

We are taught not to take ourselves too seriously when it comes to our potentialities in the Spirit.

One of the things Jesus wanted to do in our lives is clarify that very issue.

He did it for that woman. He wants to do it for all of us.

Let us be convinced by him. Anyone who thinks lowly of herself or himself cannot do the great things we are created for.

TWELFTH SUNDAY OF THE YEAR

150. The Cross Every Day

Luke 9:18–24

His cross is obvious where Christians meet, live, or are dead.

That's right. Didn't Jesus say that if we want to be considered his followers, we have to take that cross on our shoulders every day?

What does that really mean?

I know what it formerly meant to me. I know what I was taught it should mean to me. Every time something nasty happened to me, people around me would say that my pain and suffering were a participation in the suffering and death of Jesus Christ: that toothache, headache, stomach cramp, difficulties in my studies, disappointment, sickness, disaster, accident—any suffering.

They said: That is your part of his cross. That is your part of his suffering. In this kind of mysticism, some would even go so far as to say: "How happy you are that you are called to suffer. God sends crosses only to those God loves and trusts."

As a result you might be tempted now and then to shout to God: "Can you please stop loving me?"

Though it is true that in a way all human suffering relates to him, there must be another meaning to Jesus' words about that daily cross.

When Jesus spoke about his cross in Luke's text of today, the people who listened did not yet know that he would die on the cross. He knew, we know now, but they did not know. So he cannot at that point have been referring to the cross on which he was going to die. It was just *that* cross.

There is another thing. He told his followers they should carry his cross *daily*. He did not carry that cross daily. He carried it at the end of his life maybe for an hour or so, and even then he had to be helped by that man from an African town called Cyrene: Simon.

When speaking about the cross that his listeners and we have to carry every day with him, he was not just speaking about the cross you see there about the altar.

He must have been speaking about the cross he was carrying at the moment he spoke: The things he was doing day by day.

We know what those activities were. They were his constant struggle against the *sin* around him in all its forms. The sin and injustice in the temple service, where some profited from the piety and guilt feelings of the poor and miserable. The sin and injustice in human relations, as when he defended the adulterous woman against her hypocritical oppressors and told her not to sin anymore. The sin and injustice in the political field, in the economic field. The corruption, bribery, neglect of children. The breakup of families where husbands left their wives, just like that, and on and on.

Name a sin, call out an injustice, and he would be seen struggling against it—not violently, but very powerfully—every day, every hour.

It was in that way that he made enemies who would nail him on the cross. It was in that way that he carried his cross every day, long before his actual death.

It is in that way that we should follow him by refusing to be bribed and by refusing to bribe.

Yesterday I met a mother who has a daughter studying in Europe. One of her friends was flying out to Europe, and she had cooked some sweets for her daughter. She had worked very long on her gift, and packed it carefully. At the airport, a customhouse officer told her: "You are not allowed to fly that present out." They both knew this was nonsense. They both knew what was expected. She told him: "No, I am not going to bribe," and the food stayed here.

She is still so sad about it that she hasn't eaten any of it herself. We should not dramatize a gesture like that. Jesus definitely would see it in the light of his struggle, in the light of his cross.

That is what he meant with his daily martyrdom, witnessing (because that is what *martyr* means) in your pain to the reality he stood for. The reality we should stand for daily.

THIRTEENTH SUNDAY OF THE YEAR

151. Called to Liberty

Luke 9:51–62

Paul wrote: "He freed us." He meant to free us forever. Paul even added: "No law can touch you!"

We might wonder what this freedom really means. Many will say he liberated us through his death on the cross, thinking of a sacrifice, a price, a ransom paid for us.

Some get very enthusiastic about this. They burst out in chants and dance, witnessing to it. They fill radio and television programs with it, endlessly.

Is that endlessness in itself not a sign that they are slightly confused and don't know what really happened to them?

We could look at this liberation from another point of view. In Jesus, our human possibilities become visible. He showed us what it means to be a human being. He showed what it means to live from within: a life that made him—according to the gospel of today—resolutely take the road to Jerusalem, though he foresaw and foretold what would happen to him once in that town.

He also taught them the conditions that have to be fulfilled before we reach the level of his inner freedom. No nest, no hole, no resting place, no time for the past: "*Let the dead bury their dead.*" No time for the present: "*no good-bye for the family at home.*" Completely open to the Kingdom of God, without ever looking back.

That is a strange message for a leader. They rarely if ever grant such liberty, such dignity, such responsibility to others.

It is what Paul understood better than anyone else. Wasn't he the one who was in conflict about that past and that present with a leader like Peter?

Paul also knew best the dangers. "You were called to liberty, not in view of self-indulgence, but to serve and to love each other, *building the new community.*"

We are free to love, we are free to serve. We are not bound up. We are not closed in. We are not chained. We are free in the Lord.

FOURTEENTH SUNDAY OF THE YEAR

152. Seventy-Two

Luke 10:1–12, 17–20

I met a Jewish Bible scholar. We spoke about religious issues because he obviously was interested in those issues. We spoke about Jesus. We spoke about Paul. We spoke about the Bible and about scholarship. He said: "You Christians, you are lacking in biblical scholarship. You very rarely get the real meaning, even of what Jesus said or of what Paul wrote, because you simply don't sufficiently know their Jewish background." I thought about this when the gospel of today mentioned that Jesus sent out seventy-two of his disciples. Seventy-two; why seventy-two? He is sending them out in view of a harvest; he sends them out to reap and collect, to bring together and to gather.

Why seventy-two? I tried to find out in some scholarly works. I found an answer, an answer that makes the gospel of today a very revealing, very interesting, and very relevant one.

If you count all the sons of Noah's children—Shem, Ham, and Japheth—in Genesis, you come up with about seventy-two. It depends a bit on how you divide the names mentioned. The Bible says that after the flood, seventy-two people started to spread all over the world. Those seventy-two represent all the peoples of the earth. All people, though they now have more than seventy-two names, go back to that original seventy-two.

Read with this background, when Jesus sent out his seventy-two, he must have been thinking of those seventy-two sons, of those seventy-two ancestors, of those seventy-two peoples—of all peoples in this world. Those seventy-two got a mission from Jesus, a very obvious mission. They had to announce: "The Kingdom of God is near."

You know what that Kingdom of God entails. It means that sometime all people will join in one banquet prepared for all of them by their parent and life-origin in heaven.

That is not all Jesus said. Jesus also said they should consider themselves laborers bringing in a harvest. He added that the harvest is rich, ripe, and ready. The plants in the fields, the ears in the wheat, the corn on the cobs, the potatoes in the dark under the earth, the grapes shining in the sun, the oranges on the trees, the bananas between their leaves—they are all ready to be collected, but the laborers are few.

Do you see what this means?

It means that according to Jesus, within all cultures, movements and developments have taken place that make us hungry and thirsty for that meal we will have together with our Father in heaven, with God, who as a mother, the mother in the first reading of today, wants to comfort her child: humanity.

Paul, the apostle of the nations, understood this best.

Preaching in Athens, he said, referring to the same Genesis passage: "From one human being God created all races of humankind and made them live throughout the whole earth. God himself fixed beforehand the exact times and limits of the places where they would live. God did this so that they would look for him as they felt about for him."

Those seventy-two were sent to gather all of them, to collect the harvest and bring it home. We are sent out in the same way, and that is why all of us, of whatever culture, should be gatherers and peacemakers.

We are of the seventy-two.

FIFTEENTH SUNDAY OF THE YEAR

153. From Within

Luke 10:25–37

Moses wrote: "This law is not beyond your strength or beyond your reach. It is not in heaven, it is not beyond the seas. No, it is very near to you. It is in your mouth, it is in your heart."

These words Jesus took very much to heart. These words he applied before referring to anything else. These words made him look for his Father's Spirit in anyone he met, bringing out what so often seemed to be lost.

A lawyer came to him to ask: "Sir, what should I do to inherit eternal life?" Jesus answered: "What should you do to inherit eternal life?" The man didn't give his answer from within, but from without, from the law he knew so very well: "You must love the Lord your God with all your heart, with all your soul, with all your mind, with all your strength, and your neighbor as yourself."

"You have answered right," Jesus said. "Do this and life will be yours."

The lawyer then came with another question, a tricky, dangerous one: "And who is my neighbor?"

This was a tricky, dangerous question because Jesus had been accused of going further than the law. Isn't going further than the law against the law?

The law originally restricted the idea of neighbor to the members of the Jewish people and the strangers living in their country. In the time of Jesus, the group of alien neighbors had been reduced to only proselytes, drawing around the Jewish people an impenetrable, kind of magical, ring.

What answer would Jesus, who was seen healing Romans and pagans, give? *None!* He told a story.

It was the story about a Jew walking from Jerusalem to Jericho who was beaten up on his way and left behind, bruised, crippled, and slowly bleeding to death.

A Jew came along and passed. Another Jew came along and passed. A Samaritan—not a Jew, not a proselyte, not a neighbor—came along and stopped. He stopped the man's bleeding, dressed his wounds, poured oil and wine on the dressings, and brought him to a country inn for further treatment, guaranteeing payment of all the costs involved.

When the story was over, Jesus asked the lawyer: "Who was the neighbor of that man who was beaten up alongside the road?"

The lawyer thought of the ring, the magical circle his people had been drawing around itself. He thought about the law, the written law as customarily explained in a very restrictive way, and then he said from *within* himself: "The one who took pity on him!" From within himself, he broke the magical spell. He did it from within, from *within*.

And Jesus found what had been lost.

SIXTEENTH SUNDAY OF THE YEAR

154. Mary's Extra

Luke 10:38–42

Jesus arrived in Bethany. He had already been threatened. He had been hiding, he had been interrogated by the security forces. He was no longer welcome everywhere. Law-abiding citizens started to shun him.

When he entered Bethany, many windows and doors closed. Children were called home, and their parents watched him from behind the curtains.

Yet, Martha came out of her house to meet him. She welcomed him. She made him sit down, she washed his feet, she offered water to refresh his hands and face, she gave him a cool drink, and she said: "You are so welcome!"

Jesus sat down, took his drink, and was happy to be in a home for a moment.

Martha went to the kitchen and brought out the food. There was a clanging of pots and pans, the smell of baking bread, the perfume of fruits, vegetables, and wine, the noise of boiling water on the fire. It was very homely, very pleasant with the cat purring in a corner. Martha was busy, and so was her sister Mary. They both wanted to welcome Jesus as nicely as possible. They were both like good Samaritans to him.

Mary did more than serve and help. According to the original manuscripts (with the exception of only one version), Mary *also* sat down at his feet. In the translation that we used for our reading today, that word *also* is missing, but it really should have been there.

Martha was busy. Mary was too, but Mary did that something extra. Martha was like the good Samaritan. So was Mary, but Mary did more.

Jesus let both go their way. He appreciated Martha and her running up and down to the kitchen. That running was definitely a sign of her love for him, of her faith and hope. Martha is doubtlessly part of him, but when Martha starts to condemn her sister for not helping her with the serving and for sitting at his feet, he speaks out. He says that Mary was right in listening to him, in listening to the Lord, in listening to God.

We all should resemble the good Samaritan, but we should not forget that the story about him was preceded by the saying: "You must love the Lord your God with all your heart, with all your soul, with all your strength, with all your mind, and your neighbor as yourself."

We should all follow the example of Mary, who added to what Martha did. We should follow Martha, too.

To have faith means *to come down from the donkey of your ordinary, everyday life*, to help others, to demonstrate and protest, to work and to study in their favor.

It means *also* to listen to the Lord, to pray and be attentive, so we can *monitor* all our service in the direction of his Kingdom to come.

We have to serve our neighbor; we have to listen to the Lord.

We don't have enough Marthas among us, but they are certainly more numerous than the Marys.

That is not only a pity, it is something that is felt.

SEVENTEENTH SUNDAY OF THE YEAR

155. His Reservedness

Luke 11:1–13

They saw him praying. There must have been something very special about his prayer. That's why they asked him: "Teach us how to pray. Teach us to pray as you are doing it." You just heard his answer in the gospel reading. There is more to his answer than just saying the Our Father.

The gospels speak about Jesus praying, but they do not mention all his prayers.

They mention that he went to participate in the Passover feast at Jerusalem; they never speak about his participation in the liturgical prayers there.

We are told that while he lived in Nazareth, he went to the synagogue every Sabbath day, but there is no mention of his prayers in that synagogue.

We hear how he lived very piously in the circle of his family, but there is no trace of his family prayers.

What is mentioned is special, personal: He went to the desert and the mountaintops to pray.

We are told that he said: "Enter into your inner room as you pray to the Father, who is there hidden."

We were warned by him: "Don't pray as the Pharisees, who pray in public to be seen by all." Another characteristic is his *reservedness* in his prayers.

He refuses to invoke the power of God, as we so often do when in difficulty or need. When a soldier hurt him in front of the approving high priests, he responded by saying: "Don't you realize that I could call on my Father for help, and that he would send me at once more than twelve armies of angels to defend me?"

He does not do it, not even when he is caught in such difficulties and harassment that he has to shout out in anguish, "My God, my God, why did you forsake me?" Why didn't he pray as all of us would be tempted to pray, as so many of them had prayed in the Bible? "Bash their heads; let their children perish; make their women infertile; let the hills and the mountains fall over them."

Was that the reason we don't hear anything about him joining the old prayers in their temple and synagogues?

He was sure that God would have helped him. He was sure that God would have interfered with power and might against those who used power against him. He did not ask for that type of violence.

On the contrary, he asked God not to use power. He said: "Father, please, don't look. They don't know what they are doing."

How could the circle of violence he came to break ever be broken if he used the violence of his Father's power?

That is what he taught them when he said: When you pray, say: "*Our* Father." Not the Father of me and my group, but *our* Father, who can't be turned against anyone.

Thy Kingdom come, thy will be done, not in power, but in the growth we are asking for, respecting our human decisions.

Give *us* bread, all of us, not just some, but all.

Help *us* to forgive, not using violent revenge, but the forgiveness that liberates us from the past as we forgive. Lead us no longer in temptation to do otherwise.

Amen.

EIGHTEENTH SUNDAY OF THE YEAR

156. Your Money or Your Life

Luke 12:13–21

A man ran up to Jesus. He was a tortured man, frustrated, wronged, and diminished. His brother refused to give him his share of his inheritance.

He had only one idea in his head: How do I get that money? How do I get my share?

His mornings were pestered by that idea, as were his afternoons. All during his nights, he was so upset that he turned over and over, from his right side to his left side and from his left side to his right side, so he could not sleep, even for a minute.

He was so full of that question and that problem that he went all the way up to Jesus with only that idea in his head. He could not speak about anything else. So even before saying: "Hi," or "Good morning," or "How are you?" he asked Jesus: "Tell my brother to give me my part of our inheritance."

Jesus refused to speak that word, and he explained why. He told the man: "Be on your guard against avarice. It does not help a person in life. It makes further life impossible. It cuts out further possibilities. It blocks everything!"

Isn't it true that you often say the same thing to yourself?

Didn't you ever say that if you had that car, status, house, land, or stocks, you would be freer, more able to give another shape to your life?

You would be able to be moral, more liberal, and more faithful to the people who really fill your life.

It is your car that blocks you. It is your house that kills you. It is your status that strangles you. Things took over in your life.

Then he told them that other story, about a man who did get his part. He was already rich when he was blessed with an absolute bumper harvest. Fantastic, the coffee had never been so good. He said to himself: "Let me store it up for myself. Let me build a bigger barn, a bigger warehouse, an enormous safe, a strong room for all the things I have, and let me take things easy. Let me eat, drink, and sleep, having a good time. I, by myself, alone."

That is what he did. He did not look for any further possibilities in his life because of the *things* he had, because of his inheritance.

He could have done so much. He could have organized an enormous feast. He could have adopted hungry children and filled his life with joy. He could have done all kinds of things. He did not. He could not. He bound himself. His goods bound him with very strong strings. He did not make anything out of it. He could not give any real sense to his life, even not to the last task anyone has in this life, giving sense to his death. To him, death could mean only absolute and total disaster.

Did you ever hear the African story about how death and sickness came into this world? In the beginning, nobody ever died. God gave people life for some time in this world, and then after some time, God would call them over to God's Kingdom for a fuller life. God used to send a messenger, a beautiful young man or woman, with the invitation. That young woman or young man was so nice because of the beautiful invitation they brought.

Everybody was always very happy to see them, always very happy to switch over from this life to the next. Until one day, one of those messengers was sent to a man who was very rich. He had just had a bumper harvest. He had just pulled down his old storage shed and built a new one, a huge one. He had put his harvest in that storage shed, and the very night that everything was ready, the messenger came with his invitation from God. The rich man said he was not ready to go. He had still too much to eat and drink in this life.

When the messenger came back to God, God asked: "Where is the man I invited?" The messenger answered: "He did not come. He had too much to be able to come."

God became very upset, and there and then, he decided to send sickness and old age to people before God's messengers came.

God wanted to soften us up, to make us loosen slowly—through dying eyes, dying ears, and dying teeth—the strings attaching us to the earth and this life.

There was a man who came to Jesus and said: "Tell my brother to give me my share of my inheritance." Jesus refused to say that word. He did not want to cooperate in that man's losing his possibilities and in binding him in such a way that neither life nor death would make any sense to him in the end.

NINETEENTH SUNDAY OF THE YEAR

157. No Need To Be Afraid

Luke 12:32–48

We live in difficult days. The days of glamour are over, and so are the days of snug security, too. What we were able to do ten years ago, we can't do anymore.

Things are getting more and more complicated. The travels we could make without fear all over the world came to an end for many who are afraid of international terrorism. The evening walks we could take without harassment in our own neighborhoods can't be taken anymore.

There are dangers everywhere: international conflicts, national difficulties, muggers around the corners of our very own streets and squares.

Almost every week, there are rumors of new wars; almost every day, new conflicts seem to break out: car bombs, detentions, strikes, violence all over.

Even if we aren't directly involved in all this, each of us is hit. We are all paying the price. Even the most common staple foods are priced beyond reach of the masses, taxed as they are to pay for the armaments they say we need.

In all this, through all this, the good news of the gospel remains: "There is no need to be afraid, little flock, for it has pleased the Father to give you the Kingdom."

A promise, nothing more, is the only thing we seem to have. Nothing else.

Is that sufficient to assist us to survive, to help us hang on, to make us motivated enough to continue?

For Abraham it was, as you heard in the second reading of today. Because of such a promise, Abraham left the town in which he was living. Because of such a promise, he started to live as a nomad in a tent, always on his way, looking toward a city founded, designed, and built by God. He never saw that city. He never arrived at it. His whole life was full of complications, and he had very good reason to doubt.

Hadn't he been promised a descendancy as numerous as the stars? And yet, almost up to the moment of his death, he had no child from Sarah, and when he finally had his child, he was asked to sacrifice it to God.

He kept on because of his dream, because of that promise of a town, a settlement, he never saw realized in his life.

Abraham is a good example of what a promise can do in the life of a human being.

Aren't we in the same situation? Have we anything that's more than just a promise?

Yes, we have. We are further. We are nearer. We have a tangible model. We have the fulfillment with us.

We have it in a celebration like this one. We realize here and now what we cannot realize in everyday life. But here it is, and we have it.

Sometimes in a congregation like this, two families really dislike, even hate, each other. They never shake hands. Their children are told not to play with each other. They never speak to each other. They don't even look at each other. They are air, very thin, rarefied, and yet polluted air to each other.

When they enter church, the first thing they do is look to see where the others are sitting. If the others are sitting to the right, they are going to sit to the left. If the others are sitting to the left, they are going to the right.

There will be no prayer for each other. There will be no exchange of greeting. There will be no kiss of peace. But then, at the moment of the sharing of the bread, they both go to the same table. They both receive the same Lord. They both share the same wine. They both form the one body of Jesus Christ.

"There is no need to be afraid, little flock, for it has pleased the Father to give you the Kingdom!"

Not in a promise only, but a reality here and now that is not fully real, but nevertheless is the model of a better future.

TWENTIETH SUNDAY OF THE YEAR

158. His Kind of Peace

Luke 12:49–53

The problem in the three readings of this twentieth Sunday of the year is evil.

In the first reading, Jeremiah is put in a well, very deep down, cut off from the light, up to his knees or maybe to his elbows in the mud, because he fought in his town against injustice, evil, and sin.

In the second reading, we are asked not to cling to sin, but to stick to goodness, to fight the battle until the end.

And in the gospel, Jesus says: "I came to bring a fire, a purifier, and a new Spirit! I did not come to bring peace, but division, dissent and war."

Strange text. Strange to us who are accustomed to depicting Jesus beautifully, with large eyes, a shapely beard, in soft colors, carefully dressed, with a sweet glow all over him.

The warning today is clear.

He says: "Don't think that I came to bring an easy peace. I came to bring peace, yes, but I did not come to pull wool over the misery in this world, so that nobody can see it anymore. Don't think that I came to pull a blanket over all the coldness of human relations so that the shiverings no longer will be felt. No, I did not come to bring that peace. I came to bring a fight, a battle, a struggle, a fire, a sword to undo all the evil in the world. You, you should join in my fight against that evil, against that sin.''

We can join it by our sacramental confessions, which we should not only see as occasions to ask for forgiveness, but also as a means to combat and overcome sin in us.

We can join it by educating our children well, by counseling and correcting the people we live with.

We can join it by insisting on honesty and fair dealings.

There is more to that fight, to that fire, and to that sword than sin.

A strange thing happened to me some days ago. I was walking through the campus when suddenly a student, carrying some files and papers under his arm—showing himself and others that he was busy studying—rushed up to me in one terrific swoop.

He stopped short in front of me and said: ''Can I ask you a question?'' I told him: ''You are doing that already. What is your second question?'' He said: ''Why do you mention sin and iniquity before you wash your hands during Mass? What is the difference?''

I am afraid my answer was not very clear. It was too quick, too unexpected.

Why that double-up when speaking about evil: sin *and* iniquity?

There is a difference. Sin is not the only evil that terrorizes this world. There are other things for which nobody seems to be responsible: our sick political system, the armaments race, our competitive educational system, the differences between the rich and the poor, the bureaucratic setup of administration, industrial relations, the world's economic disorder. All evils for which nobody seems to be personally responsible. An evil like witchcraft, bewitching so much of our world.

When we join Jesus in his invitation today, we are facing a great and necessary mission, indeed. That iniquity also has to be overcome!

Alone, we can do nothing, but together and with the fire he brought—the fire of the Spirit—we can purify and cauterize this whole wide world.

TWENTY-FIRST SUNDAY OF THE YEAR

159. The Gate Is Narrow

Luke 13:22–30

Through towns and villages Jesus went teaching, making his way to Jerusalem, where he was going to be murdered.

He must have known that. In a sense, it was the reason he went. He was going in through that narrow door, death, over the narrow path leading to it. While he was thinking of all this, there came a man who asked: ''Sir, will only a few be saved?''

Jesus did not answer the question directly. He never does. He hardly ever could. His frame of reference was too different from that of his questioners. He only said: "The gate is open, it is narrow, but it is open. Everyone should be able to pass, nobody should be left behind."

He said that even though he had told them before that it would be easier for a camel to go through the eye of a needle than for some to go through that narrow gate.

According to some exegetes, one of the gates leading into Jerusalem was so narrow that a big, *richly loaded camel* could not pass through that gate. The gate was nicknamed the "needle's eye," just as we now call some roads "bottlenecks."

The gate is narrow, but it is open. The man wanted to ask, "How many will you let through? How many will your Kingdom-of-heaven immigration officers stop? Who will get a visa, a passport, a green card, a residence permit, an identity card, a social security number, or an alien's registration?"

Jesus' answer was: The gate is open. Free entry. No formalities, no restrictions, no bribes, taxes, complimentaries, watchmen, guards. Nothing, but once more, *the gate is narrow*.

What did he mean? It was the richly loaded camel that could not pass.

Did you ever hear the story about the man who was warned in a neighboring country: "The police are looking for you? The Central Intelligence Agency, the Criminal Investigation Department, they are all looking for you. You are *persona non grata*. Disappear. There is still time, the road is open, be quick!"

He postponed and postponed, because he wanted to arrange all kinds of things before: hide his car, bury his gold, get his money from the bank. Suddenly it was too late. He was picked up and disappeared.

During the Second World War, families would be warned: "Get out, disappear. You cannot take much, the luggage margin is very narrow, one piece only. Be ready tomorrow." Some were not ready. They had not been able to make up their minds about what to take and what to leave. They were taken and perished.

How many will be saved? The door is open, but it is narrow. The path leading to it is narrow, too.

Only persons can pass, but only persons matter.

So let us not make all kinds of things our worry and burden. Let us live a human life to the full. Invest all you have in that human life of yours and that of others. Live simply and soberly, generously and carefully. Do not care about what others say. Live just and chaste, humble and uncomplicated, but do live! It is the only thing you are and have: your life. Live, caring for the only thing that will pass with you through that narrow door. That is what he did on his way to Jerusalem, walking the narrow road, the road less traveled, to that narrow gate of his cross and the life and glory to follow.

TWENTY-SECOND SUNDAY OF THE YEAR

160. Be Gentle in Your Business

Luke 14:1, 7–14

The gospel of today contradicts itself. Twice advice is given, and the two pieces of advice contradict each other. It is as if Jesus says: "Go," and at the same time, "Don't go." It is as if Jesus says, "Do this," and at the same time, "Don't do this."

Let's start with the second saying. He recommends: "If you prepare a feast, don't invite all kinds of guests who can and will repay you. Don't calculate that way, but invite those who will not be able to do anything in return. Invite disinterestedly, and your feast will be grand. If you invite only those who are going to reinvite you, then they will say to one another: 'He invited us only because he wants something in return,' and your feast will be no feast at all. Be wise, don't calculate; be generous, and all will go well."

In his first piece of advice, it seems that Jesus suggests calculation. He says: "If you want to be honored, don't take too high a place at the table, because you will be humiliated when the host comes in. Don't even take the place that is yours, because you will not be honored, either. Think, calculate, be clever; take too low a place, and when the host comes in, he will walk up to you in front of all them, and he will say: 'Oh, don't sit there, come higher up.' And all the guests will say: 'Look at him, what a noble man, and so humble.' " There must have been something else behind all this. There must have been a hidden intention, and there is.

When we invite those who cannot repay us, our invitations are according to the lines of the Father's heavenly banquet. Our invitation runs according to the lines of Jesus' Kingdom. Isn't that also true when we sit down with the poor and the smallest, with the miserable and the wretched, when we take their place, their stand, and their position? Isn't that what he did?

Mind you, this should not mean that we all become like Sister Teresa from Calcutta, or that we all start to hand out all we have to the poor.

It doesn't even mean we should start soup kitchens and all kinds of charitable associations. All those things are necessary now, because there is something else we did not do. The something else indicated in the first reading of today: *"My son and my daughter, be gentle in carrying out your business, and you will be better loved than a lavish giver."*

Jesus Sirach advises us to carry out our business in the office, family, traffic—in everything—gently. That is to say, taking into account the weak, the poor, the small. We will be loved the better for it, because then the whole world would change to the extent that all the aid and the handouts would no longer be needed.

Everyone, every single widow, every single orphan, and all the marginal ones, would find their places at the tables of this world.

One of the great analyzers of our modern world, Karl Popper, wrote that society will only heal when it takes the interest of the weakest of the weak among us *first*.

In a Third World country, we are accustomed to aid, to help, to assistance from the rich countries, from outside, from overseas. If those rich regions, those other worlds, would be more gentle *in their business*, if they would sit down with the poor, as Jesus suggested and practiced, wouldn't everyone find her and his place more easily here, and in the Kingdom to come?

TWENTY-THIRD SUNDAY OF THE YEAR

161. His Revolution

Luke 14:25–33

The gospel of today sounds very harsh at first hearing. It seems too much to hate your father, your mother, your wife, your children, your brothers, your sisters, even your own life and all your possessions in order to follow him.

To understand it, we must consider in what kind of context Jesus was saying all this. He was on his way to Jerusalem. He was on his way to the cross. He was going to be murdered, and he knew that very well. And there they were, the hundreds, the thousands, following him on his way to that cross. He knew where this road was leading him, but they did not know at all.

That is why just this once, he turned around, stopped them, and asked: "Do you really know what you are doing?"

In fact, they were following him for completely different reasons. They wanted a change. There were the hungry, who wanted to be fed; the sick, who wanted to be healed; the poor, who wanted to become rich; the dead, carried by their relatives, who, according to those relatives, wanted to be revived.

They followed him enthusiastically, full of hope and very interested in the good things of life.

He turned around, he stopped them, and he said: "Are you sure that you are willing to walk my way? Do you know where I am going? Did you count the costs, and are you willing to pay them?"

There was misunderstanding between him and his followers. They were following him the old way. They had not changed their options in life. They wanted to profit from him, to get more things, a better position in the old order, to get rich, to get healthy, to get security that this world had never been able to offer.

He wanted to give them another life, with another option, from within another vision.

He wanted a change. They, too, wanted a change, but they wanted a different one than the one he was thinking about. They were thinking only of themselves, their families, their lives, their possessions.

He was thinking of the Kingdom of God, the kingdom of people, the kingdom of the whole of humankind. He was thinking of humanity as God's family on its way to a final outcome. He was thinking of a totally different change than they were.

Nowadays, too, many people are thinking about a change, a very radical one. They have not only been thinking about this. Profiting from this deep desire, leaders have been organizing revolutions. Almost half of humanity is living in a postrevolutionary age.

Did those revolutions really change things? The names of the leaders changed, yes. The names of the leading groups changed, yes. The portraits of the presidents in the public buildings and local bars changed, yes. Did the human condition change? Did our option change? Did we become less selfish?

There was a country far from here with a terrible dictator. He was really sucking the blood of the poor. The farmers in that country got very upset. They organized themselves and shot the old dictator. They appointed their own leader as the new one. After some years, that new leader was really a dictator. He was sucking the blood of the poor. The farmers got upset. . . .

Jesus turned around to all those who followed him and asked: "Did you change your option when you decided to follow me? Are you willing to think in terms of the Kingdom of God? Are you willing to give up your old ways, your own self, your corruption, your own life, your possessions?"

Can you do that?

Do not try to build a new city, if you are not willing to do that. You will shed blood, much blood, and it will all be in vain.

Do not try to start a revolution or a war, if you are not willing to change. Nothing would be won.

TWENTY-FOURTH SUNDAY OF THE YEAR

162. They Were Very Angry

Luke 15:1–32

They were angry with Jesus, very angry—the good ones, the clean ones, the law-abiding, well-washed, learned, faithful, regular temple goers.

They were angry because he sat down at table with the bad ones, the dirty ones, the disobedient, careless, stupid, faithless ones, those who were never seen in the temple or synagogue.

They made no secret of their thoughts. They complained bitterly. They blamed him.

And then he tells them those three strange stories. About a man who leaves ninety-nine obedient sheep alone to look for one crazy one. About a housewife who does not bother about the nine coins in her apron pocket, but who turns the whole house over to look for one lost one. About a father who organizes a party for his good-for-nothing prodigal son and who forgets to inform his faithful son about it.

They were angry. Why?

Just imagine Jesus sending us a heavenly messenger—Gabriel, Michael, or Raphael—to inform us that he was coming here to Nairobi to visit us at the end of the month. Don't you think all the churches would prepare? The choirs would renew their repertoire. The buildings would be repaired. Everything would be freshly painted. The paint would be donated. Large churches and small ones, old ones and independent ones, would wash their stoles, their vestments, their cassocks, their albs, their banners, their flags, and their streamers, and everybody would live in expectation. Then he comes. He really comes. But he does not go to All Saints Cathedral, he does not go to Holy Family Cathedral, he does not go to the Deliverance Church. He does go to the drinkers in bars and pubs, he sits down in nightclubs with town girls, and he invites bribers, thieves, and smugglers to his table.

What would the reaction be? What would your reaction be?

Their reactions were clear: They could not stand it. They thought they were the sacred ones, the privileged, chosen, and saved ones. Luke wrote somewhere else in his gospel: "They were sure of their goodness and they despised anyone else" (Luke 18:9). They thought they had fulfilled the law. They were the sheep that had always been obedient. They were the coins that had always remained in the purse. They were the son who had always stayed at home. And now they were not even invited, informed, or preferred.

In the end, they killed him to prove they were right and he was wrong, that they were the blessed ones and he was the cursed one. Under the cross, they shouted: "Now save yourself. Let us see whether God is going to save you!"

They killed him because he had forgiven the others, because he had invited those others to his table.

They could not stand that God was greater than their hearts. They could not bear the thought that God is good to the wicked. They thought they had done everything because they had reduced God's life style to their own law.

They did *this* so many times; they did *that* so many times; they went to the synagogue every Sabbath; they prayed all the prescribed prayers; they never ate pork; everything was kosher; they were all right. . . .

Did you ever realize the nature of Jesus' prescriptions? They cannot ever be completely fulfilled: Forgive seven times seventy times; if anyone slaps you on the right cheek, turn to him your left cheek.

His measure will never be reached by any one of us. We will always depend on him who is looking for the stray sheep, the lost coin, the prodigal son—for us, who are all invited to that table of his.

TWENTY-FIFTH SUNDAY OF THE YEAR

163. On Dirtying Your Hands

Luke 16:1–13

The notice came in the morning. The manager just heard that he was going to be probed. He had a moment of panic. It would mean his dismissal. His double-dealing would be discovered, he had no doubt about that. A court case was unavoidable.

He sat down behind his desk. He had no time to lose. Friends would be more necessary than ever before. He needed protection. He needed help and support. He called those in debt to his master and told them to sit down. He explained his predicament. He said: "Now the books can still be changed. Tomorrow will be too late. What percentage will you give me if I change them?" Amounts were mentioned. Some haggling took place. Affairs were settled. Erasers were used, and finally the books were closed. Everything had been dealt with in time.

After having told this story that was known all over Jerusalem because it had really happened, Jesus said that he admired the presence of mind of that accountant. He did not panic. He did not faint. He did not lose a minute. He stayed wide-awake. He did not lament, but took action immediately.

He asked them: "Why don't you act like that caretaker when it comes to the Kingdom affairs I entrusted to you?"

He did not mean to say that we should act unfairly in view of the Kingdom. He asked us to act as quickly and as efficiently as that caretaker in the situations we meet.

He foresaw an obvious objection we might make in deciding not to act in this world.

Isn't this world a place of darkness? Aren't all its structures corrupt? Isn't everything tainted with evil? Wouldn't it be better if we retired totally from public life—socially, politically, and economically? Shouldn't we keep ourselves pure and without stain?

His answer was: "No, you should not abstain. Use money, use all you have, tainted as it is, to win you friends, and thus make sure that when it fails you, they will welcome you in the tents of eternity."

We cannot escape from the evil of this world. We cannot keep our hands clean, but we are not allowed to keep them in our pockets, either. We have to take the risks he took in order to change us all.

TWENTY-SIXTH SUNDAY OF THE YEAR

164. On Not Dirtying Your Hands

Luke 16:19–31

Jesus said: ''There was a rich man.'' We often add that he was mean. Jesus did not say that; besides, he did not seem to be mean at all. He spent his money lavishly. He spent it on himself: dressed in purple, according to the latest fashion, underwear of the finest linen, beautiful meals, ten-course dinners, candlelight all over, soft music in the background, vintage wines, ice-cooled imported beers.

He was not mean, but he was not hospitable, either. He seems to have wined and dined alone.

Jesus did not say that he was bad. We often add that he was bad. In fact, that rich man was not bad at all. He allowed poor Lazarus to lie at his door day and night, notwithstanding his sores and sicknesses. Who of us would allow that on our own premises? Wouldn't you call the police?

Jesus does not say that Lazarus did not get the scraps that fell from the man's table. We say so, but not he. In some translations, it is added that no one gave him those scraps, but maybe this meant he had to fetch them himself, creeping under the table with the dogs when the servants came to clean up after the meals.

Jesus described the poor man Lazarus as totally destitute, totally helpless. He lay, since he could not sit or stand. He was full of sores, and the dogs— while waiting for the scraps—came to lick his wounds, which means he didn't have the strength to keep the dogs away from himself.

Though he wasn't bad, and in the eyes of himself and the others, he was very tolerant and charitable, the rich man made one mistake.

He did not want to dirty his hands. He did not take any action to improve the poor man's lot. He allowed him on his property, he allowed him to search for scraps in his trash cans, but he overlooked the point the dishonest character did not overlook last Sunday: He did not make friends. He did not really care for the life process that was dying in the running sores of Lazarus.

It was that lack of care that created a distance between him and Lazarus, one that grew from day to day, though they lived in the same world and in the same compound.

When they both finally died, that distance still separated them.

The rich man had not shared his life with anyone. He had not been mean, he had not been bad, he had been alone, even though the other was there, too.

He had not wanted to dirty his hands, and now even the tip of a finger he asked for was refused.

The distance had become too great.

TWENTY-SEVENTH SUNDAY OF THE YEAR

165. Your Faith Suffices

Luke 17:5–10

The gospels were written for the first Christians. They were written to encourage them. The gospel of Luke is no exception; his gospel was written to encourage the Christians he knew. It is in that light that we have to read the gospel of today.

The people around Jesus went to him and told him: "Please, give us more faith. We haven't enough of it. We can't do anything as we are. We can't even start. Please help us. We are very weak. We are beginners. You are so holy. We aren't, but we would love to be like you."

They were like a businessman who says: "I don't have sufficient money. Wait until I have some more, and I will start." Since he doesn't do any business, he never will start.

They were like a farmer who says: "I haven't sufficient seed to sow all my land. Wait until I have some more, and I will start." As he does not sow the seed he has, he will never get any more seed, and he will go hungry.

The disciples came to Jesus. They asked: "Give us more faith, and we will work wonders," implying that their faith was so small they couldn't do a thing.

Jesus, in a sense, does not listen to their request at all. He does not promise them more faith. He does not pledge them anything at all. Jesus said: "Even if your faith would be very small, smaller than the smallest seed, you would be able to move mountains, to move trees, to move that tree over there," and he pointed at a mulberry tree, a tree famous for its age—it can live to be more than six hundred years old—and its very tenacious rooting system that can break rocks into pieces.

Jesus just said: "Start with the little you have, and you will work all you want."

He unmasked in them, and he unmasked in us, one of the ways we use to escape our responsibilities. We can't pray, because we haven't sufficient faith. We can't be charitable, because we are very weak Christians. We can't organize ourselves for justice because we are only beginners. We can't stop drinking because we haven't sufficient grace. . . .

Jesus objected: "Don't kid yourselves. Don't speak like that. Don't even ask for more, but start with what you have!"

Some years ago a woman died who was considered by many a living saint. Her name was Dorothy Day. She started all kinds of activities: a newspaper, *The Catholic Worker*, which still exists; houses of hospitality for vagrants that still function; feeding programs; Christian communal farms; and so on.

Many admirers came to visit her, to have a look at her, to cherish her, to speak to her, to touch her, if possible.

Sometimes they would tell her: "*You are a saint*," or she would overhear others saying of her, "*She is a saint*." She would get upset, turn to the speaker, and say: "Don't say that. Don't make it too easy for yourself. Don't escape this way. I know why you are saying: 'She is a saint.' You say that to convince yourself that you are different from me, that I am different from you. That is easy. In that case you can go your own way. I am not different from you. I am not a saint. I am like you. You could easily do what I do. You don't need any more than you have; get kicking, please."

Amen.

TWENTY-EIGHTH SUNDAY OF THE YEAR

166. Deeper Than the Skin

Luke 17:11–19

There they were, standing the prescribed distance from him. Misery had brought them together, nine Jews and one Samaritan. They were not allowed to approach him. From a distance they shouted: "Heal us, please, heal us!"

Jesus kept to the rules that time, and he said: "Go to the priests and show yourselves."

They turned around and went, and on their way, they were healed.

One of them came back. He fell on his knees before Jesus and thanked him at the top of his voice.

That is why everybody almost always tells us that this gospel episode teaches us that we should be thankful. Definitely: Thankfulness is a very great virtue. It shows what a person is worth.

Yet, is this story really about thankfulness?

They were ten. One is called a stranger by Jesus, a Samaritan. When they asked him for his help, he sent them to the priests in Jerusalem, to the temple's skin-disease check point.

They went, and they were healed on their way. It was only then that the Samaritan remembered he could not go to those priests. He would have been most unwelcome. He certainly would have been kicked out. That is why he left those others and turned the only way he really could go.

He came to Jesus to thank him, but that is not all that happened.

Jesus asked him: "Where are the others? The nine others, where are they?"

Of course, he knew where they were.

One had been a shopkeeper before his sickness hit him, and an hour after having obtained his healing and his healing certificate, he was back in his shop, doing the accounts. Another had been a farmer, and next day he was milking his cows. Another had been a lecturer at the university, and he, too, returned directly to his job, and was seen in the Senior Common Room drinking with all his academic friends.

They all had been touched by Jesus. Their skin, the surface of their bodies, had been healed, but for the rest it had all remained the same.

Now and then, surrounded by their friends and family in the evening hours with a glass of wine in their hands, they would witness: "Look at my skin. Once it was one pimple and ulcer and wound. Jesus touched me, he healed me, alleluia, alleluia, praise the Lord." For the rest, it was as if nothing had happened at all.

The Samaritan came back, and Jesus said: "Stand up, go on your way. Your faith has saved you."

Not his skin, but him; not the surface, but his heart; not his epidermis, but his mind. He really followed him.

Number ten came back. He did not return to his old life and his old world. He lived a new life with him.

We, too, are touched by him. If we had not been touched, we would not be here.

How deep did it go? Are we like the nine, or are we like number ten?

The nine were tested in their old world, according to the old rules of the temple. They were declared clean and healthy on the surface of their skins.

Number ten was tested by Jesus, who said: "You are healed and changed." Number ten never returned to his old life.

TWENTY-NINTH SUNDAY OF THE YEAR

167. Saturation Prayer

Luke 18:1–8

Our prayers to God often seem to be heard by human beings. While Moses asked God for a victory over what he considered to be the evil in this world, *his soldiers* fought that victory.

The widow in the gospel must have asked God that *the judge* would hear her prayer.

Take the student who is praying for success in his examinations. Isn't he praying that he himself may succeed? Isn't he praying that he may spend the necessary time behind his desk? Isn't he praying that he may use the techniques needed to retain what he studied and to reproduce what he knows?

Think about a sick person who has to undergo a serious operation. When she, her surgeon, the nurses, and her family pray for a successful operation, isn't that prayer going to be heard through their attention and care?

Take that other life issue for which so many people are praying at the moment all over the world: The end of the armaments race, disarmament, peace to the world.

There are going to be more and more peace demonstrators chanting peace slogans, missile sites will be more and more surrounded by people who pray to have those missiles removed.

Don't you think that if all the people in the world were to pray seriously for peace, those prayers would be heard?

Don't you think that if all people in the world were to pray seriously for an end to the armaments race, that race would stop?

In the gospel of today, Jesus speaks about the necessary consistency in prayer, about the needed insistency.

He explains how prayer works. He explains how prayer is heard.

The widow who wanted justice done to her went again and again to the judge who despised her and did not want to help her since she was poor and uninfluential.

She kept coming, once a day, twice a day, three times a day, for one week, a second week, a third week, a fourth week. She filled the mind of that unjust judge with the idea that justice should be done to her. Every day, she added a new reason. Every day, she showed a new aspect, until that judge's mind was totally saturated with thoughts of her. Up to the point that he could think only of her when waking up in the morning, all during the day, and late at night. So he decided to do her the justice she wanted and deserved.

It works like that glass of water in which you start to dissolve sugar. You add one spoon of sugar, you stir, the sugar dissolves; you add more sugar, you stir, it dissolves—right up to the point that the water gets oversaturated. It cannot hold any more sugar. At that precise point, you only have to add one more grain, the smallest crystal of sugar possible, to have the whole situation change. Suddenly all the sugar crystallizes out of the water in one abrupt movement.

This is what will happen if we pray enough for the real issues of our times. The issues that, if solved, will fulfill so many of our prayers for our own employment, health, family, food, drink, and career.

This is what will happen if we, all of us, raise our hands high enough and long enough, praying for justice, peace, unity, and love.

Praying like that, we are saturating our minds and spirits with those divine desires, more and more, up to the moment that will be suddenly heard by ourselves with the help of God.

That is how it will work. That is what Jesus tells us today, adding a warning: Will this growing faith be found on this earth?

It should be, until the end.

THIRTIETH SUNDAY OF THE YEAR

168. On Churchgoing

Luke 18:9–14

The story Jesus told us today is about us. It is about people who go to church.

Luke gave this story an introduction; he gave it an intention. Luke says that Jesus told it because some glorified in their justice and consequently despised others. Because of Luke's preface, we run the risk of being biased when listening to Jesus' parable. Because of Luke's introduction, we will condemn the Pharisee as a hypocrite, even before we have heard the end of Jesus' story.

Modern commentators tell us to listen to the story without taking into account Luke's use of it.

The story is about us here in church today, and it is about those who did not come. Many people did not come. If they all had come, there would not have been room left in the church today. We would have been over six thousand in this parish, but we will be only about two thousand.

Those who did not come sometimes harass us for having come. Some days ago, the University Young Christian Students Association had a meeting. In that meeting, this kind of accusation was heard. Someone said: "People go to church with very pious faces, a Bible under their left arm, a hymnal under their right arm, they sing alleluias with high-pitched, excited voices, they receive Holy Communion very devotedly, *but* they are hypocrites. As soon as they are out of church, they forget all about what they did in church. As soon as it is Monday, they will be bribing in their work again. They will be corrupt and faithless. They will be just like all the others. They will be no different from us who did not go to church because we don't want to join their fake games."

Have you ever been told that you are a hypocrite because you go to church?

In how many homes did the husband stay in bed while his wife was preparing to go to church? While she was putting on her Sunday dress, while she was arranging her Sunday bonnet, looking for the Bible that got lost during the confusion of the week, he said from the bed: "There she goes with her Bible and her hat, with her piety and pretense! Hypocrite, don't you remember how you behaved last week? How you gossiped and slandered, how you nagged and lied? Hypocrite, I am not going to join you in that game, in that show, in that spectacle," and he turned over to go back to sleep.

How often have we read in letters to editors: "All Christians are hypocrites. They are pretenders."

How often do people say: "Churchgoers are no better than those who do not go. In fact they are worse. They are pious frauds. Pharisees."

All this implies that only the holy ones should go to church—the totally just, the completely chaste, the fully sincere, those in whom there is nothing but goodness, fairness, divine beauty, and virtue. In fact, those who do not need God's mercy or help at all.

Jesus told them a story about two people who went to the temple. They were two different persons. One was good, sincerely good, in a way, even too good. He never robbed; he never treated anyone unjustly; he never broke the sixth commandment; he fasted one hundred four days a year, though only one day was prescribed; he paid church tax on everything, though he only had to do it on cereals, oil, and wine.

This man was so holy that he definitely could go to church. He belonged there. He was no hypocrite. He lived up to his ideal.

In the back of the church was the other one, a tax collector, a robber, very unjust, greedy, adulterous. A man who should *never* have gone to church. The hypocrite! What was he doing there? Who did he think he was? Out!

Jesus did not judge like that. Jesus listened to his prayer. Jesus recognized how his prayer started with the beginning of Psalm 51:

> Be merciful to me, O God,
> because of your constant love.
> Because of your great mercy
>   wipe away my sins!
> Wash away all my evil
>   and make me clean from my sin!
>
> I recognize my faults;
>   I am always conscious of my sins.
> I have sinned against you—only against you—
>   and done what you consider evil.
> So you are right in judging me;
>   you are justified in condemning me.
> I have been evil from the day I was born;
>   from the time I was conceived, I have been sinful.
>
> Sincerity and truth are what you require;
>   fill my mind with your wisdom.
> Remove my sin, and I will be clean;
>   wash me, and I will be whiter than snow.
> Let me hear the sounds of joy and gladness;
>   and though you have crushed me and broken me,
>   I will be happy once again.
> Close your eyes to my sins
>   and wipe out all my evil.
>
> Create a pure heart in me, O God,
>   and put a new and loyal spirit in me.

Do not banish me from your presence;
    do not take your holy spirit away from me.
Give me again the joy that comes from your salvation,
    and make me willing to obey you.

How could a man praying like that be called a hypocrite? Jesus did not do that, either. Jesus did not say that he should not be in the temple. On the contrary, Jesus said: "This man went home a better man, he went home changed and justified."

If we prayed in this way, who would be able to call us hypocrites? And should not those remaining home because they think us hypocrites and themselves sinners, join, too?

THIRTY-FIRST SUNDAY OF THE YEAR

169. Come Down

Luke 19:1–10

When Zaccheus heard that Jesus was going to enter town, he closed the drawers of his desk and locked them. He closed the door of his safe and locked it. He closed the door of his office and locked it. He closed the door of his house and locked it. He closed the gate in front of his house and locked it. Zaccheus had used almost a dozen keys before he left his house. He was a money man; all he thought of was money. He dreamed about money. His money made him so security conscious.

He went into the street. He wanted to "see" Jesus, that was all. He wanted to "observe" him. He did not want to be touched by him, he did not want to be pulled, pushed, admonished or converted by him.

He wanted to "observe" only. He did not even want to be seen. He definitely did not want to get involved. And, therefore, before the street filled up, he climbed a tree, and there he sat on a branch, waiting and thinking about his favorite subject: money.

All of us often resemble Zaccheus on his tree branch, only observing: The Church should have done this; the theologians should have said that; the bishops should have written a letter; the intellectuals should have started some research. Others, others, others. . . .

We are sitting in a tree above reality, looking down on others, speaking about the pope and what he should do, about the cardinal and what he should not do, about the bishops and what they should do, about the priests and what they should not do, about the Catholic press and what they should do. We don't really involve ourselves, we observe coolly, like Zaccheus wanted to do. *He did not succeed.*

Jesus entered the street. People were milling around him. He stopped under Zaccheus's tree, and at first, Zaccheus was happy about that. Now he would be able to see Jesus in action. Then Jesus looked up and saw Zaccheus in the tree. Zaccheus wished he could make himself invisible. Jesus called him down: "Come down, and hurry!"

Zaccheus almost fell out of the tree, and he joyfully received Jesus. He became so enthusiastic that even before Jesus had said anything, he started to respond to him, spontaneously, but, of course, only in the terms he knew, in terms of money.

Zaccheus said: "I will give half my capital to the poor, I will restore everything I stole fourfold." Money. He spoke only in terms of money.

Then Jesus took over, and Jesus acted as if he had not even heard the word *money* mentioned. He spoke about the person, that human being, his own creation, Zaccheus. He gave him a name. He called him: son of Abraham. That name opened in Zaccheus—that short, one-dimensional, money-making, money-lending, money-loving, money-smelling, money-man—quite another dimension. That name "son of Abraham" spoke of him in terms of eternity, infinity, and an eternal promise of divine life, of heaven and other realities.

The same invitation is addressed to us today: Come down, join me, open yourself up to your real dimensions and possibilities.

Let us not restrict ourselves to being observers. Let us not restrict ourselves only to money and our biological needs.

Everything around us, the papers and the advertisements, the radio and television, the conversations at the bars, try to convince us we can be reduced to food and drink, to gold and silver, to pizza and hamburger consumers, to clothing and sex, to a car and a house, to beer and Coke, to soaps, to grants, to loans.

We are larger, we are bigger. We are absolute, we are divine, we are sons and daughters of God. Even heaven is not our limit, God himself is our destiny.

If that is true, let us come down and respect, in ourselves and in each other, that heavenly country, that divine echo.

THIRTY-SECOND SUNDAY OF THE YEAR

170. Laughing about Life after Death

Luke 20:27–38

They came to Jesus snickering. They were sure they were going to catch him with his own words. Why hadn't they thought of this one before?

The question was about life after death. The issue was the resurrection. They had decided among themselves that there was no life after death, because they reasoned: "The consequences of life after death are ridiculous, totally absurd.

Where would you put all those people? How would you feed them? How would you be able to cater to all those human relations messed up so thoroughly here on earth?''

They had found the example of that poor lady who, seven times in succession, embraced a dying husband in her bed, only to see him depart before any fruit had set.

They did not start with their real issue. They started with that widow and those seven husbands, one after another.

It was only at the end that they said: ''Now what is going to happen after her death and resurrection and after the resurrection of those seven? How is she going to manage? How is she going to divide her time?''

They laughed before they had finished, knowing that he would not be able to answer.

He did not.

He even overlooked their question. He asked them another one. He asked them about four people who went before them: Abraham, Isaac, Jacob, and Moses. He asked them: ''Do you really think those men of God died? Do you really think God made them disappear into clouds of nothingness, into the dark of oblivion? Do you really think that God, who loved them so much, who influenced their lives so intensely, would have forgotten those even you remember? Do you really think that God is a God of dead people, of only some life moments, of some green wood that dried up to be thrown away and be burned in a fire to turn into dust and ashes? Are you trying to tell me that God will disavow them, overlook them, or forget them? You must be joking!

''Is that what you think? Wouldn't that be absurd? Wouldn't it be unbelievable? Can you think of yourself as being overlooked in the end after your struggles, your frustrations, your moments of happiness, and your moments of real greatness? You must be kidding!''

Listen carefully to the names he mentions: Abraham, Isaac, Jacob, and Moses. Listen carefully to what he says: ''Those who are judged worthy!''

Let us not deceive ourselves about Jesus. Let us not deceive ourselves about ourselves. The life that awaits us hereafter is our own life, the consequence of what we *did* here on earth.

On earth, we should live as Abraham, Isaac, Jacob, Moses, and Jesus Christ did—lovers of human life—and we will live forever and ever.

THIRTY-THIRD SUNDAY OF THE YEAR

171. The End of the World

Luke 21:5–19

The idea and the belief that the end of the world and the return of Jesus are very near has often played havoc in the lives of many.

Even this year, many students did not qualify for entry into a university because they had been walking around with small booklets, printed in the United States, that said the end would come this year. They failed because they stopped studying to prove they believed. Besides, why study if you believe a thing like that?

When we hear such a story, we often laugh. Should we laugh?

The tellers are definitely in very good company. Everybody can read in the letters of Paul how he believed, in the beginning of his apostolic career, that Jesus would return during his lifetime.

Some Bible experts hold an even more remarkable theory: That Jesus also expected the end very soon. But the date, he said, he did not know.

It is on the point of that date that those Christians who know it all seem to go wrong. They say they know. It is proved again and again that they do not know.

They forget, or they never understood, that time is a very strange reality. We have the time of our clocks and watches, where every minute has sixty seconds, every hour has sixty minutes, every day has twenty-four hours, and every week seven days.

This is the time we project into space.

My past is far away, behind me; my future is far away, too, in front of me. This is time in which every hour has the same length, the time by which we can indicate dates and years.

Then there is another time, our own psychological time, the time in which we live, in which a minute can last a century and five hours hardly a second.

Take your own experience as an example. You have to leave on a Kenyan bus. The bus is ready. The motor is turning. You need a ticket from the counter at the office. The man behind the counter says: "I have to drink this coffee first; wait a second." Outside, the bus threatens to leave. The driver is hooting, the passengers are waving at you. You have to wait half a minute, one minute, two minutes, and it all seems to last a hundred years, eternity.

Then you go to a party, a real swinging, beautiful party with lively company, full of joy and swing. You arrive, you enjoy it, you dance, you drink, you eat, you chat, and then your girlfriend or boyfriend comes to you and whispers in your ear: "Shouldn't we go home? It's two in the morning." And you say: "Two in the morning? How is that possible? We came in only a minute ago."

You forgot the time.

It is in that psychological time that Christians can be so shocked by the situations in which they have to live that they feel that Jesus has to come back very soon to rule the nations with fairness.

Don't you think Christians who are persecuted might expect him very soon because of that?

That soonness is not as much connected with a date—December, January, or the year 2000—as with their hope and their belief.

We, too, should have something of that hope and belief.

The end is near. It must be near. He will be coming soon. We should not sit down, fold our hands, and wait.

Paul did not do that. Jesus did not do that, either. We should go on, working and building, doing the things that really matter, because the end is very near.

THIRTY-FOURTH SUNDAY OF THE YEAR

172. Kingdom Seen

Luke 23:35–43

It was a very sad group of people going to the execution place that afternoon: Jesus, two criminals, policemen, soldiers, the henchmen and their assistants.

It was a very glad group of people, too: the priests, the scribes, the dignitaries, and magistrates who had him condemned to death. Then there was the crowd that so easily assembles on such disastrous occasions.

The group was even sadder once they were hanging on their crosses, Jesus in the middle, the two robbers on each side. One on the right and one on the left.

In conformity with the prevailing regulations, the reason for their condemnation was mentioned above their heads. The inscription above the man on his right read: *robbery with violence*. The inscription above the man on his left read: *robbery with violence*. The one above his head read: *Jesus, King of the Jews*.

The priests were laughing at him. They paid no attention to the two others. They were not interested in them. They were there only to see Jesus die, the man who had threatened their setup and their income.

The rest of the people were just standing there, looking at the three, but they, too, looked especially at Jesus.

There was no trace of beauty in him anymore. He had been mangled too badly during the last twenty-four hours since his arrest.

The priests had given up on him long ago. The people were doing that now. After his death, they would go home in utter silence, beating their chests in horror and despair. They could not see any good anymore in the one who had not stopped seeing good, a trace of divinity, a trace of God's Kingdom in all of them, even in the smallest, the poorest, the most sinful, the most terribly handicapped, the ones screaming with all kinds of evil spirits in themselves.

When that prostitute came in and everyone said: "She is very bad, a real sinner," hadn't he said: "I don't agree. There is good in her, one will speak of her until the end of time because of that goodness in her!"

Hadn't he been the one who called Zaccheus down when he was hiding in a tree, convinced of his sinfulness, saying: "Zaccheus, don't be silly, come down. You are the son of Abraham. I want you to be my host, I want to be your guest."

Now death reigned. Evil seemed to have overcome. Hope was definitely squashed. God seemed to be absent.

Did he himself not shout: "My God, my God, why have you forsaken me?"

The priests started to jeer. They shouted: "Let God help you. Where is your God?"

The soldiers joined them in their cheap fun. Even the robber on the left did the same.

Now the sun started to disappear. Dark clouds gathered between the cross and the sun, the source of light to the world. It became darker and darker. People had to light torches to see one another, though it must have been only about three in the afternoon. The earth started to tremble, as if in despair, and no voice, no voice was heard from above. God remained silent.

A darker scene had never been observed.

When all hope seemed to have gone, the one on the cross at his right looked up at him—*God only knows why*—was it in answer to his cry?

Looking up, he said: "I see some Kingdom in you. I see some humanity in you. Please, when you arrive in your Kingdom, think of me!"

Jesus lifted his head, he looked at the one who at that moment saw something in him, and he said: "Of course, there is a Kingdom; of course, you will be there with me, today!"

Sisters and brothers, it sometimes seems that all is very bad, that everything turned against us, that all is dark, that there is no hope. The older you are, the more you must have experienced this in your lives.

Light is gone, darkness reigns, death looms, our enemies are laughing at us, we have shouted in vain for the Father to come.

Let us pray that we may always find someone to tell us what the good murderer told Jesus: "I see some Kingdom in you. I see some divinity in you. I see some light in you. I see some hope in you. I see some humanity in you!"

Those words meant salvation to the robber. They meant salvation to Jesus, too. They were the foundation of the Kingdom he started with that robber that very day.

Let him reign, together with us, for all time to come.

The good murderer found what seemed lost. He did what Jesus had been doing all his life. Hope drawing near!

REFLECTION ON SOME RECURRING CELEBRATIONS

ALL SAINTS/ALL SOULS

173. Praying for the Dead

Matthew 25:31–46

You must have been at many funerals. You must have heard very many speeches and talks at those occasions.

You might have noticed something very peculiar about all those words at those occasions. I did, but you must have, too.

There was that funeral of a man who only thought of his business day and night. A man who thought so much of making money that he almost looked like a bank note, thin and green as a dollar. At his funeral, nobody said a word about that. He was, they said, such a loving husband and so caring for his children, and like an open hand to all those in need. And one simply starts to wonder!

Suddenly there is no doubt about his goodness. There is no hesitation about his mercy. There is no doubt about his charity. (S)he should go straight to heaven.

Yet, when the tears are dried up and the coffin is covered with sand; when the flowers start to whither in the sun and the last visitor has left; when everyone has returned to the world in which that beloved person had lived for so long with them, they will find in that world the harm he did, whether the eulogist at the funeral mentioned it or not.

We really face a problem when we see the life of that man in the light of today's gospel.

Was he good, or was he bad? Was he a sheep, or was he a goat? Is he a saint, or is he a sinner? Does he belong to the right, or does he belong to the left?

He did feed some hungry during his life, but he refused to feed so many others. He did quench the thirst of some, but he left so many thirsty. He did visit some prisoners, but he refused to visit others. He did dress some who were naked, but he did not dress them all. He did meet Christ in some, but several times he refused to meet him in others. What will Christ do in such a case, sitting there as a judge on his high throne before the whole of humankind? Confronted with that mixture of good and bad, splendor and squalor, half-sheep, half-goat, what will he do?

Will not all of us be in that very same situation? Are not all of us that mixture? Do we not all know that we are surrounded by those who are hungry, thirsty, naked, and imprisoned, while we help only some of them now and then?

That is why all of us, once we stand before that throne, will be but too willing to forgive those who did real harm to us in this world.

Because we are all guilty, we are all at fault, we all betrayed each other, we all need forgiveness, and without that forgiveness, all of us should be standing on the left, with only his mother, Mary, and maybe Joseph standing on the right.

Today we commemorate all souls. We pray for those we think might not yet be in the full company of God, as their sins here on earth are still with us and even now frustrate our lives.

The teeth kicked out by them are still missing. The scars of the wounds made by them did not yet heal. The psychological harm they did still mars our minds.

Today we pray for them, but our prayer makes sense only insofar as we are willing to forgive them and ask God to do the same.

All Souls is a day of mercy, of universal mercy, a day of forgiveness. But it should also be the day to review our own lives in such a way that goodness and sanctity prevail more and more.

ASSUMPTION OF THE BLESSED VIRGIN MARY

174. Assumption Is Acceptance

Luke 1:39–56

Isn't it strange that we have as our gospel reading today, at this feast of the assumption of the blessed virgin Mary into heaven, the meeting between Mary and Elizabeth?

That meeting does not seem to have anything heavenly about it at all. An aunt and a niece meet each other.

The heavenliness of their story seems to depend on their heavinesses: They are both filled with something from heaven. Mary with Jesus, and Elizabeth with John.

But from that meeting, we may learn what this feast of the assumption means.

When those women meet each other, they do it in a special way. They admire each other. They admire each other not in a way that creates a distance between them, but in a way that brings them very near to each other.

They embrace each other. They lay hands on each other. They say: "You, how is it that you are here, how is it that you came to me, you of whom I think so highly, how glad I am that you came!"

They meet like friends. No power play, no false pretense, no jealousy, no hidden motives, open and clear, attention for each other, and joy, *acceptance*, friendship.

Elizabeth is so touched that she reacts with her whole person, not only spiritually, but with her body, too. The fruit she is carrying in her womb jumps up with joy. Mary reacts in the same way. She opens her mouth and sings: about herself and her place, about being small and yet great, about her God and her thanks, about being *accepted* by God as a human being, a person, a woman, a mother with *spirit* and *body*.

We might come to very moralizing conclusions that this is the way we should meet each other, that this is the only way of giving each other the opportunity to find our place in this world and in God's plan.

That does not seem the point today.

The point today is the assumption, God's acceptance of Mary—her whole mind, her whole spirit, every single organ in her body.

God did not use her. She was neither God's vehicle nor God's means. She was not a surrogate mother. She was she, she was accepted as she had been made, with her history, her strengths, and her weaknesses—because she, too, was now and then in doubt, angry, upset, and afraid.

What Elizabeth did to Mary, what Mary did to Elizabeth, at that very simple meeting somewhere in the Holy Land's bush, is what God would do to her, the mother of Jesus. Celebrating this, we should take her as our *model*. That is how we are treated by God; that is how we are going to be treated by Mary's son.

CORPUS CHRISTI

175. Body of Christ

John 6:51–58

The feast we celebrate today is called *Corpus Christi*, the Body of Christ.

After having celebrated the Holy Spirit on Pentecost and the Trinity on Trinity Sunday, we are invited to come back to that other dimension in him, that other dimension in us: *body*, matter, the basics—a matter that matters very much.

We are of one Spirit, we are of his Spirit. We are of one Body, we are his Body.

You can see that and experience it when you look at what happened that evening when he took the bread, when he took the wine, and said—*while sharing that bread, while sharing that wine*—"This is my Body, this is my Blood!"

When he was holding up that "bread" and that "wine," it was his Body, it was his Blood. It was our Body, it was our Blood when they shared that "bread" and that "wine."

Some days ago I was in Washington, D.C., in the National Shrine. A dozen or so pilgrims came out of the grandiose basilica. They had just participated in a Mass. They had just received Holy Communion, communion with him. Communion in him and with one another, forming with him his Body, his Blood.

I saw them. I even saw that a blind man received communion with them.

They came out of the church together with him. He walked among them, tapping the pavement in front of himself with his cane. I could see them from the other end of the circle in front of the church.

He did not see them, since he was blind. He must have been aware of them all talking excitedly, feeling a bit lost in a strange place.

They did not see him, either, though they were not blind. They were busy with themselves. He ended up in the midst of them. Someone stepped on his cane, bending it, while he was pushed on. They left him alone, trying to straighten his cane.

They all had been to Holy Communion together in Jesus, who said of all of them: "This is my Body, this is my Blood!"

Yet, when it came to everyday life, that reality got lost. The body did not seem to have formed. They were not really in communion. They did not really form his Body, our Body. Did they?

Do we?

MAUNDY THURSDAY

176. His Final Will

John 13:1–15

Jesus knew that his hour had come: The hour to pass from this world to the Father, to pass this world on to the Father.

He knew. They did not know. In the beginning, even he did not think much of the end. You don't think of the end, not even at the beginning of a *farewell party*.

There are too many things to be taken care of: the invitations, the seating of the guests, the drinks, the food, and the talk. But then, when the party is on its way and almost over, there is a moment when the conversation stops, the moment everybody was afraid of, including him.

He knew he was going to be betrayed, arrested, beaten up, tortured, crucified, and killed in the middle of the day on a cross.

Knowing all this, he rose from his seat at the end of the meal. They all looked up. The conversation stopped. They had a feeling that something was going to happen: Judas had left in the dark of the night. What would he do? Call them together for some last admonishing words, like a dying African father would do, speaking to his sons and daughters?

What would he do?

Ask for a paper and pen, to write in clear, bold script: "I bequeath my home, my land, my cattle, and my share . . ."?

He took a bowl, a jug full of water, and a towel. He went down on his hands and knees and washed their feet, not even looking up. He washed all of them, one by one, thoroughly. He washed the feet of all of us, believers and unbelievers, old and young, saints and sinners, pimps and street girls, popes and bishops, rulers and ruled, rich and poor, filled and hungry, dressed and naked. He washed and washed, without even looking at whose feet he was washing. *He never intended to stop*, because he said: "Do you understand what I am doing? I gave you a model of what you should do: Wash each other's feet, and after that, break your bread, sharing it all over the world, all over humanity until I will be with you again in the Kingdom to come."

GOOD FRIDAY

177. Delivered into the Hands of Men

John 18:1-19, 42

John's gospel makes it very clear: Jesus delivered himself *freely* into the hands of man. When the mob came to meet him, he asked them: "Whom are you looking for?" and when they answered: "Jesus of Nazareth," he made them all tumble on their faces in the mud of the wicked earth on which they had been standing. He let them taste the bitterness of the earth's lot.

After that, he delivered himself to the corruption in their temple, to the intrigues in their politics, to the jealousies in their lives, to the injustices at their courts.

They took him, grabbed him, detained him, interrogated him, caned him, and crowned him with thorns.

We took him, grabbed him, detained him, interrogated him, caned him, and crowned him with thorns, shouting for his end, calling for his blood, demanding his death: *hoping for light, but preferring the dark.*

John's gospel makes it very clear where this deliverance into the hands of men led him. John makes it very clear where the deliverance of the just, of those who strive after righteousness, into the hands of men will lead them.

You know it. I know it. We know it. What was the end of Oscar Romero, the archbishop of San Salvador in March 1980? Where are Martin Luther King, Mahatma Gandhi, Tom Mboya, and so many others? Where are those hundreds, thousands, and millions who were shot for the sake of justice, for the sake of an alternative?

It is the evangelist John who speaks about Jesus' death in the most explicit way.

He not only reports how Jesus hung on the cross, how he bled empty, how his lungs collapsed, how he bent his head, how his body twitched for the last time.

He also tells us how a soldier looked up at him, and how he took a spear and pushed it through his chest into his heart and out flowed—it is John who testifies—his blood and the last drop of moisture.

He was dead, absolutely and totally dead. That soldier added a full stop behind the story of that glorious life.

They all went home, after having killed—they thought—all goodness in this world, after having given up their most deeply rooted hope, trying to convince each other: "Didn't I tell you this type of life cannot survive in this, our world? Didn't I tell you? Let us forget about it. Let us forget about him. Let us be realistic. We have to learn to live the life we have, corrupt and violent, harsh and treacherous."

And when they all were at home, insofar as they had homes in this homeless world, Mary, his mother, Joseph of Arimathea, Nicodemus, and a few others took him down and buried him in a tomb with a stone in front, sealed and blocked.

The sun darkened. The curtains in the temple ripped apart. The whole earth shook in vehemence when it received his body: its origin and its end.

JUNE 29

178. Peter and Paul

Matthew 16:13–19

Saint Peter and Saint Paul are always celebrated together. That is remarkable, not only because less-important Christian ancestors have their own private and personal feast days, but also because Peter and Paul had difficult times in each other's company. They discussed, dialogued, fought, and avoided each other for days and days, and then faced each other again in power and force.

Yet, it is good, I suppose, that we celebrate them together, because Peter and Paul kept each other in balance, a very necessary balance.

Saint Peter was the churchman, the typical churchman. Jesus called him the rock, the stone on which the community was going to be built. He might also have called him the rock because of Peter's tendency to solidify, to petrify. Peter wanted safety and a well-protected house.

Think of his attitude on that mountaintop, when in front of Peter's eyes, Jesus changed, developed, transfigured, and glorified. Elijah appears, Moses appears, and Jesus speaks to them about what he is going to do; he is talking about his passover, about a new life. And Peter said: "Stop, keep it, hold it, this is super, alleluia, let us build something around it, let us keep it safe and warm, within walls and under a roof.''

Peter, the rock, the brick and stone believer, the churchman, the builder, the contractor. Saint Paul was his exact opposite.

While Peter tried to close doors to the uncircumcised and people like that, Paul threw them open again.

While Peter insisted: ''Law, law; order, order,'' Paul wrote about the glorious liberty of the children of God. He wrote: ''Where the Spirit of God is, there is freedom.'' And he then added a thing rarely quoted by church leaders: ''Why should freedom depend on somebody else's conscience?'' And in his difficulties with Peter, he shouted: ''Liberty, brothers; liberty, sisters, you are called to liberty!''

Peter and Paul keep each other in balance.

With Peter alone, we would be a rock; with Paul alone, we would be an open door.

Both worked, notwithstanding their difficulties, with the same vision, and both got that vision from Jesus himself, although in very different ways.

Paul got his like this. He was sitting on a horse, fiery as ever, a kind of spiritual cowboy, with his sheriff's star under his lapel and a list of people in Damascus in his pocket.

He was going to arrest them and bring them to court because they were subversive, they were spreading false rumors about a resurrection from the dead, about an ascension to heaven, about a new way to be taken, about an ax at the root of the old tree of life, and other rubbish. Paul was out, as the Acts of the Apostles say, to *slaughter* them.

There he was on his horse, in a hurry, because he wanted to arrive before the news of his coming arrived.

Suddenly there was light all around him. His horse fell, he fell, and he heard a voice that said: ''Paul, why are you persecuting *me*?'' Paul thought of the names on his list and said: ''You, who are you?'' The voice said: ''I am Jesus of Nazareth.'' Paul was very surprised, because that name was, of course, not on his list. Jesus was exactly the one who was rumored to have been executed, risen, and ascended to heaven.

Then suddenly he started to understand, Jesus identified with the people on his list. He got his vision there and then, as he declared afterwards: ''Jesus is the Head and we are the members.'' He got his vision, the vision of Jesus bound up with us. Afterwards he said again and again: ''I have only one thing to announce, it is that we are all ONE in Christ Jesus!''

Peter got that very same vision in another way. Jesus asked: ''Peter, do you love me?'' Peter answered: ''Yes, Sir, you know that I love you!'' Jesus asked a second time: ''Peter, do you love me?'' Peter answered: ''Yes, Sir, you know that I love you!'' Jesus asked for a third time: ''Peter, do you love me?'' Peter said: ''Please, Sir, stop it. You know that I love you!''

And Jesus answered: ''In that case, take care of the others, take care of all the others!'' He got his vision, the vision of Jesus. A vision in which Jesus, God's offspring, sees the whole of humankind belonging together: ''I am the trunk, you are the branches.'' He is the Head, we are the members. According to Jesus, we belong together, we form one body. There is only one human being: Humanity.

That is his vision. It's also his working plan, his organizational project.

It is not only a vision. If this is really true, if we really belong together, then the bag man and the bag woman in the street, with their rags and their missing social background, belong to you, to us. If they are sick and hungry and miserable, then we are sick and hungry and miserable, until things are changed, until the vision of Jesus is translated into reality.

If we are to be one—and we are to be one, just as Peter and Paul finally were one—then we have to break our bread. We will have to break our bread.

Index of Gospel Texts